IMAGES
of America

WATCHUNG

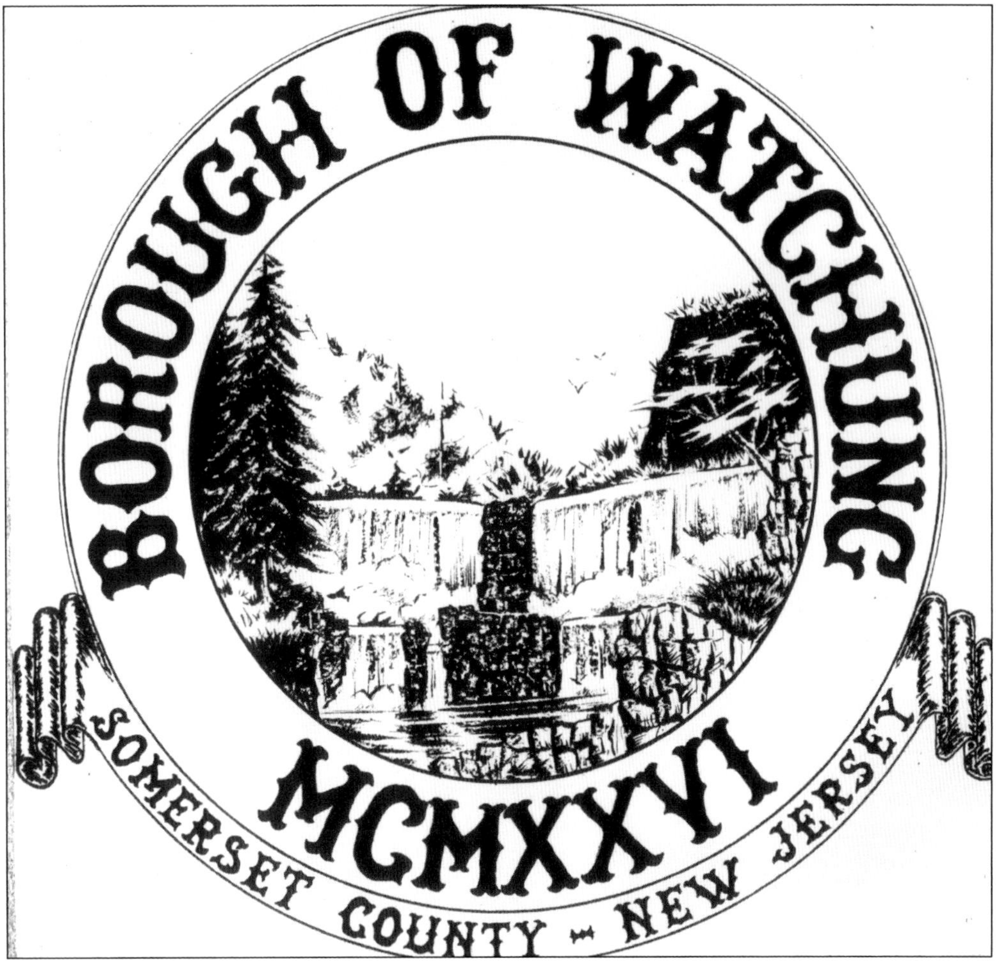

THE BOROUGH SEAL. Although the history of this area can be traced back to the 17th century (when Native Americans and Dutch settlers lived here), Watchung was not incorporated as a borough until May 6, 1926. The center of the borough seal features Wetumpka Falls, located on the Stony Brook, which passes through a notch in the First Watchung Mountain.

IMAGES
of America

WATCHUNG

David B. Page

ARCADIA
PUBLISHING

ISBN 978-0-7385-0959-4

Published by Arcadia Publishing
Charleston, South Carolina

Printed in the United States of America

Library of Congress Catalog Card Number: 2001093044

For all general information contact Arcadia Publishing at:
Telephone 843-853-2070
Fax 843-853-0044
E-mail sales@arcadiapublishing.com
For customer service and orders:
Toll-Free 1-888-313-2665

Visit us on the Internet at www.arcadiapublishing.com

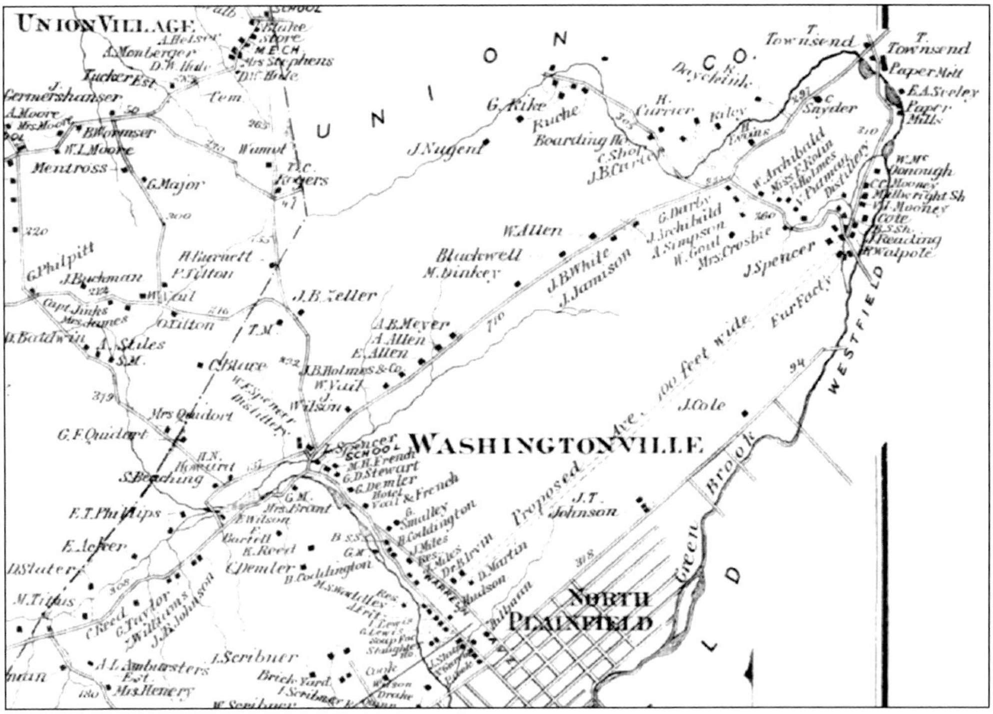

WASHINGTONVILLE. As shown in *Atlas of Somerset County, New Jersey* (published by Beers, Comstock & Cline in 1873), Watchung was named Washingtonville in the late 18th century and was part of North Plainfield Township. When an application for a post office was filed, it was discovered that there was another town named Washingtonville, and so the town was renamed Watchung.

Contents

Acknowledgments		6
Introduction		7
1.	The Land and Its Legend	9
2.	Business and Industry	27
3.	Borough Services	53
4.	Residences	67
5.	Schools and Churches	87
6.	Disasters	103
7.	Community Life	113

Acknowledgments

I would like to express my sincere appreciation to the many individuals who generously shared their photographs and information to make this book possible.

Special thanks are due to the Watchung Historical Committee and the Watchung Chemical Engine Company for their support and access to their extensive collections. In particular, I would like to thank Barbara Diem, member of the Watchung Historical Committee, who also shared her personal collection of photographs; Catherine Ilchert, president of the Watchung Heritage Coalition; Gary Greves, historian for the Watchung Chemical Engine Company; and Judy Page, who helped with the research.

I would also like to sincerely thank Mayor Anthony Addario; Betty Aldrich; Paul Arts; Betty Black; Phyllis Blackadar; Mario Caruso, Joann Kohler, Bruce Ryno, and the North Plainfield High School Alumni Association; Tom and Steve Castronovo, Edgewood Pharmacy; Ginny Cooper; Miriam Crum, New Jersey Department of Transportation; John T. Cunningham; Tom D'Amico, Somerset County Cultural and Heritage Commission; Bernadette DeCastro-McDonald; Bob Duykinck and the Optimists Club of Watchung; Sheila Duykinck and the Watchung Arts Center; the Echoes-Sentinel; Susan Feibush; Laureen Fellin, Watchung Borough Municipal Clerk; Rino and Jeanette Ghidella; Jim Girvan and John Merry, Somerset County Planning and Engineering; Fire Chief Charles Gunther, Watchung Chemical Engine Company; David Haddon, director, Camp Brett-Endeavor; Bill Halsey; Emi Havas, chairperson of the Watchung Historical Committee; Muriel Jacobs; Jane Kipe, Valley Furniture Shop; Barbara Linder, Washington Rock Girl Scout Council; Sister Mary Innocent and Sister Laura, Mount St. Mary's Academy; Gerry Mobus; Dwight Newell and Mark Schellhorn, O'Connor's Beef 'N Ale House; Fr. Brian Nolan, Henry and Maria Albert, St. Mary's Church–Stony Hill; Bob Nunn; Astrid Ost, Julie Schenck, and Rev. J. Ronald Miller, Mary E. Wilson Memorial Union Church; Alan Page; Plainfield Courier News; Harlan Pratt; Helen Rebmann; Chief Robert Reilly, Watchung Police Department; Jim Richardson; Dr. Catherine Rock, Watchung Public School superintendent; Mike Ryan, New Jersey Department of Environmental Protection; Cindy Scalera; Alan A. Siegel; Dorothy Stratford; Dr. Philip J. Tama; Bobby Thomson; Andrea Tingey, New Jersey Historic Preservation Office; Watchung Boy Scout Troop 32; the Watchung Public Library; Watchung Whispering Leaves; Bob Weldon III, Weldon Materials; and Tiby Wotherspoon.

Finally, I would like to acknowledge the many individuals, both living and deceased, who have contributed to the Watchung Historical Committee's collection, as well as all those who helped to identify people in photographs.

—David B. Page

INTRODUCTION

In the 1600s, members of the Lenni Lenape tribe lived in small villages where the hills gave protection from winter winds and where valleys provided good soil for their crops and a stream for their canoes. Such a place was the tranquil valley between the First and Second Mountains near the gorge where the Stony Brook passes. This beautiful land would be known as Browsetown, Green Valley, Washingtonville, and, finally, as Watchung, New Jersey.

The Lenapes willingly shared their lands with the early settlers. However, they believed that any individual or group could not own land and resources. In contrast, the European settlers believed that land could be owned and improved by human effort.

A series of four land purchases in 1681 ended Native American ownership of land in Somerset County, where Watchung is located. It was under 24 proprietors to whom East Jersey passed in 1682 that Somerset County began to be permanently settled. All of Somerset County was made one township in 1693, when townships were first established in New Jersey.

Watchung's history has been shaped by its geography. Approximately six square miles, Watchung holds parts of the first and second ridges of the Watchung Mountains, a valley of rolling farmland between them, two lakes, and streams leading into the lakes. These natural resources and the beauty of the area attracted early Dutch, English, and German settlers, who had large farms. George Washington spent time in and around the area, as nearby Washington Rock provided an excellent lookout point.

In 1806, Warren Township, including what is now Watchung, was formed from Bernards and Bridgewater Townships. Watchung remained part of Warren Township until 1872, when it became part of North Plainfield Township. The Borough of Watchung consisted of the little village of Washingtonville and about 800 people when it voted to separate itself from North Plainfield Township in 1926.

Much information is known about Watchung from the mid-19th century on, and photographs of the area from the late 19th century through the present are included in this volume. Watchung has been home to a diverse set of businesses that existed here, including several quarries, ice harvesting, gristmills, a tannery and glove manufacturer, fur hat manufacturer, cider mill, sawmill, blacksmith, and florists. Residents also found time to relax, enjoying the Watchung Lake Swim Club, ice-skating, events sponsored by the Improvement Society, and an annual pie-baking contest. As many as 300 people would come from New York and elsewhere on a Sunday afternoon to enjoy the fresh mountain air on Johnston Drive.

There has been an interesting evolution of building and lot use in Watchung. The original flour mill became the tannery. Once closed as a tannery, it was used for social activities. The building was razed, and a new municipal building was constructed, including garages for the

Watchung fire department. Later, the fire department built its own location and then a second. Similarly, the Texier House on the Watchung Circle was originally the home of Hippolyte Texier, who owned the tannery. Later, the house became headquarters to the Watchung Police Department. Following a fire, it was restored as a location to house borough offices. Finally, the schoolhouse built in 1898 was expanded by having the original two rooms lifted and placed above two new rooms. The entire building has since become home to the Watchung Arts Center, an active cultural group.

By 1940, the population of Watchung had grown to 1,158. In the 2000 census, the population was found to be 5,613. Although located only 30 miles from midtown Manhattan, Watchung remains an area of natural beauty, with its lakes, streams, and rolling hills. The town is largely residential, and typical properties of one and one-half acres add to the sense of seclusion and tranquility. Today, the primary commercial section has moved to the edge of town on Route 22.

Several fires and floods have destroyed some former landmarks featured in this book. The Washington House, originally an inn from the early 1700s, was destroyed by fire in 1962. The Moldenke Castle, an unusual home constructed between 1900 and 1930, was damaged by fire in 1969 and then razed. Other buildings damaged or destroyed by fire were the Texier House, Hydewood Hall, and Mount St. Mary's Academy. A flood in 1885 destroyed the blacksmith shop, while the flood of 1973 washed away parts of Wetumpka Falls and Somerset Street.

Watchung has a small-town atmosphere with friendly people, while being located close to major highways and cities. It has an excellent school system, involved residents, and an active borough government. The publication of this book, coinciding with the 75th anniversary of the borough's incorporation, provides a tribute to this beautiful community.

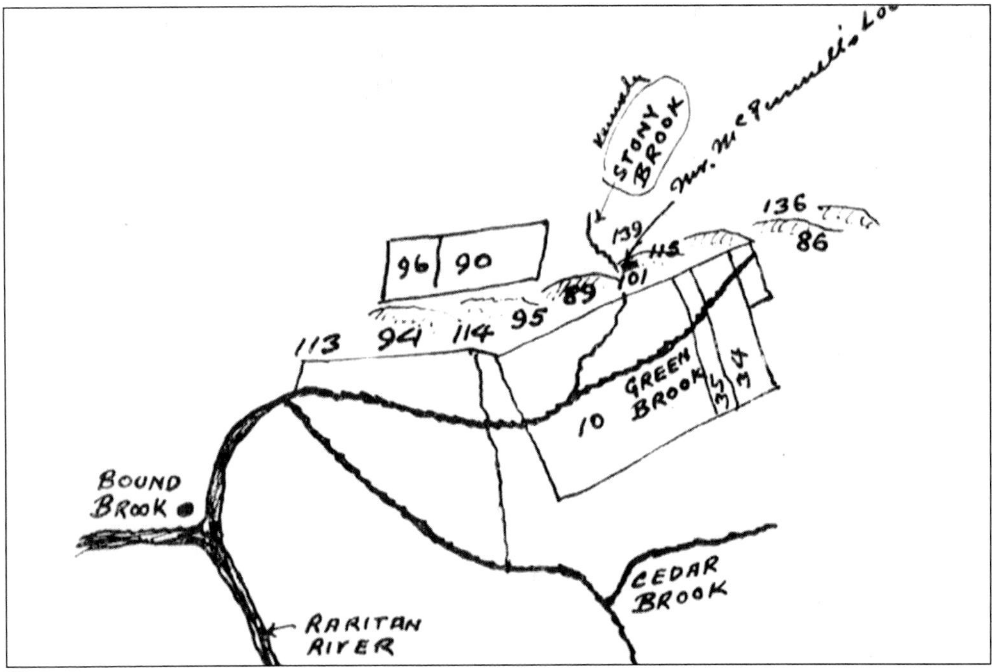

THE ELISABETHTOWN BILL OF CHANCERY. H.R. Kennedy traced this map in the early 1900s from the "Elisabethtown Bill of Chancery," printed in 1747, which recorded all purchases of land. Three transactions for land in current-day Watchung were recorded: No. 89, James Alexander, 76 acres at Blew Hills, top of the First Mountain in 1723; No. 101, Joseph Jennings, 4 acres in the First Mountain at the falls of Stony Brook in 1727; and No. 115, Elisha Smalley, 22 acres at Blew Hills on Stony Brook in 1736.

One

The Land and Its Legend

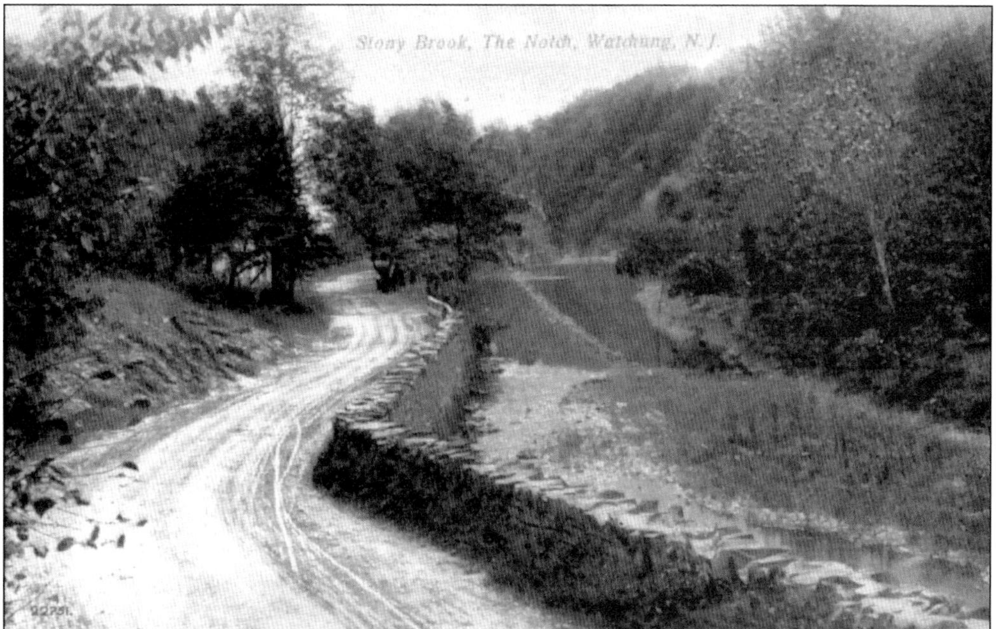

STONY BROOK. Members of the Lenni Lenape tribe traveled by dugout canoe on the Stony Brook, which took them into the Green Brook and then the Raritan River on their way to the seashore. Running along Stony Brook, Somerset Street passed through a notch in the first ridge of the Watchung Mountains. Originally, it was a Native American trail and later developed into a rough wagon road, serving as the main route down from the Watchung Mountains.

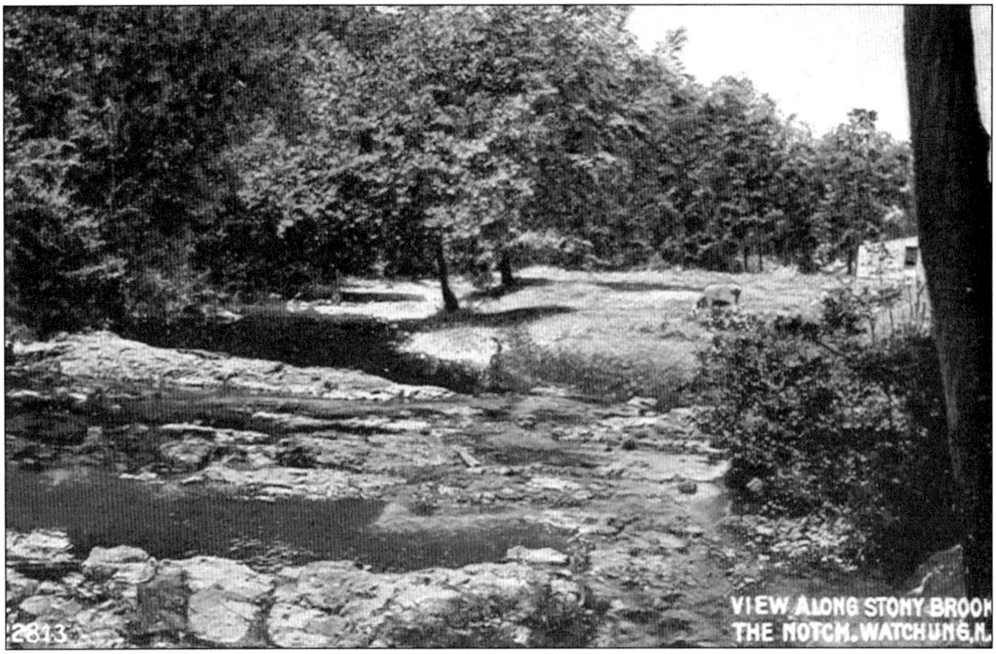

BROWSETOWN. During the early 18th century, Watchung was known as Browsetown (or Browstown) because farmers from the Plainfield area drove their cows through the notch in the summer months to browse on the grass along Stony Brook.

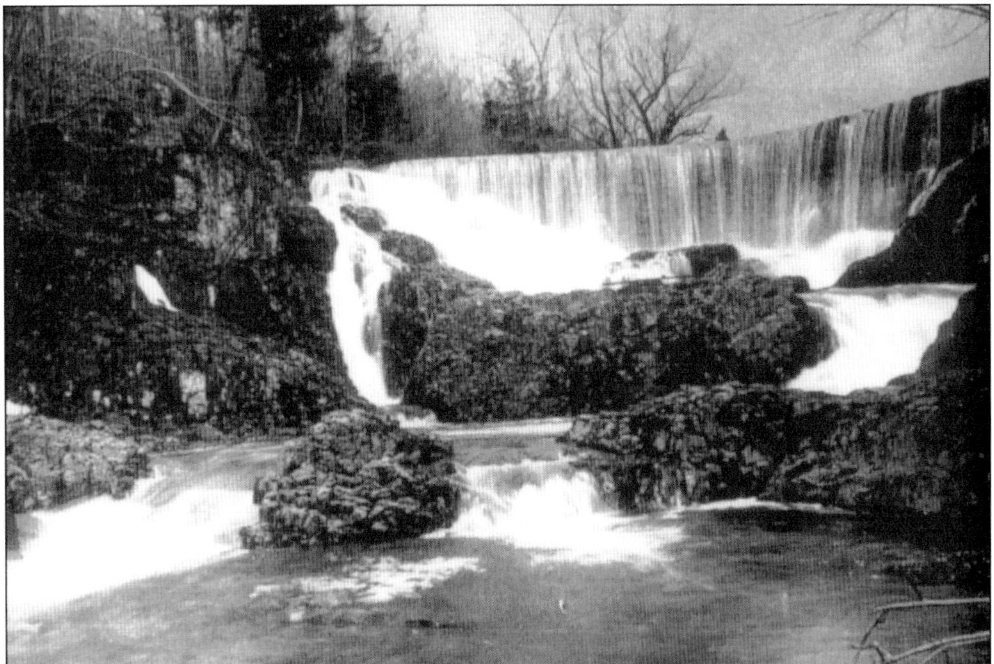

WETUMPKA FALLS. The name of the falls, located on Stony Brook, can be traced back to the Lenni Lenape word *wetoompka,* meaning "friendly sounding water." In 1900, employees of the Crescent Embossing Company of Plainfield, which featured the Native American Princess Wetumpka in its calendar, are thought to have named the falls while on a picnic there.

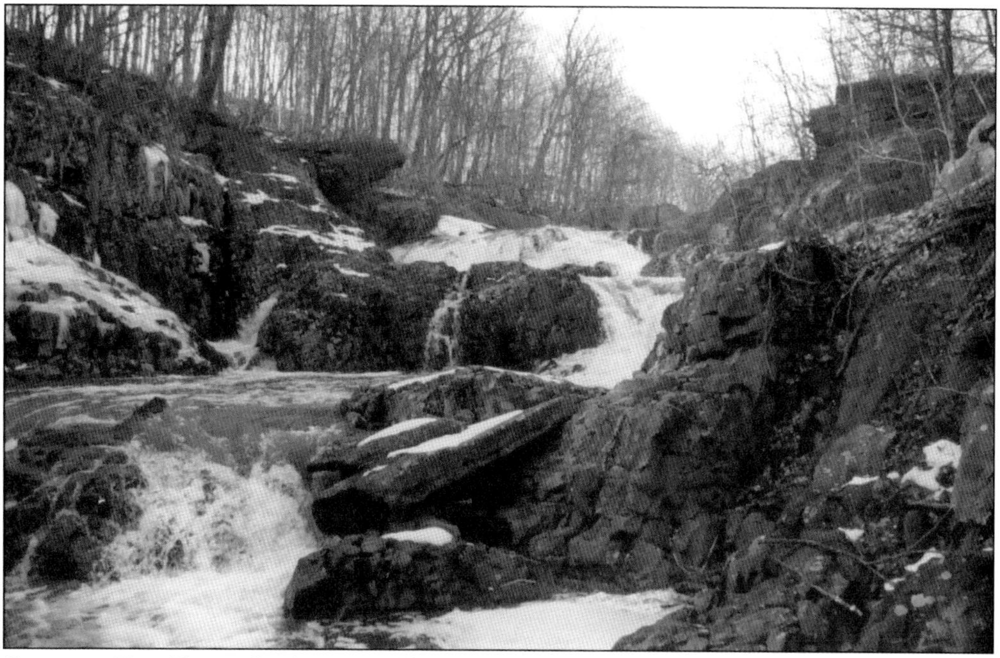

Current-Day Falls. In August 1973, a raging flood swept through Watchung and North Plainfield, severely damaging Wetumpka Falls. The falls were originally built to provide power for a quarry that operated across the road. With the quarry closed, the need for the falls was eliminated, and they were not rebuilt after the flood.

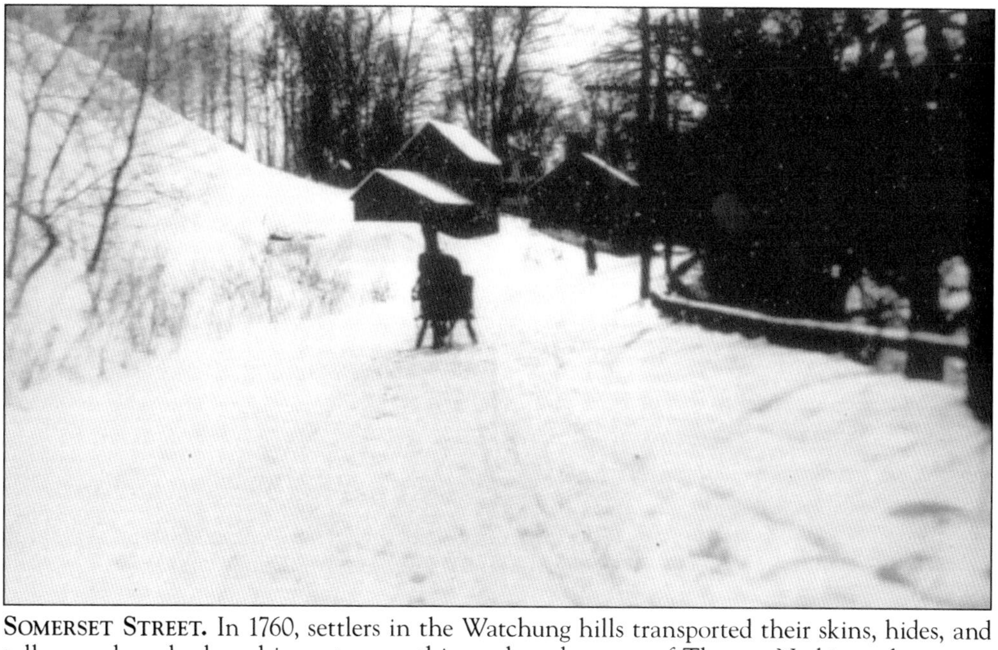

Somerset Street. In 1760, settlers in the Watchung hills transported their skins, hides, and tallow on horseback and in carts over this road to the store of Thomas Nesbit at the corner of Somerset and Front Streets in Plainfield and traded them for cloth, powder, shot, and other necessities. In 1890, this road was still a dirt road. Horse-drawn wagons and carriages were the principal conveyances of the time.

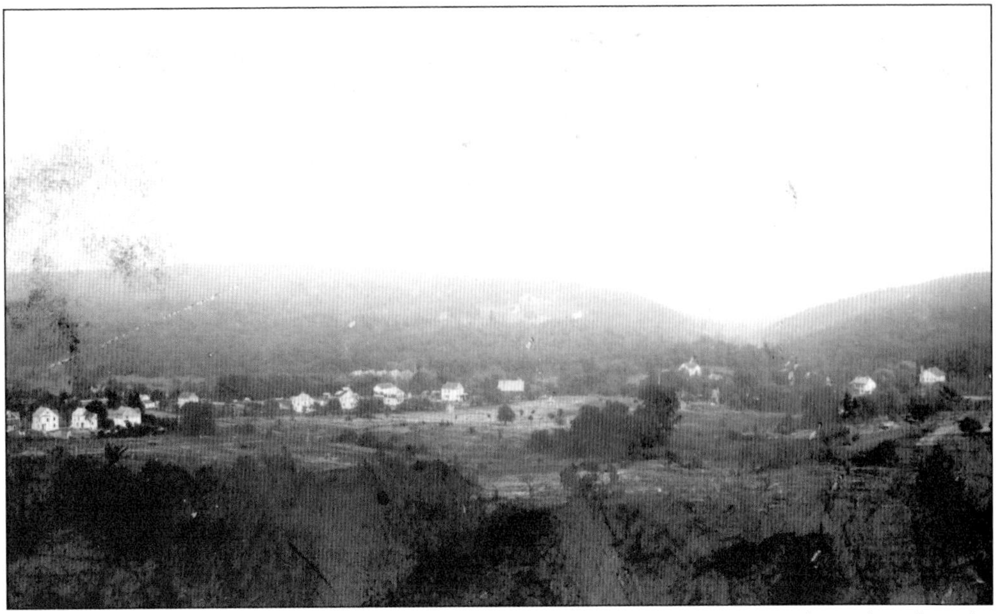

THE HIGH HILLS. "Wach Unks," or High Hills, were the Lenni Lenape words used to describe this area and the origin of the name Watchung. Approximately six square miles, Watchung contains parts of the first and second ridges of the Watchung Mountains and a valley of fertile, rolling land between them.

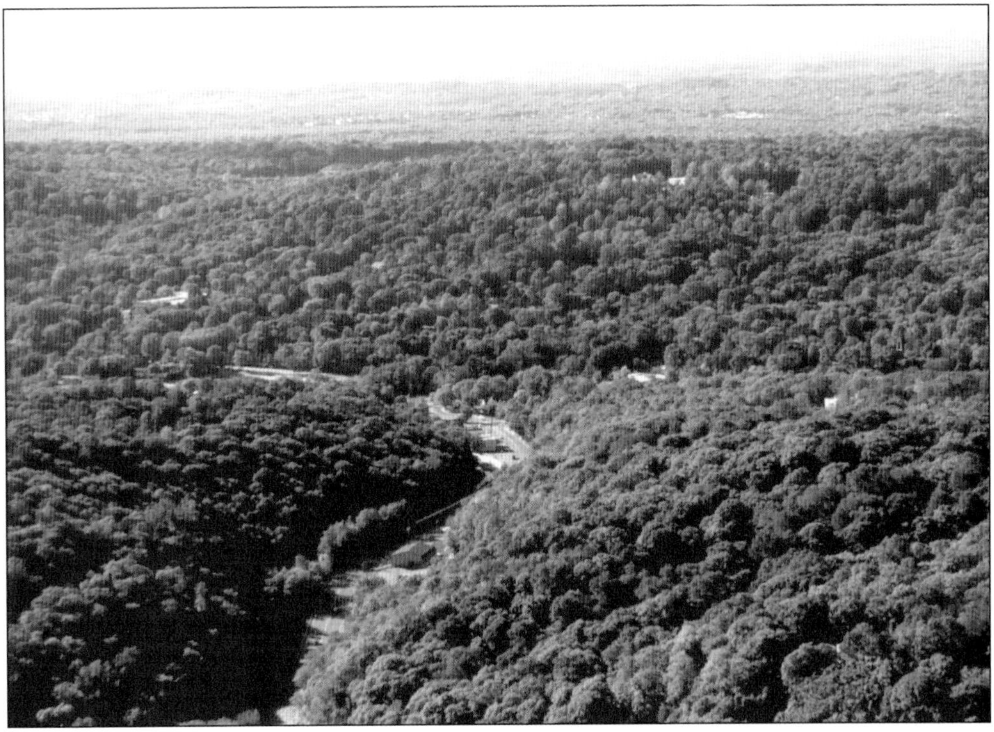

THE BLEW HILLS. In the 1700s, the mountains were referred to as the Blew Hills, which were "stony and covered with wood." Around the 1860s, the Blew Hills changed their spelling and became the Blue Mountains. They started to be called the Watchungs c. 1900.

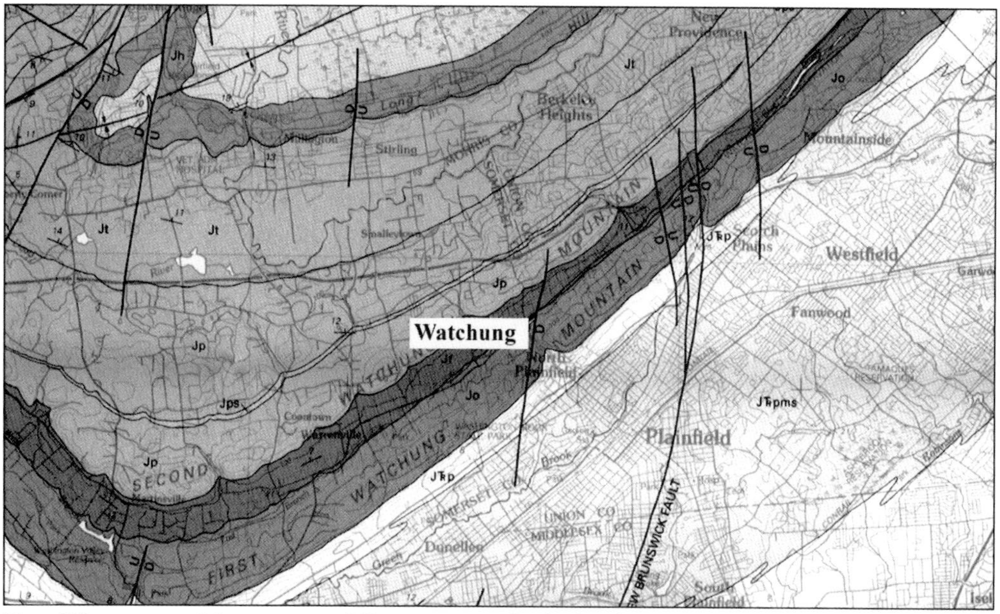

The Watchung Mountains. This portion of a bedrock geologic map shows Watchung in the center of the map, positioned between the First and Second Watchung Mountains. During the late Triassic and early Jurassic periods, at least three major periods of volcanic eruptions occurred here, resulting in the accumulation of extensive basaltic lava sheets, which formed the Watchungs. The horseshoe-shaped outline of these mountains readily identifies them on a topographic map.

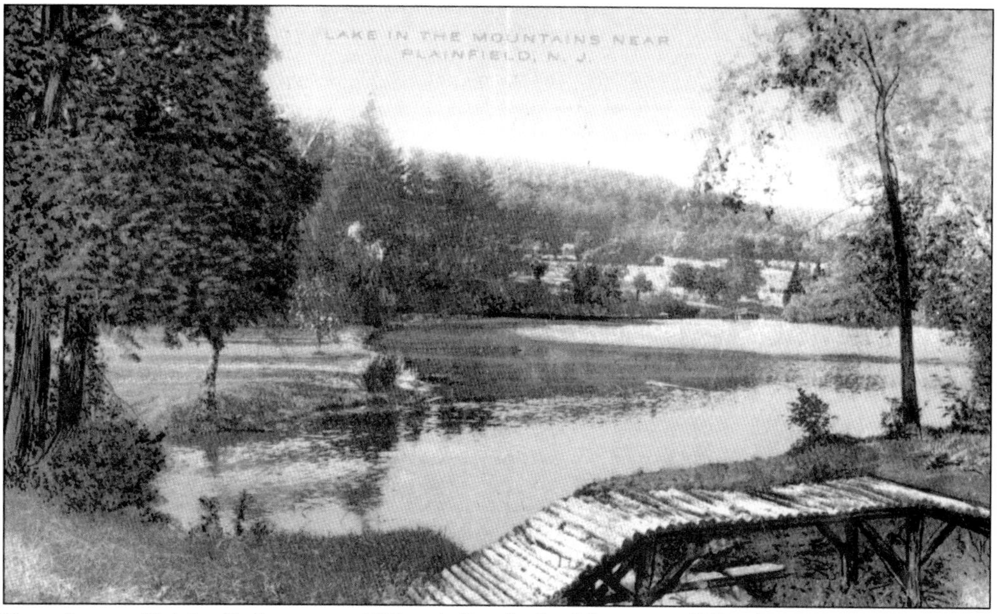

Best Lake. Originally known as Wilson's Pond, the lake east of Watchung Center was built by John Wilson c. 1860 for ice cutting. When the property was left to his son Andrew Howat Wilson, Wilson's Pond and the surrounding property became known as Burnhead, the name of his mother's farm in Scotland. Burnhead is Scottish for "top of the stream." Later renamed Best Lake, the property was purchased by the Borough of Watchung in 1966.

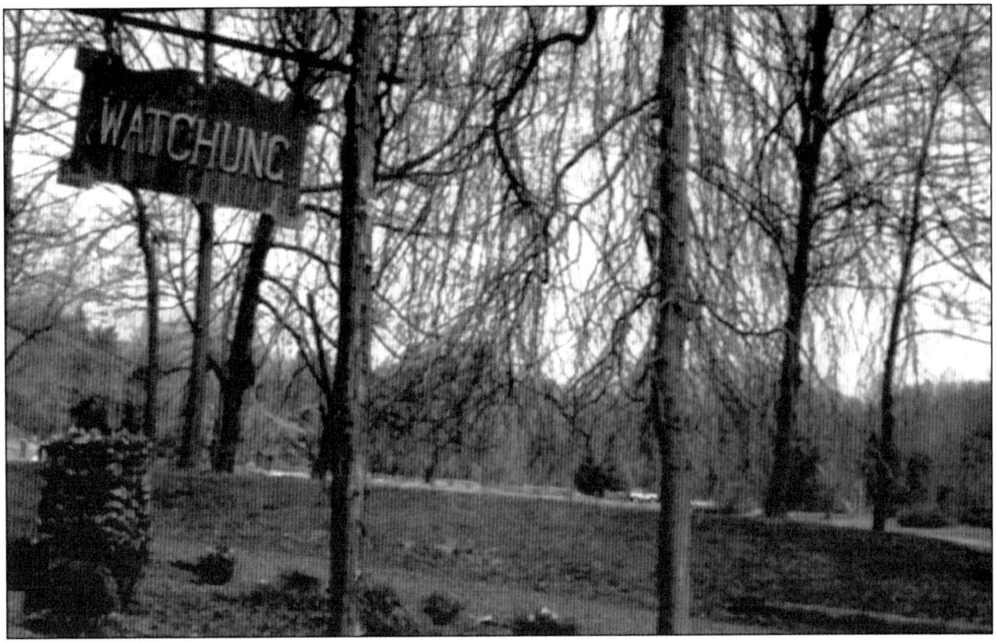

WATCHUNG SIGN. This sign near Best Lake was designed and made by Oswald Carliss *c.* 1935. At one time, signs like this one could also be found on Valley Road, Somerset Street, Stirling Road, and Mountain Boulevard, marking the borders of Watchung. Behind the sign is a gatepost made of native stone, originally used as one of the boundary markers for the Burnhead estate in the early 1900s.

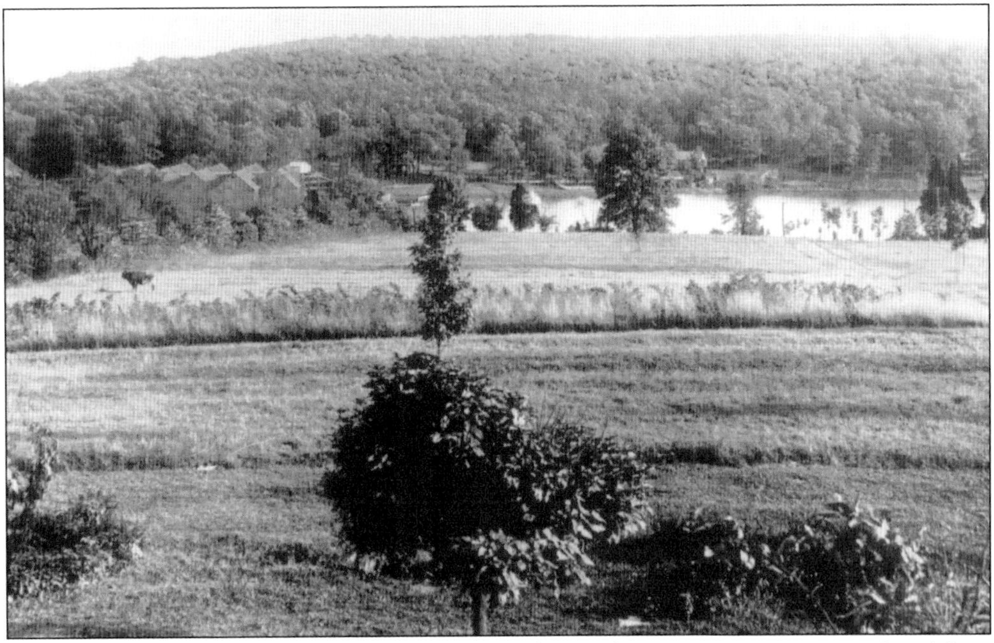

WATCHUNG LAKE IN 1907. Watchung Lake, which is today 22 acres in size, started its life in the mid-1800s. When known as Texier's Mill Pond, it was about one fifth the size of the current lake. Located in the center of Watchung, the lake is seen here in 1907 in a view looking south from the old Hughes farm.

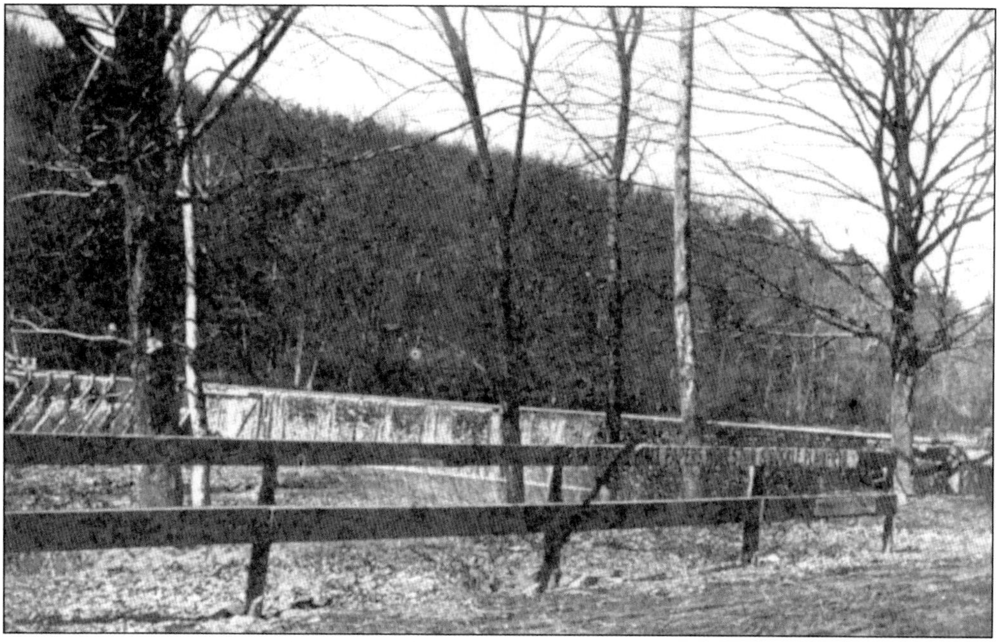

THE WASHINGTONVILLE DAM. In 1894, a concrete dam was constructed and the lake was enlarged to its current size. Water from the lake ran through a raceway to a waterwheel across the road, used as power in an early gristmill.

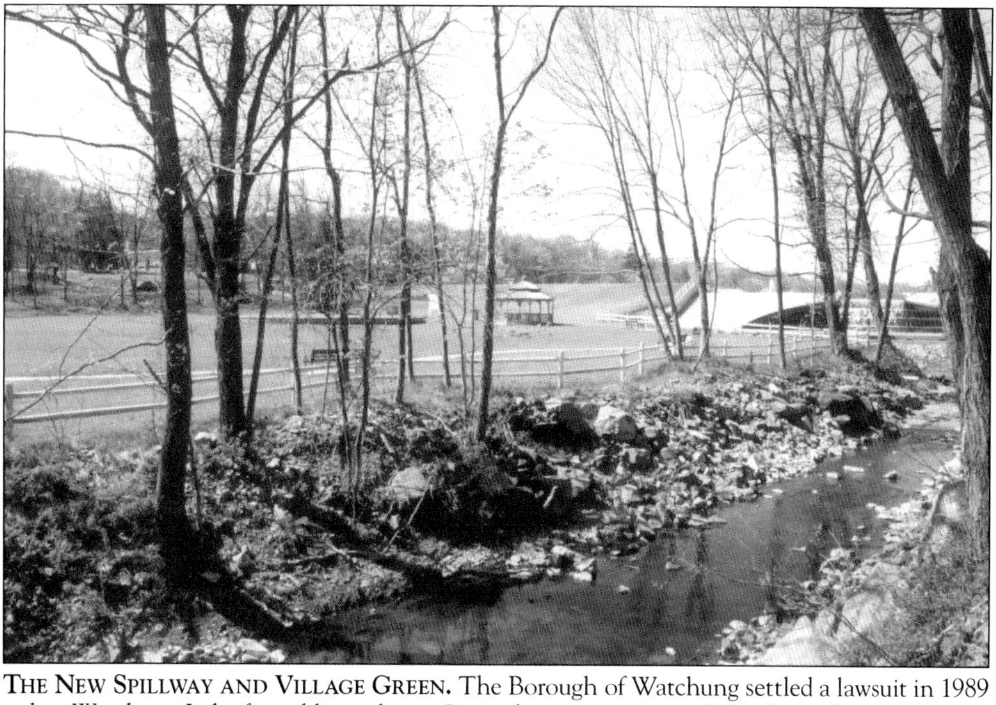

THE NEW SPILLWAY AND VILLAGE GREEN. The Borough of Watchung settled a lawsuit in 1989 to buy Watchung Lake for public park use. Since then, extensive work has been done to improve the property. A new concrete spillway was completed in 1999, replacing the original dam. The area below the spillway has been converted into a village green, helping to preserve the beauty and natural scenery of the community.

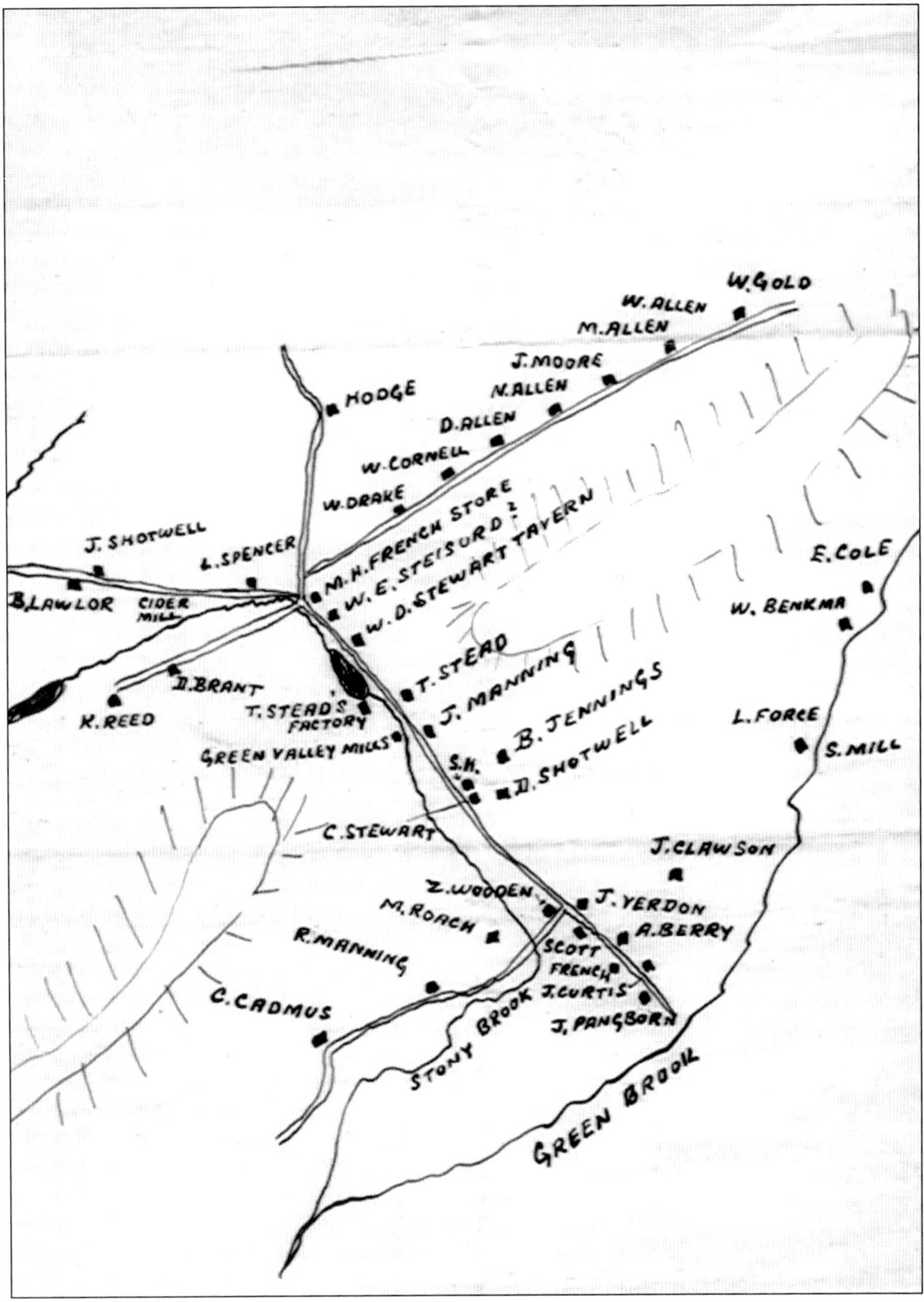

AN 1850 MAP. Traced by H.R. Kennedy in 1907, this map was taken from an 1850 map of Somerset County by Otley, Van DerVeer, and Keily. Early settlers located along today's Valley Road, running east from Watchung Center, along Somerset Street running south along Stony Brook, and along the bank of the Green Brook. Note the location of a cider mill near Watchung Center.

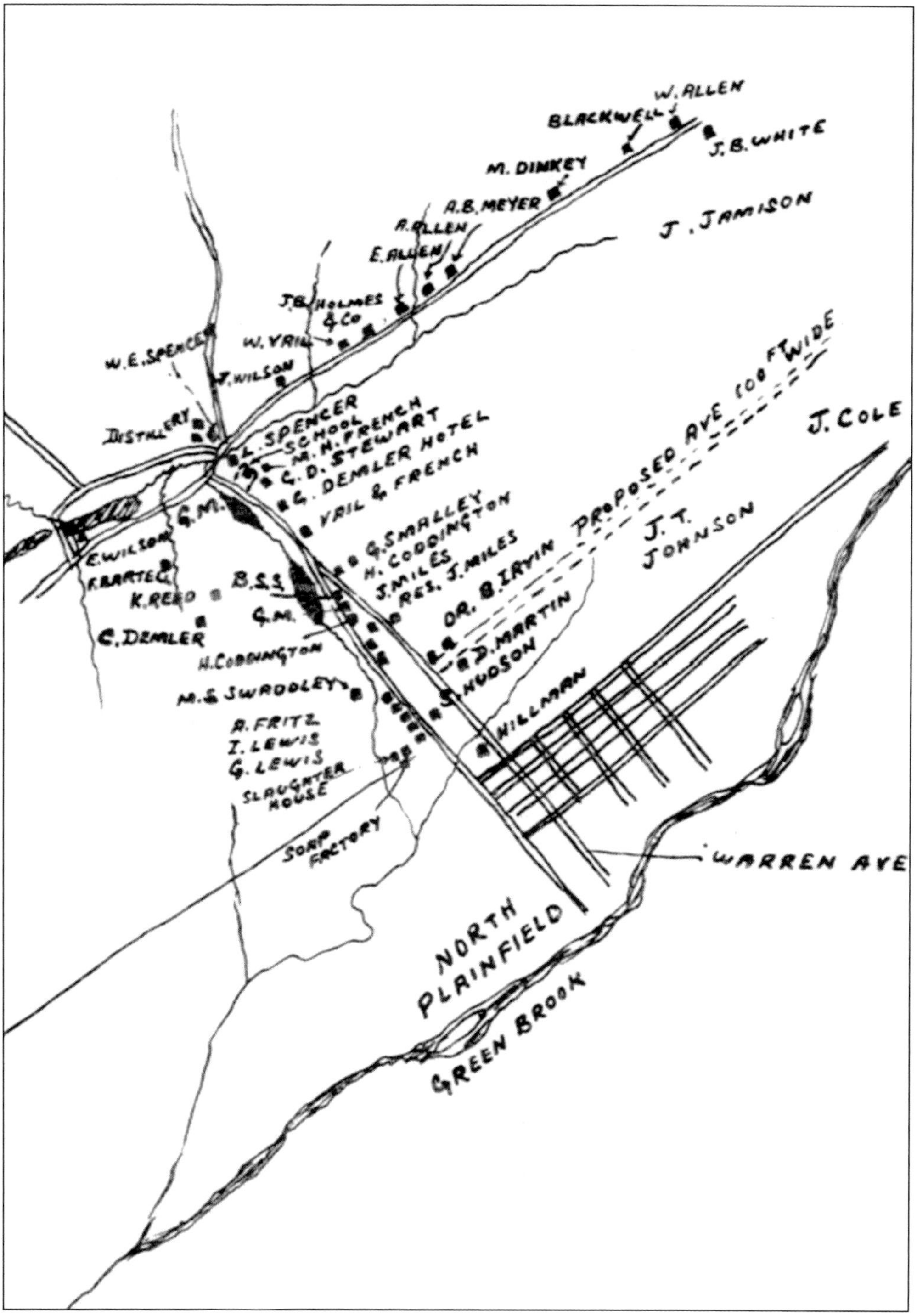

An 1873 Map. This section of *Atlas of Somerset County, New Jersey* was also traced by H.R. Kennedy in the early 1900s. Compared to the 1850 view, this map shows growth along Somerset Street and the parallel Watchung Avenue. Watchung grew slowly through the 18th and 19th centuries, with about 70 homes within the present borough limits in the 1870s.

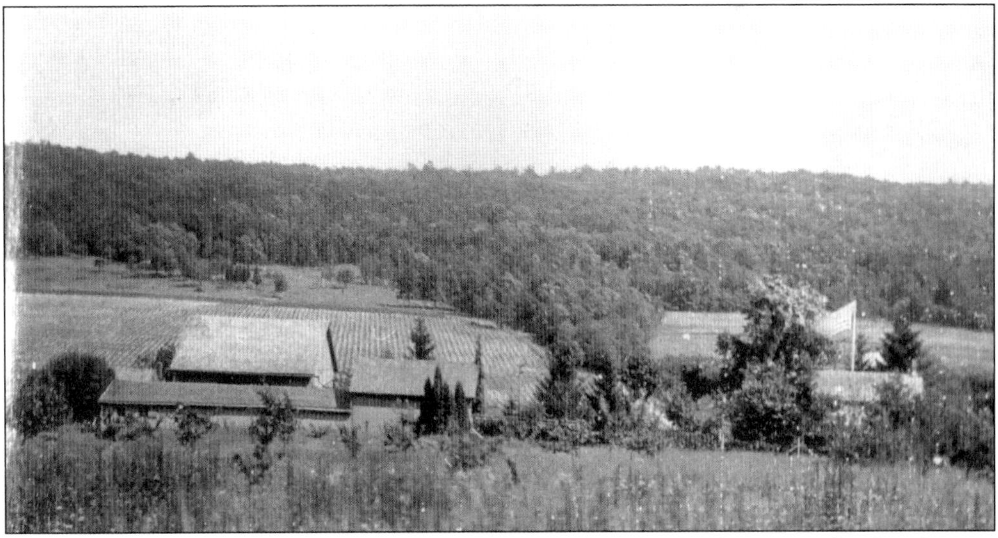

VALLEY ROAD TO THE NORTH. Rev. Edward Moldenke bought this farm on Valley Road to use as a camp for his Sunday school children from New York City. Shown in 1894, "the Homestead" was purchased from a farmer, whose original house was built about 100 years earlier. Reverend Moldenke divided the land among his three sons, with Alfred claiming the old farmhouse.

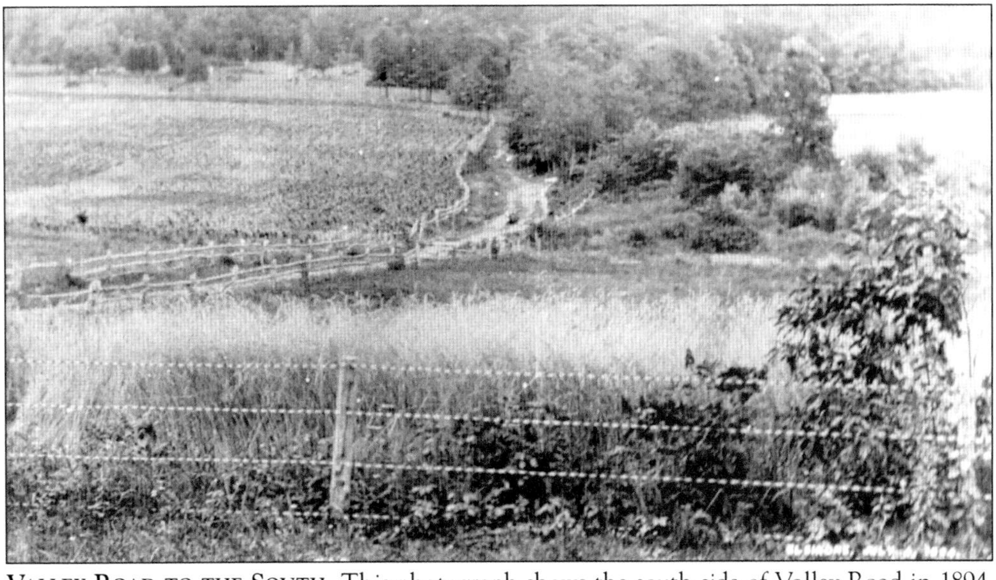

VALLEY ROAD TO THE SOUTH. This photograph shows the south side of Valley Road in 1894. Part of the farm purchased by the Moldenkes, this land would become the eventual site of Castle Elsinore, built by Dr. Richard Moldenke, son of Reverend Moldenke.

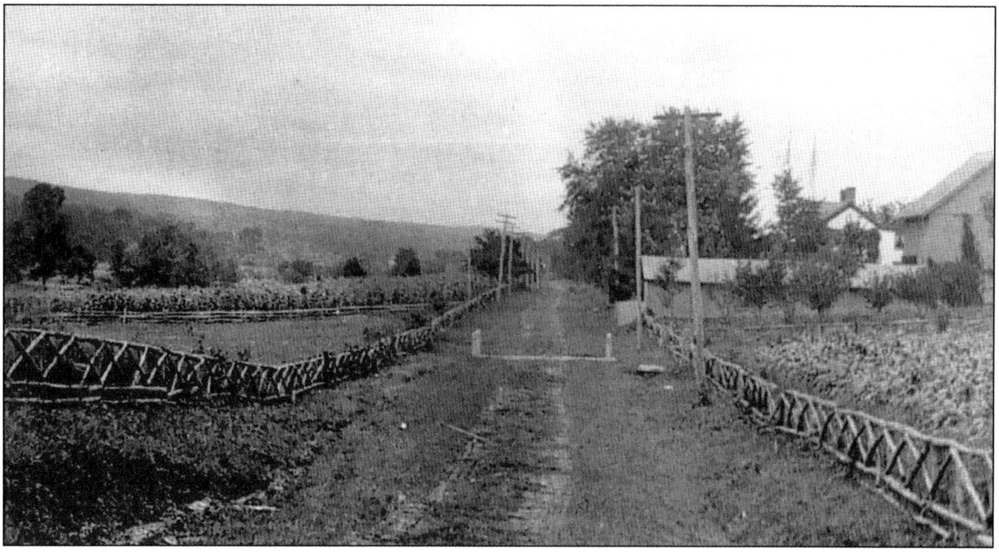

Valley Road to the East. A view of Valley Road looking east *c.* 1900 shows a wooden fence along the Moldenke property, which has cornfields on the right. During the Revolutionary War, George Washington was known to have been in the area and is likely to have passed through Watchung. On a map of Green Brook Valley, this road was identified as "Gen. Washington's Route (to Morristown)."

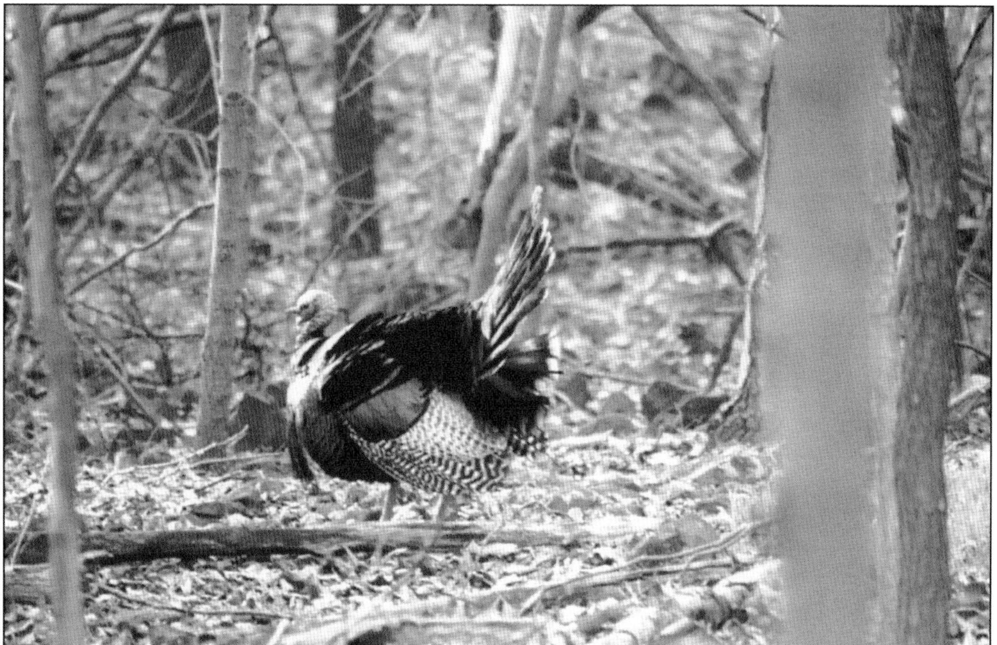

A Wild Turkey. Wild fowl, especially geese and remarkably large turkeys, increased early settlers' impressions that they had come to a land of plenty. Many wild turkeys still wander through the woods of Watchung, as evidenced by this specimen. Other animals common in this area were deer, panthers, elk, foxes, wolves, wildcats, squirrels, weasels, skunks, bears, otters, mink, raccoons, and beavers. Only cattle and beasts of burden were lacking, and horses, cattle, sheep, and pigs were imported.

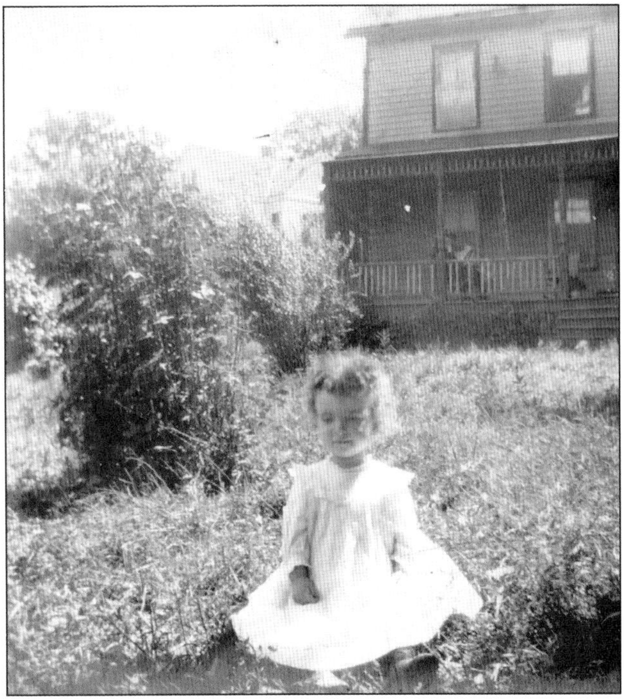

THE SPENCER FARM. The large Spencer farm was located at the center of Watchung, including land now occupied by the medical building and Valley Furniture Shop. Homes of the Spencer family were shown on both the 1850 and 1873 maps of the area. This photograph shows Margaret Walker (who lived nearby) in front of one of the Spencer homes.

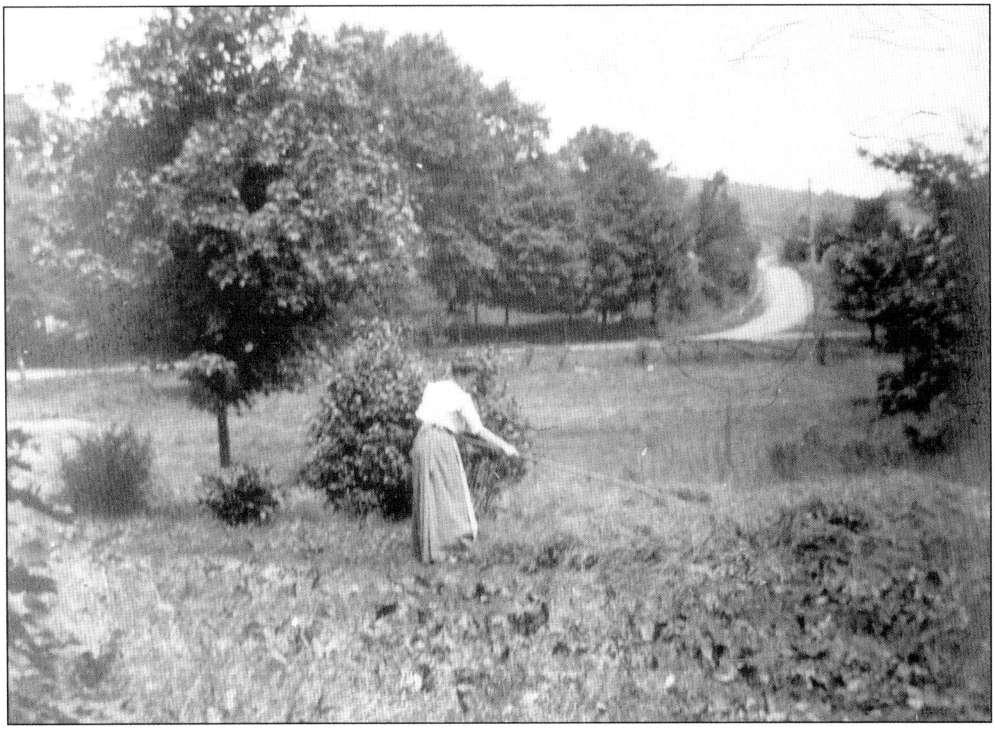

THE DUGWAY. Frances Rendall is shown *c.* 1908 near the Dugway, known today as Hillcrest Road. The Rendall family lived at 121 Valley Road. A family member, Kenneth Rendall, was captain of the Rutgers football team in 1917. While a senior, Kenneth played on the same team with Paul Robeson, a sophomore at the time who played left end.

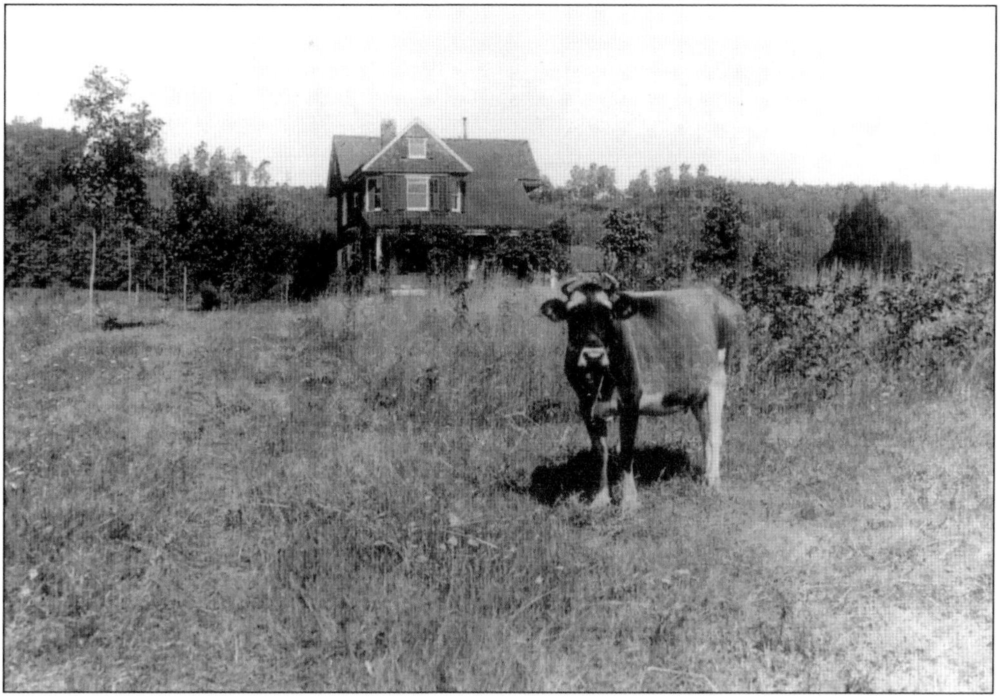

The Hughes Farm. Just west of the Spencer farm was the home of the Hughes family on land that overlooked Watchung Lake. Shown *c.* 1907, the house is located today on Hughes Lane. The signature of a wallpaper hanger was dated 1899, but the actual building date is unknown.

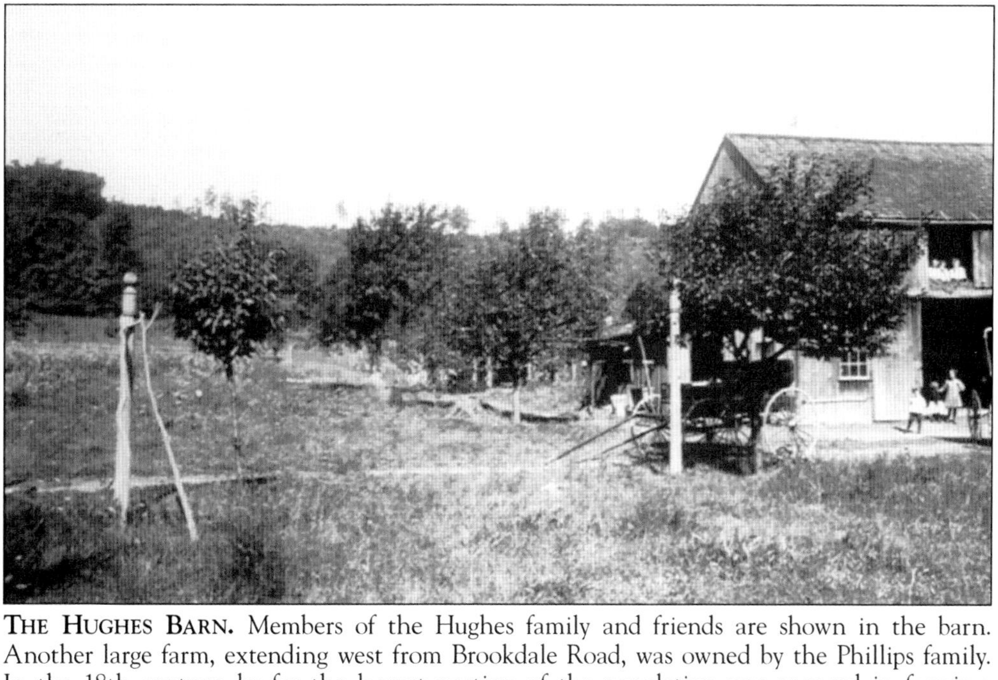

The Hughes Barn. Members of the Hughes family and friends are shown in the barn. Another large farm, extending west from Brookdale Road, was owned by the Phillips family. In the 18th century, by far the largest portion of the population was engaged in farming. The average farmer raised a great variety of crops, most of which were consumed within his own family.

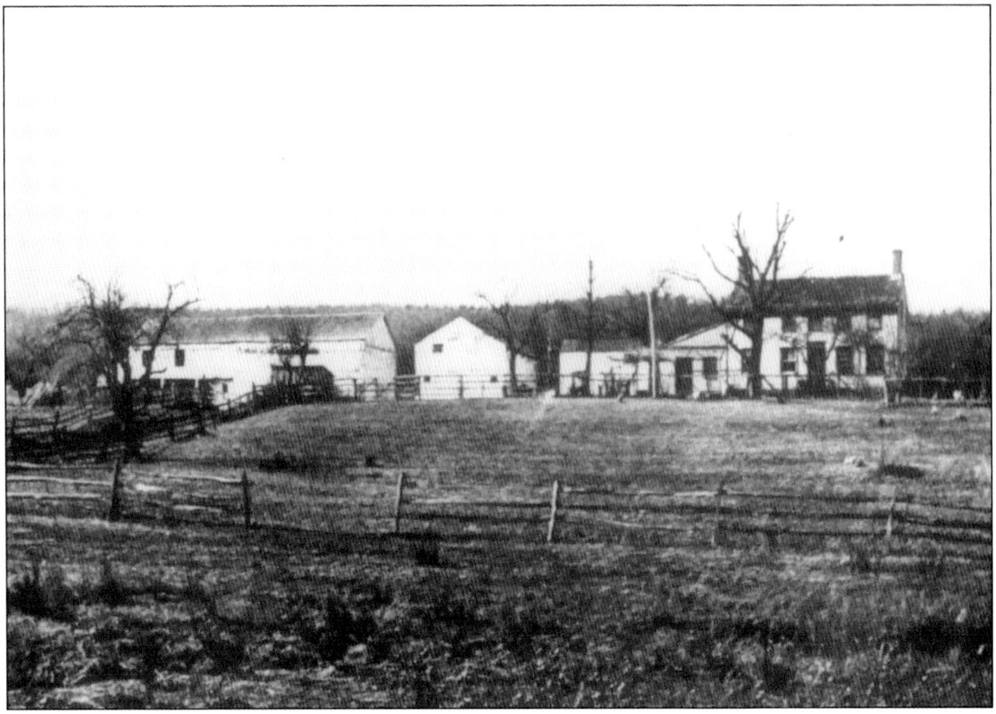

THE ACKOR FARM. The Ackor farm was a large tract on the north side of Mountain Boulevard, which appears on the 1873 Beers map. The 1830 census showed that Phillip Ackor, born *c.* 1771, owned the farm at that time. Along the valley, farming was the chief occupation, with farms averaging between 60 and 80 acres. This land was later to become a golf course as part of Twin Brooks Country Club.

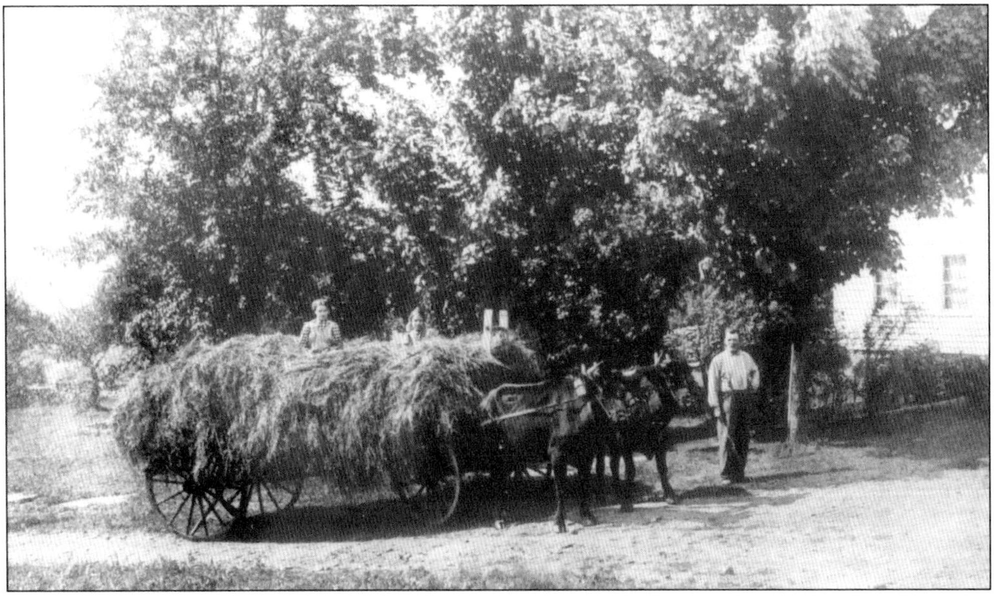

HAY WAGONS. These hay wagons are shown on the Ackor farm in the late 1800s. Oxen were used rather than horses because of the rough terrain. Horse carts were not used until the 1880s. Farmers transported their products to Plainfield on horseback, in crude carts, and on foot.

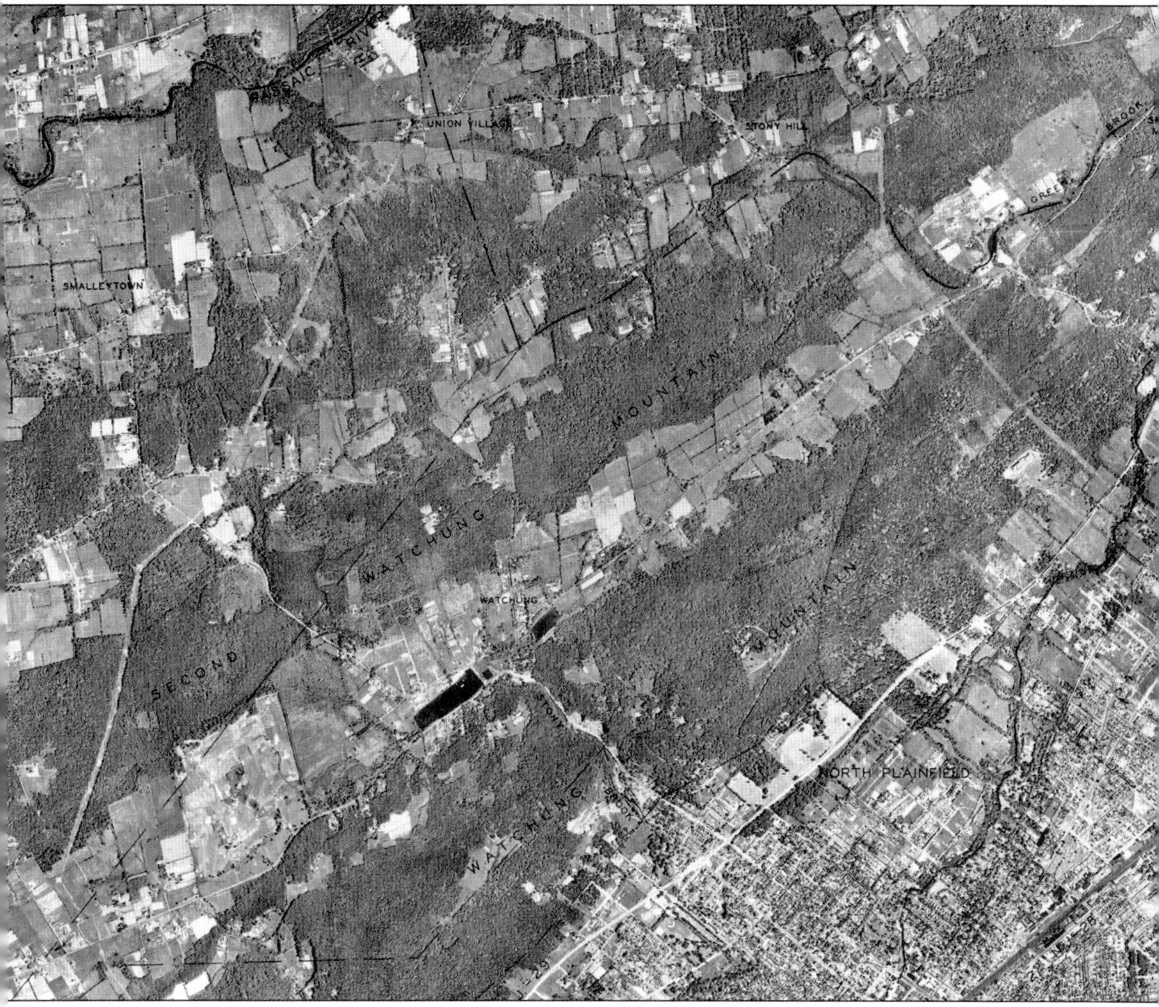

An Aerial Map of Watchung. This aerial photomap of Watchung was taken in the early 1930s. The dark rectangular spot in the middle of the map is Watchung Lake. The large farms along Valley Road to the east and Mountain Boulevard to the west are visible on a diagonal across the map. Little development had taken place at that time on the First and Second Mountains, which run parallel to the valley.

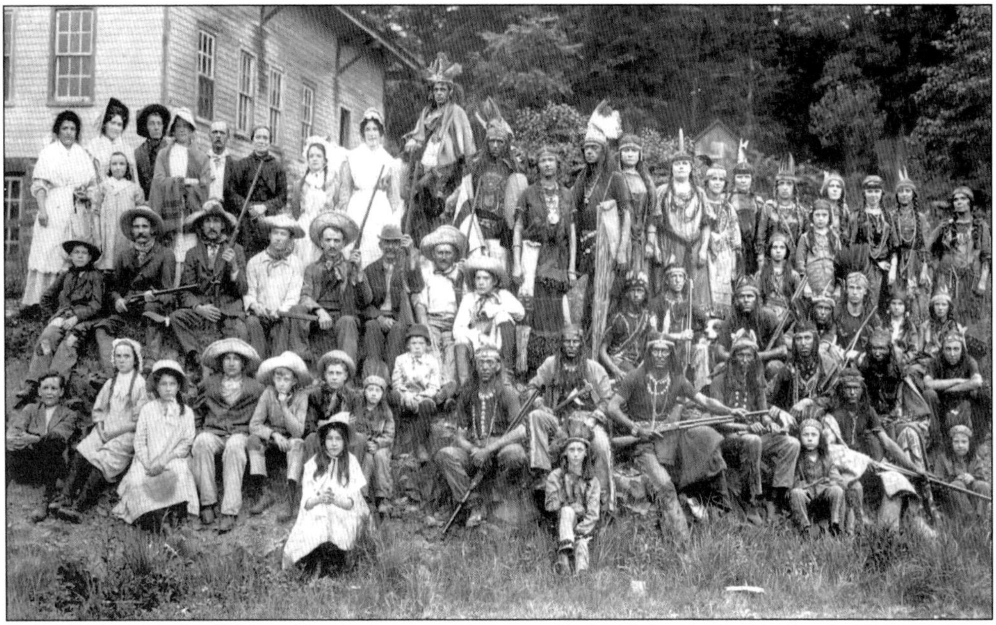

THE 1914 CAST OF THE PAGEANT. The *Indian Legend of Watchung* was written by William de La R. Anderson and first presented by townspeople in 1911. The performances, given by more than 100 persons, were staged among the tall trees along Stony Brook and Wetumpka Falls, a natural amphitheater. The pageant included two original songs, "Wetumpka," with words and music by Charles E. Spier, and the "Settler's Song," with words by Anderson and Spier and music by Spier.

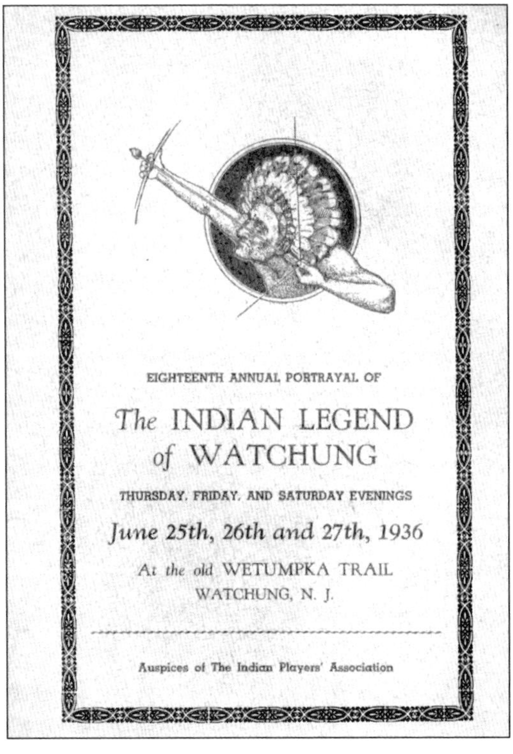

EIGHTEENTH ANNUAL PORTRAYAL OF

The INDIAN LEGEND of WATCHUNG

THURSDAY, FRIDAY, AND SATURDAY EVENINGS

June 25th, 26th and 27th, 1936

At the old WETUMPKA TRAIL
WATCHUNG, N. J.

Auspices of The Indian Players' Association

THE 18TH PORTRAYAL. Between 1911 and 1936, the *Indian Legend of Watchung* was portrayed by townspeople 18 times. After the 1936 production, the pageant was not portrayed again until 1964 during the New Jersey tercentenary celebration. The legend states that a band of settlers set camp one evening on the banks of a stream that "boils through the gap in the first ridge."

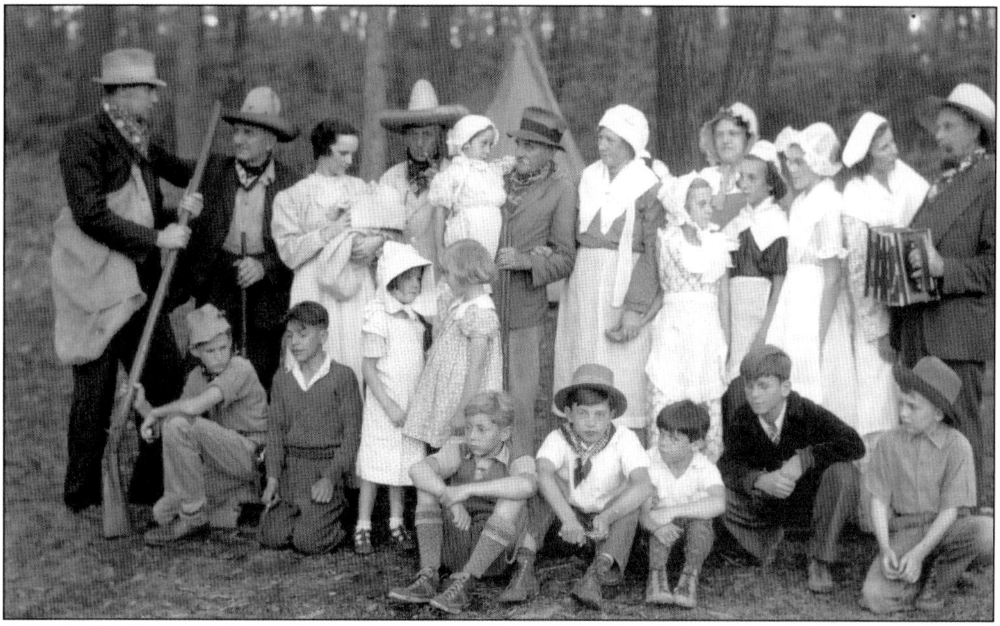

THE 1936 *INDIAN LEGEND OF WATCHUNG* PAGEANT. Settlers from the 1936 production included, from left to right, the following: (front row) David Miles, Salvatore Grievo, Barbara Adams, Barbara Barrett, Jerry Loizeaux, Dale Flocker, Leroy Nunn, Tony Santo, and Stuart Crockett; (back row) Melvin Dahlin, George Mobus, Mrs. Edward Snoden, Fred Ivamy, Jacquelyn Snoden in the arms of Lewis Snoden, Anna Nordheim, Alma Snoden, Mrs. Emil Perret, Nathalie Ault, Lorraine Perret, Jean Rutt, and Frank Winn.

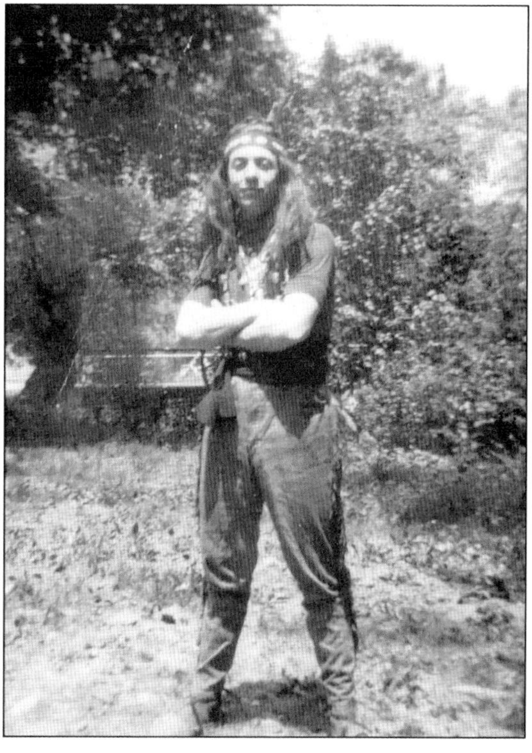

DEER PRONG. According to the legend, a Native American scout, Deer Prong, came upon the settlers' camp and was fired upon. After the settlers made a hasty departure, Deer Prong got a message to Chief One Feather, who devised a plan to entrap the settlers. The plan was successful, and Captain Michaelson, leader of the settlers, and Wetumpka, a Native American princess, were among the captives.

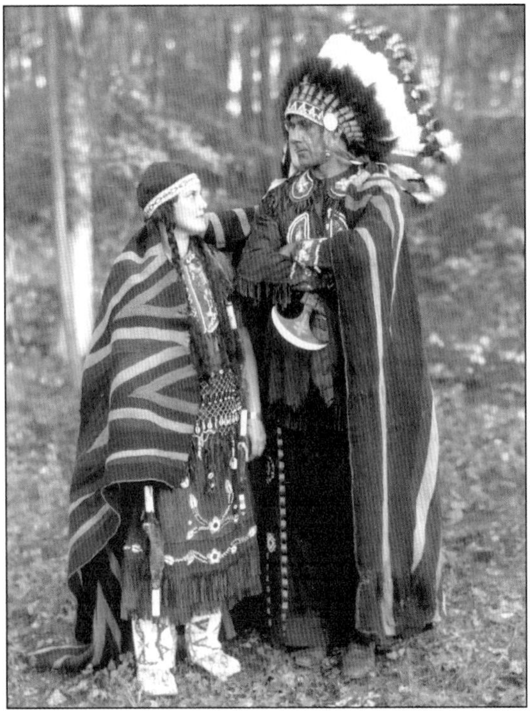

WETUMPKA AND CHIEF ONE FEATHER. Princess Wetumpka, played by Mrs. John Hartley in 1936, had previously saved the life of Chief One Feather, portrayed by Arthur Winn. She managed to set Captain Michaelson free and, disclosing herself to the Native Americans, pleaded for the release of the settlers.

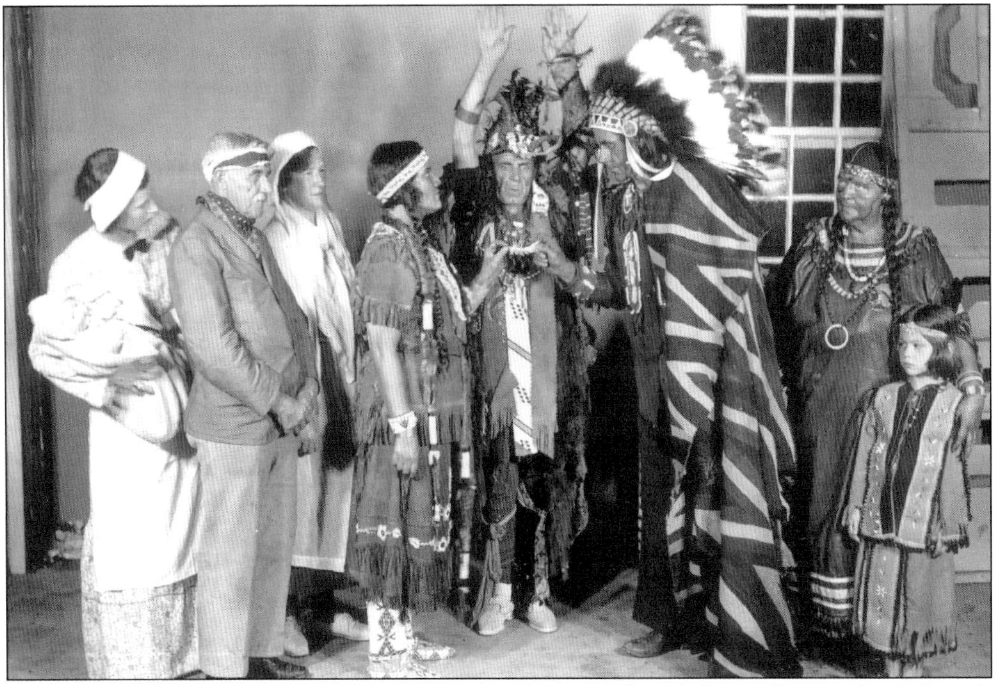

WEDLOCK. Chief One Feather assembled the grand council, and the lands were divided, with the settlers receiving the west and the Native Americans receiving the east. Then, as fate would have it, One Feather and Wetumpka joined their hands in wedlock. Shown in this scene are, from left to right, Jean Rutt, Lewis Snoden, Anna Nordheim, Mrs. John Hartley, Percy Van Ohl, Arthur Winn, unidentified, and Joan Hartley.

Two

BUSINESS AND INDUSTRY

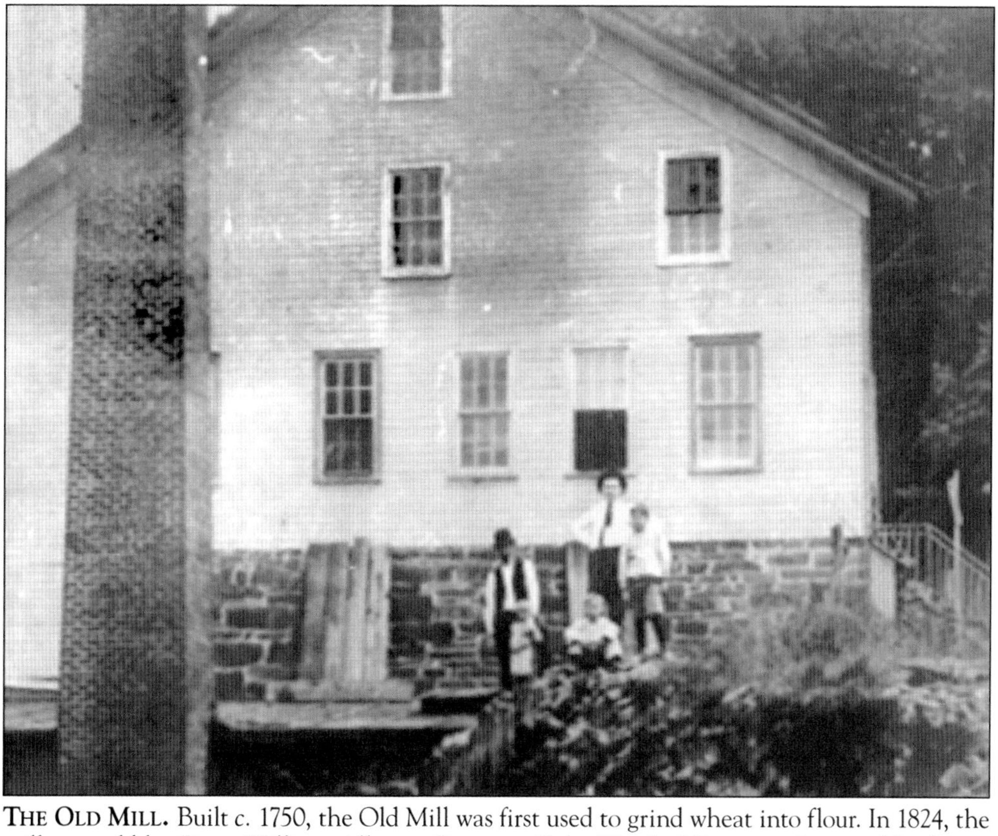

THE OLD MILL. Built *c.* 1750, the Old Mill was first used to grind wheat into flour. In 1824, the mill was sold by Capt. William Allen to Freeman Cole. The building was destroyed by fire in 1870 and rebuilt by then-owner Moses French. After 1910, the mill was home to the Watchung fire department.

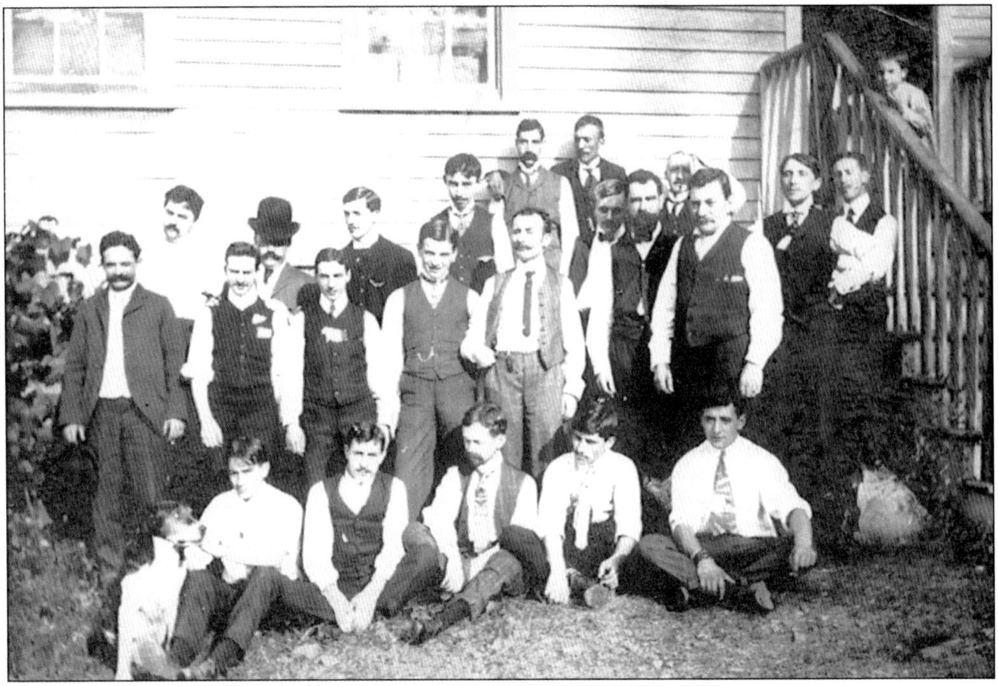

THE GLOVE FACTORY. Born in France, Hippolyte Texier bought the mill building *c.* 1890 and made gloves there until 1910. Texier, a couple of his sons, and employees of the plant are shown in front of the factory *c.* 1902. Texier is the man with a mustache standing behind the first man on the right seated on the ground.

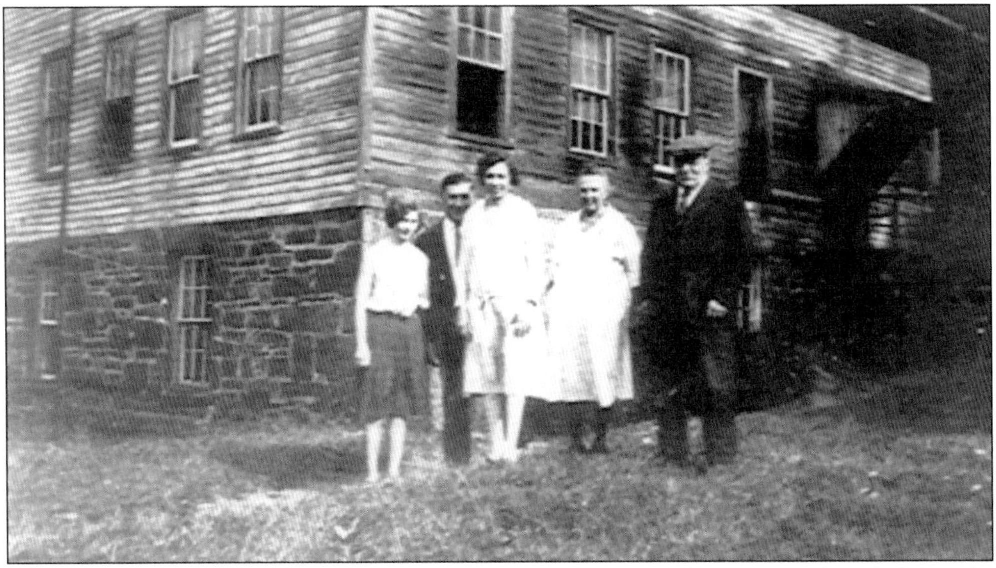

THE TEXIER FAMILY. This photograph shows, from left to right, two unidentified people, Hippolyte Texier's daughter, Leontine; his wife, Leontine; and Texier in front of the glove factory. At one time, Texier tanned and processed his own leathers in this building. By 1910, he started to buy the leather already processed and stopped using the plant. The Old Mill then became the site of dances, Halloween parties, and community dinners until 1929, when the borough hall was built on the site.

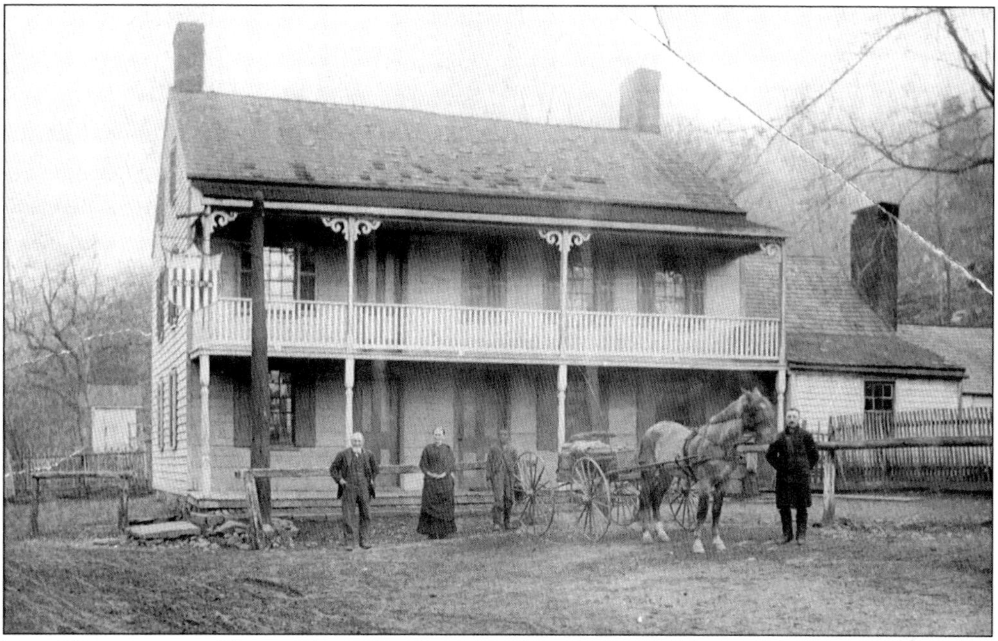

THE WASHINGTON HOUSE. In 1738, Hugo Maul owned a popular inn located on Somerset Street near Wetumpka Falls. By 1806, it was known as David Stewart's Tavern and, in 1848, it was Demler's Hotel, owned by George Demler. Later, it became the immensely popular Washington House until a fire in 1962 brought its long history to an end. Today, the Watchung Public Works facility is located on the site.

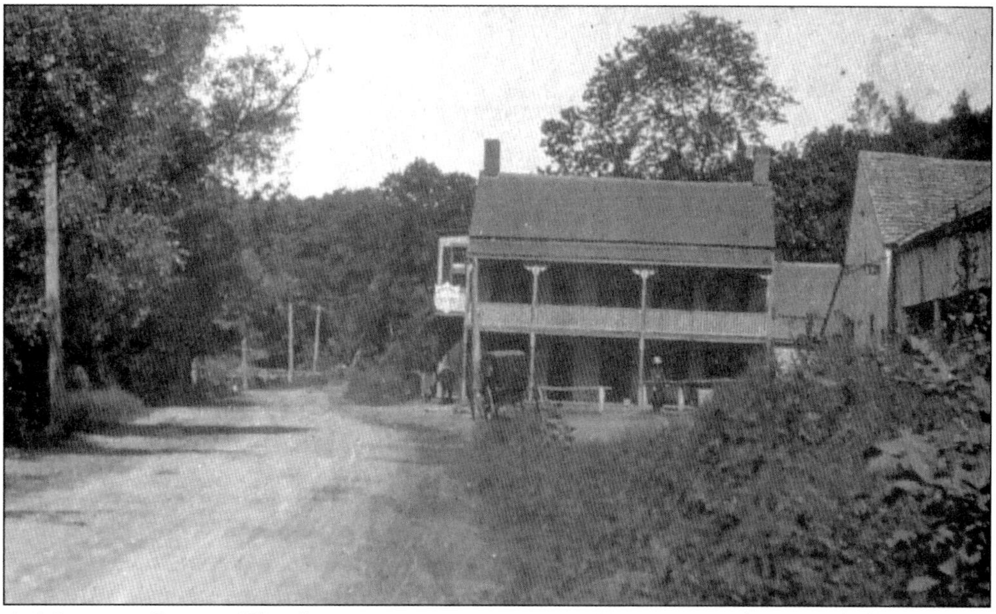

A MEETING PLACE. The first meeting to organize Warren Township was held at David Stewart's Tavern in 1806. The tavern was used as the official township meeting place until 1872, when Watchung became a part of North Plainfield Township. In 1910, a group of men gathered at the hotel decided that a fire company was sorely needed. At that meeting, they formed the Watchung Chemical Engine Company.

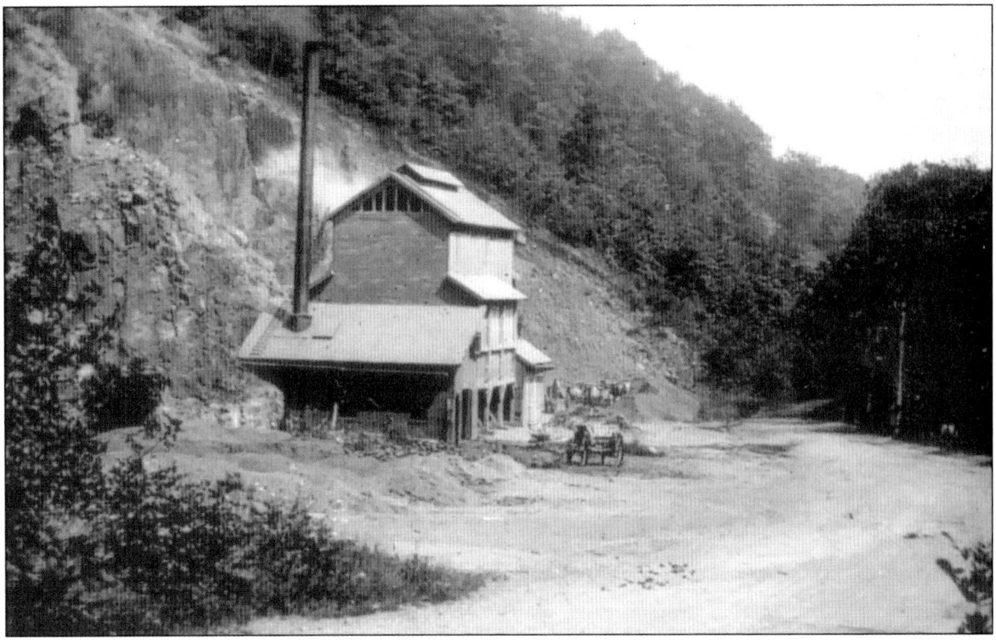

WILSON'S QUARRY. Work began in the winter of 1865–1866 at a traprock quarry located in the notch at Somerset Street. Quantities of rock and gravel were produced from an apparently unlimited source. J.Y. Wilson purchased the quarry c. 1885, and the traprock industry thrived under his supervision.

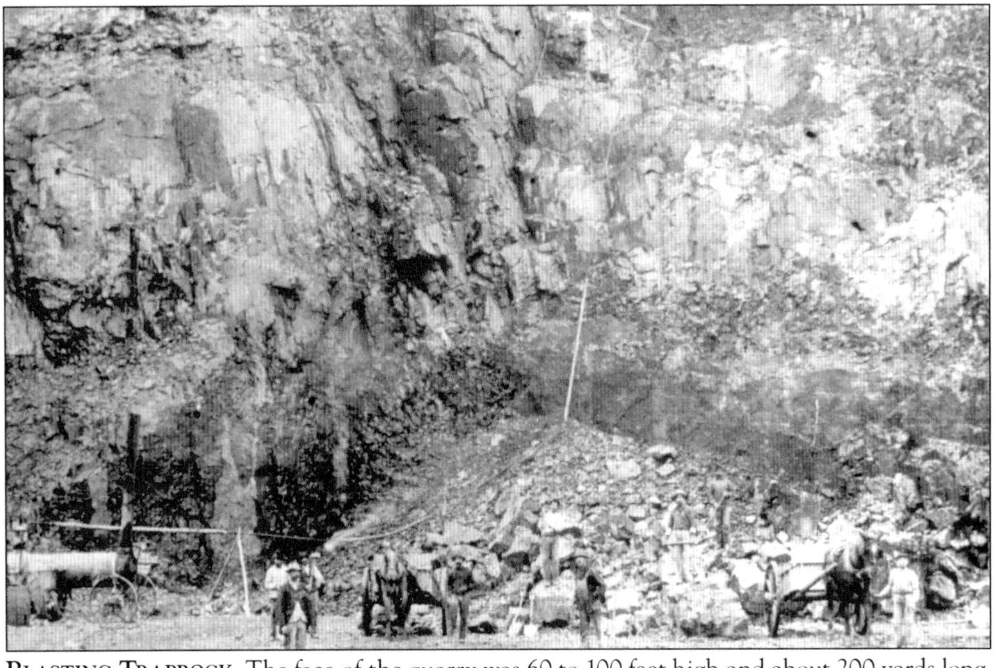

BLASTING TRAPROCK. The face of the quarry was 60 to 100 feet high and about 200 yards long. Traprock, or basalt, is volcanic in origin and is well-suited for use in road construction. The rock used to be blasted with dynamite. Travelers were stopped on both sides of the quarry, so that the blasted rock would not hit a passerby.

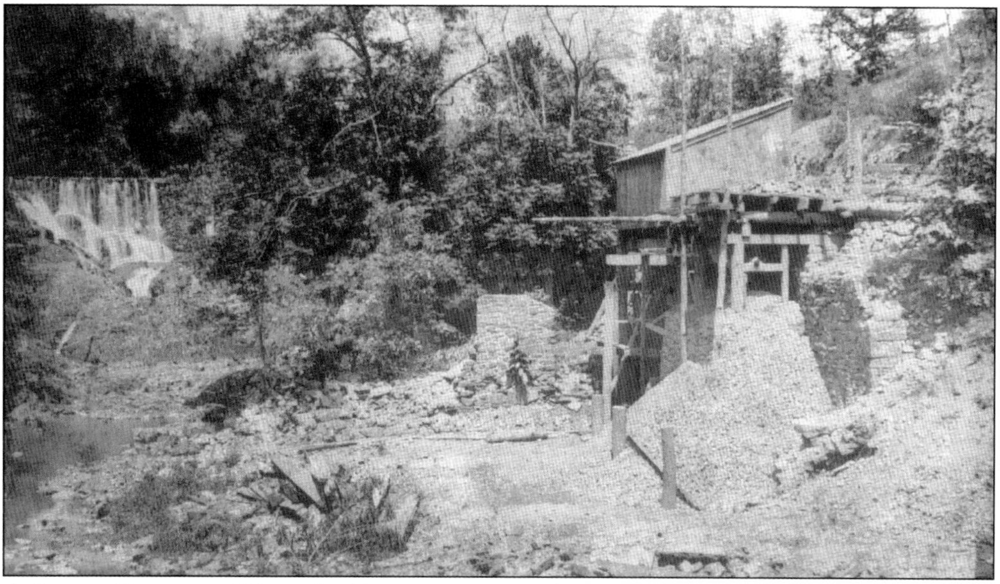

A STONE CRUSHER. When the blasting was over, the traprock was carted across the road in dump carts to this stone crusher, shown in the late 1800s. Wilson dammed up Stony Brook, creating Wetumpka Falls (left), which supplied the power for the crusher. The quarry, later known as Somerset Trap Rock, operated until the 1950s. The site is now the home of the Watchung Police Department headquarters, dedicated in 1999.

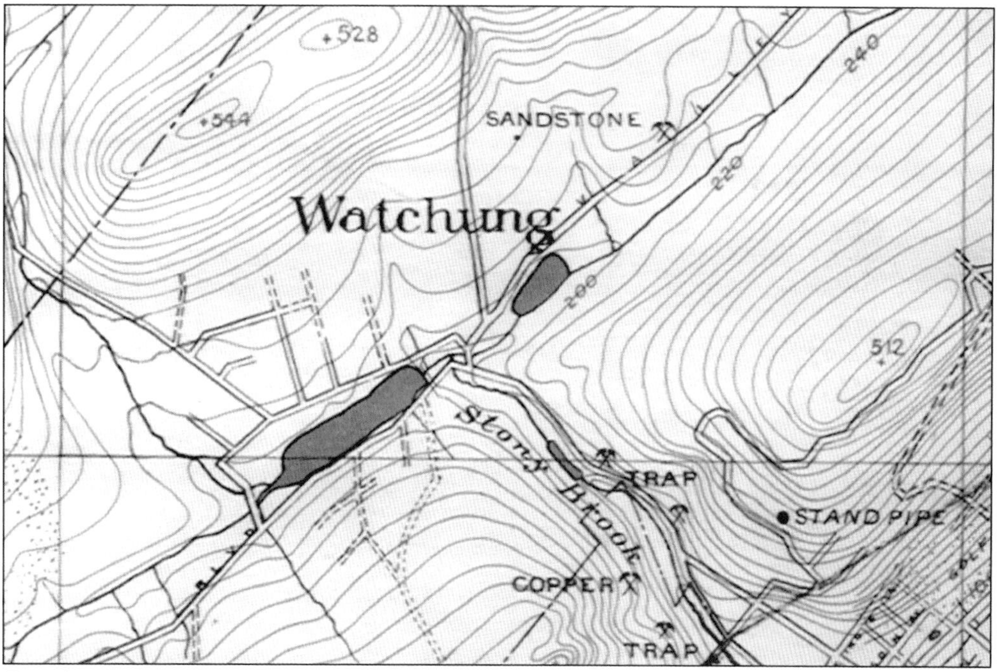

THE COPPER MINES. Extensive explorations were made on both sides of Stony Brook gorge in the early 1800s, and a copper mine was in operation in 1866. Workings on the east side were those of the Green Valley Copper Company, and the New Jersey Copper Mining Company operated mines on the west side of the gap. The longest tunnels on each side were reported to be 400 feet.

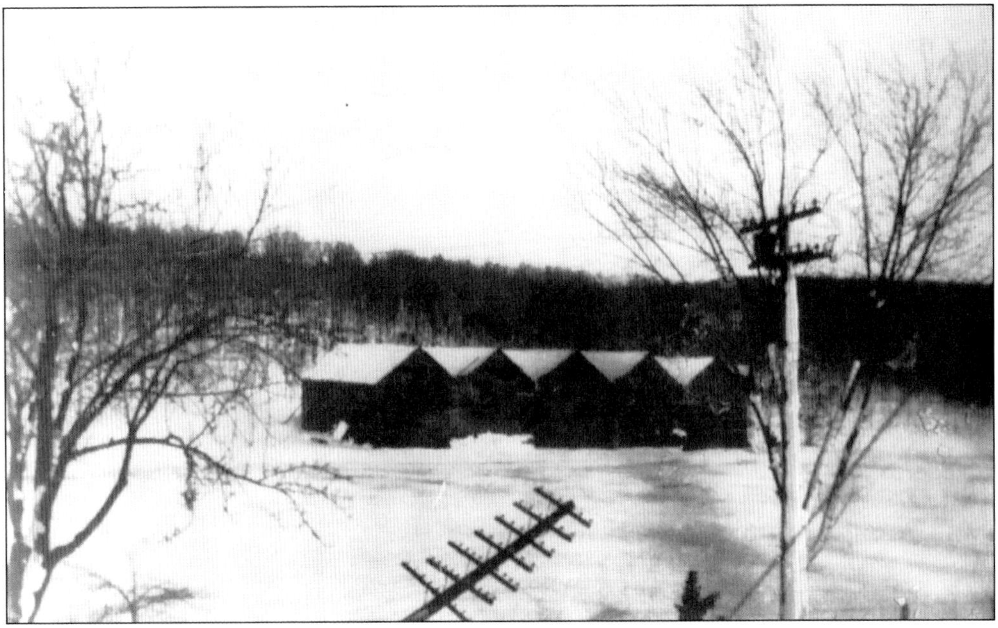

ICE HARVESTING ON WILSON'S POND. In addition to running a quarry, John Wilson started the Natural Ice Company c. 1880 on his pond, known today as Best Lake. Wilson dug out the pond, raised Valley Road for better flooding of the pond site, and built an ice business complete with five icehouses, shown here in 1913. His was the first ice business to serve the area, including the Netherwood Hotel in Plainfield.

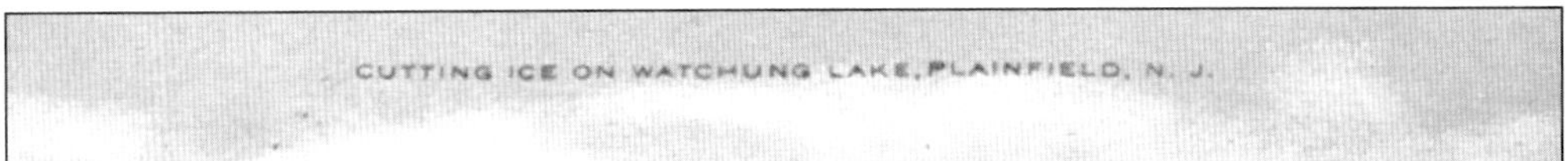

ICE HARVESTING ON WATCHUNG LAKE. The Natural Ice Company and, later, the Plainfield Ice & Supply Company, owned by Andrew Wilson and William H. Titus, operated on Watchung Lake. The ice, able to support a horse team, was cut into cakes that weighed between 250 and 300 pounds. As the slippery chunks of ice were floated to the icehouse, children would jump from one chunk of ice to another in a game called "tickley bender."

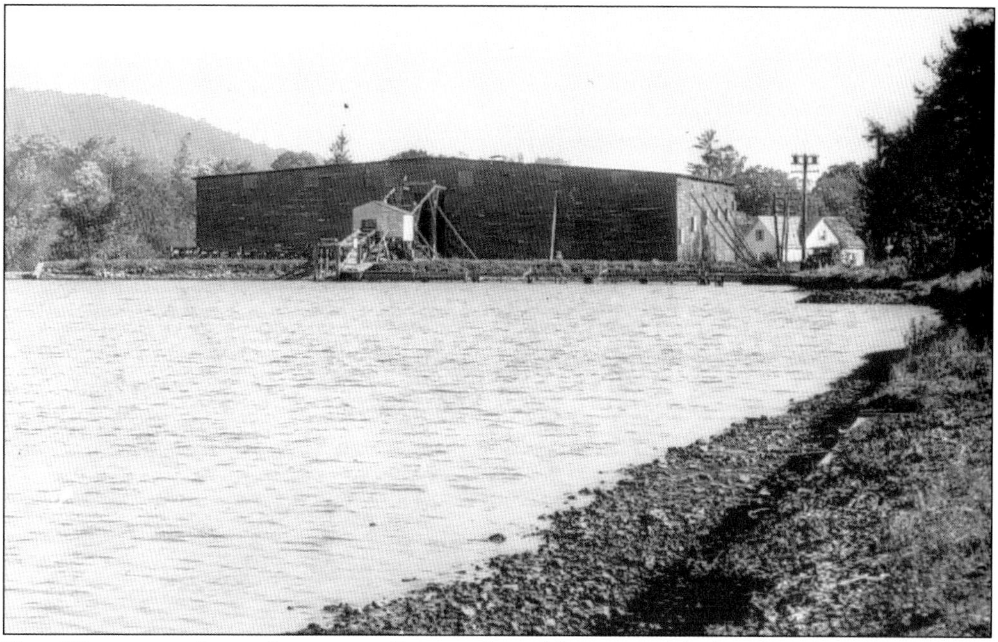

THE WATCHUNG LAKE ICEHOUSE. During the cold winters, blocks of ice were cut in huge quantities and stored in the wooden icehouse with sawdust and hay to keep the air from the ice. A channel was kept open so chunks of ice could be floated to the icehouse. Pike poles, some 16 feet long, were used to guide and push the cakes.

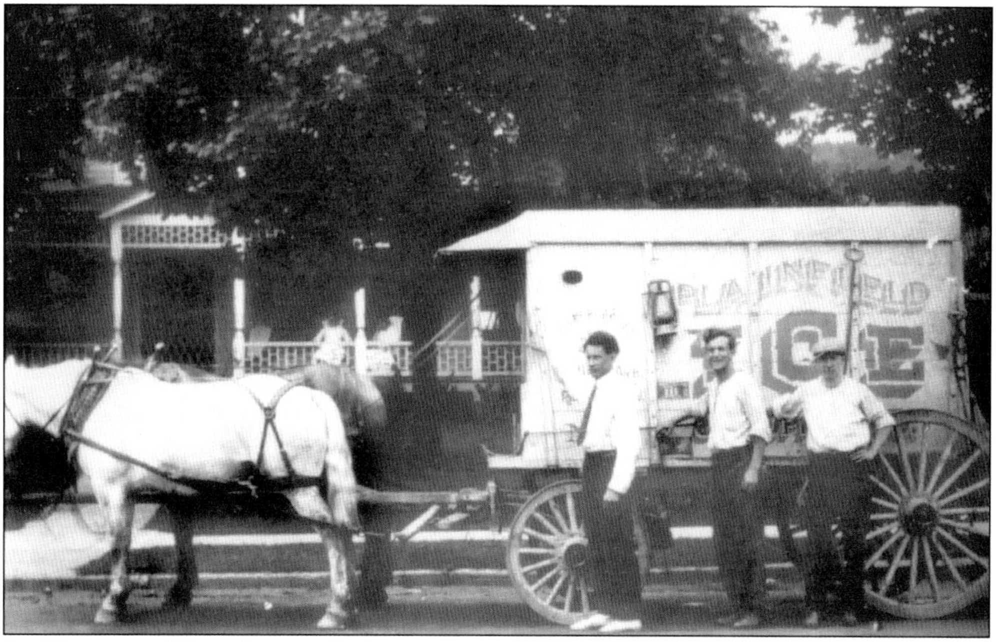

ICE DELIVERY. This photograph shows an ice delivery to Front Street in Plainfield. Ice was sold to restaurants in New York City and Philadelphia, as well as to taverns and restaurants throughout central New Jersey. The Plainfield Ice & Supply Company had average daily sales of approximately two tons of ice. The person on the left is Frank Decker (a cousin of Anna L. Titus), who owned the house at 990 Somerset Street.

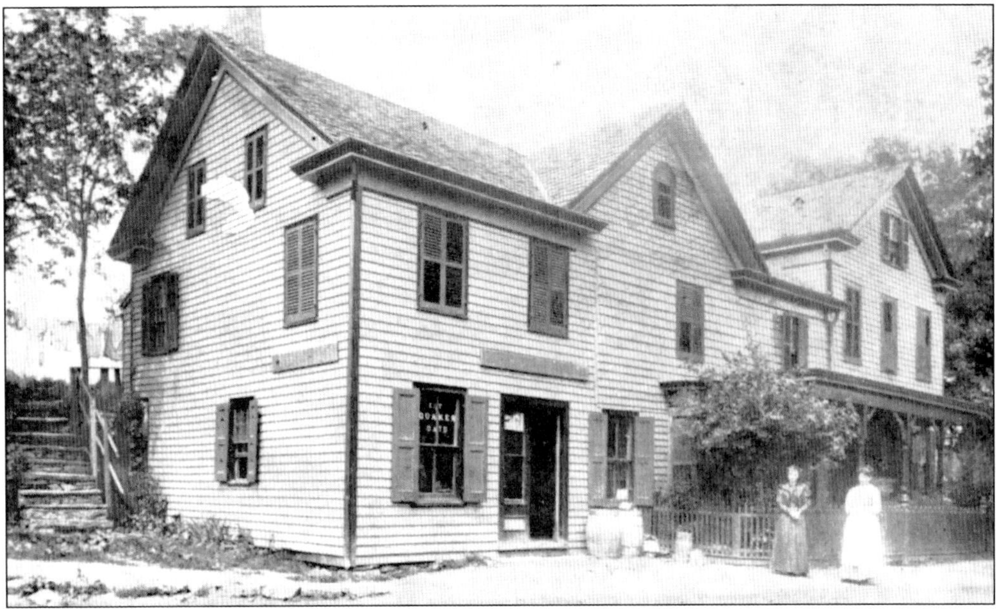

French's General Store. Shown on the 1850 map as one of the few businesses in the area, the general store was originally owned by Moses H. French. Purchased by William H. Titus and Frank Decker in the early 1900s, it became known as the "Honeymoon Apartments," where many early residents started out their married lives. This building, located facing Somerset Street just below the Watchung Rescue Squad building, was torn down to make way for the Watchung traffic circle.

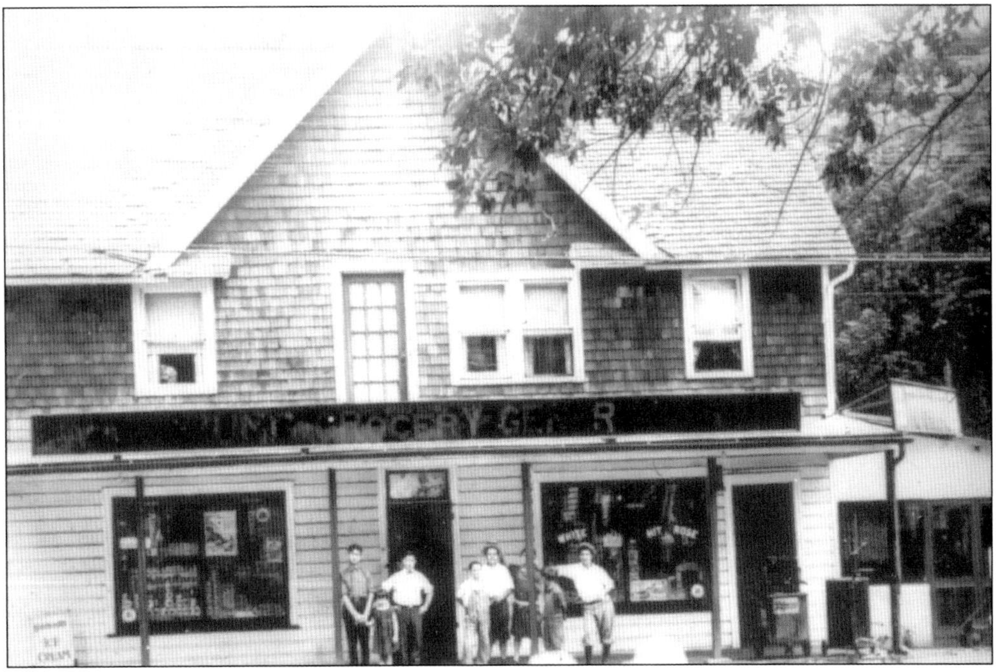

The Grocery Store. Directly across the street from the general store was the Watchung Grocery Store, owned by the Grobois Brothers. This was one of the businesses that frequently changed hands.

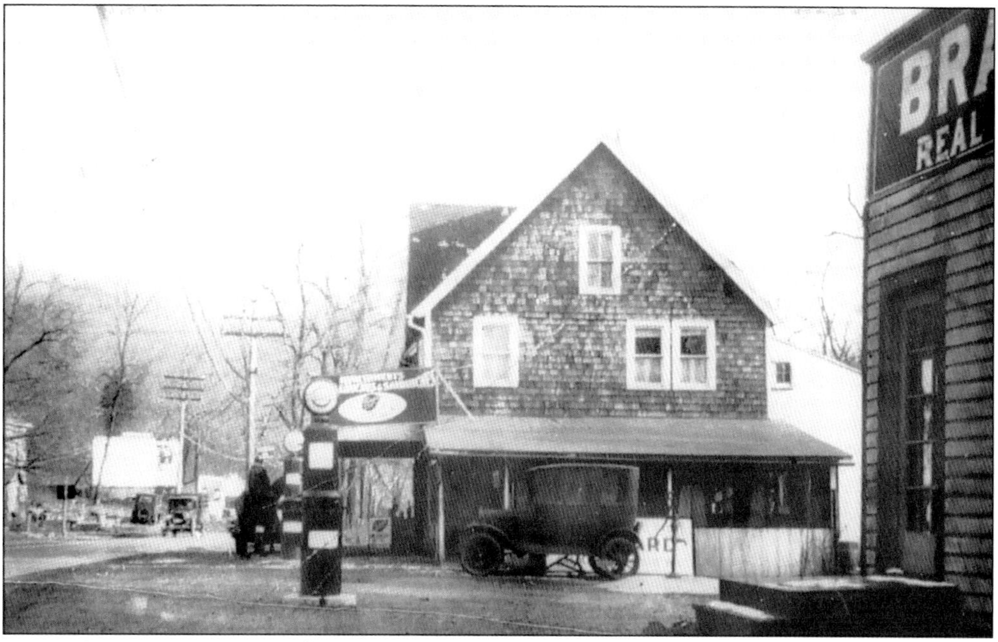

UPPER SOMERSET STREET. This is what Somerset Street looked like in a view facing south from Watchung Center *c.* 1949. On the far left is a house dating from 1750, while a real estate office is on the far right. In between is a gas station and the grocery store offering "Refreshments, Lunches and Sandwiches." Note also the man on horseback in front of one of the pumps.

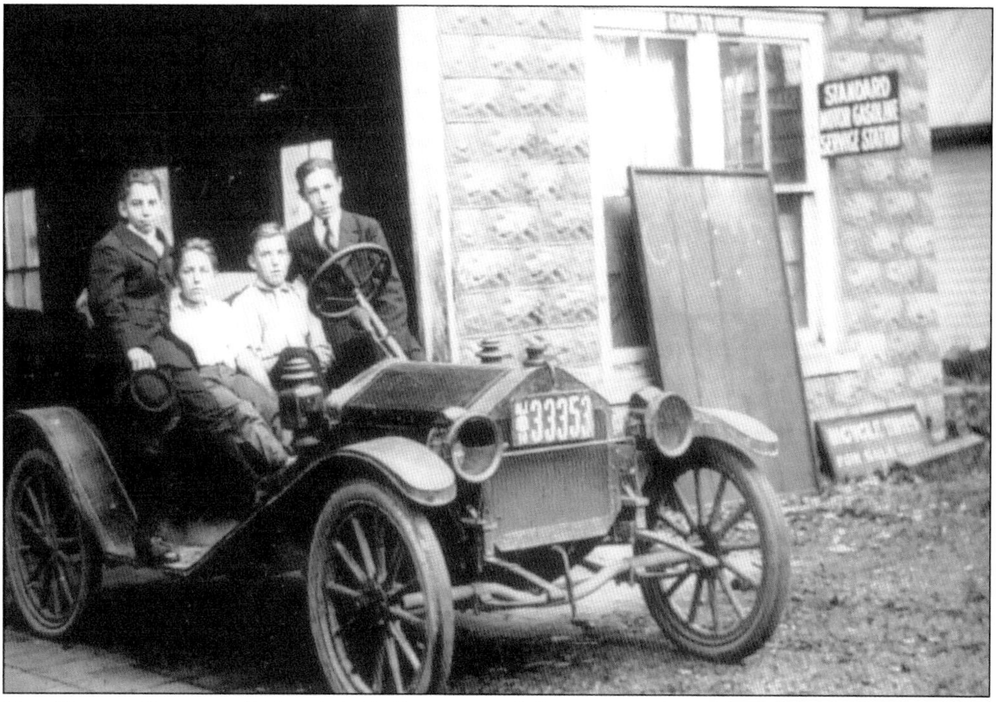

THE BELLIS GARAGE. Richard L. Bellis operated this garage, located at 688 Somerset Street. He also served as a councilman and, in 1926, was appointed police chief, a position comparable to today's police commissioner.

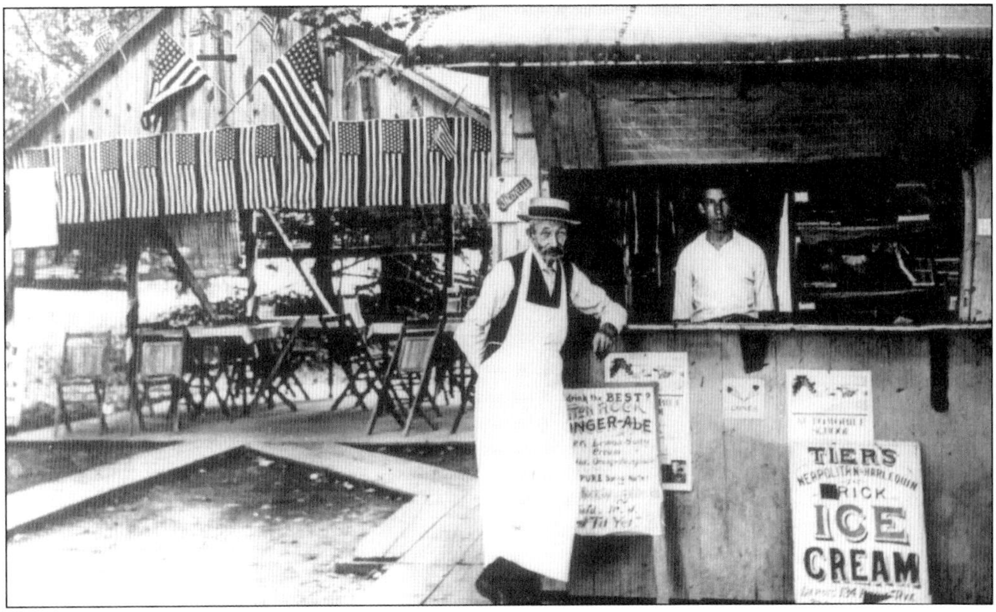

MILES STAND. This luncheonette, owned by Frank Miles (left), was located at the northeast corner of Somerset Street and Johnston Drive. People going to or from the Plainfields via the trolley car that operated on Somerset Street would stop at Miles Stand for ice cream or a soft drink while waiting for the trolley or to rest before walking up the hill to Watchung Center.

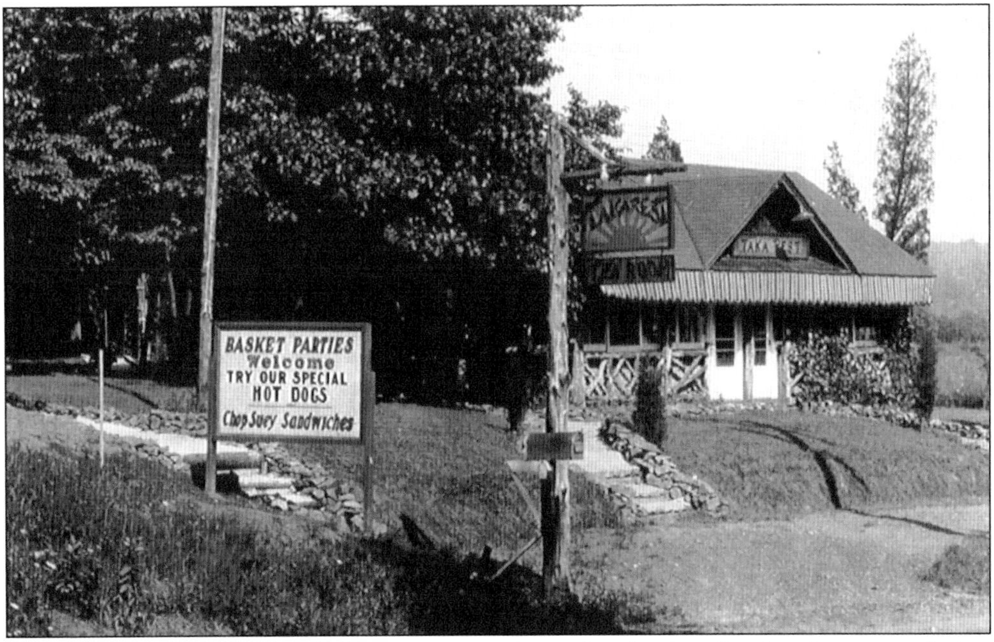

THE TAK-A-REST TEA ROOM. This tearoom was located on Stirling Road at the corner of what was then a driveway and is now Dogwood Lane. Today, the building is a private home. Featuring hot dogs and chop suey, the tearoom was operated by two sisters and was popular with women.

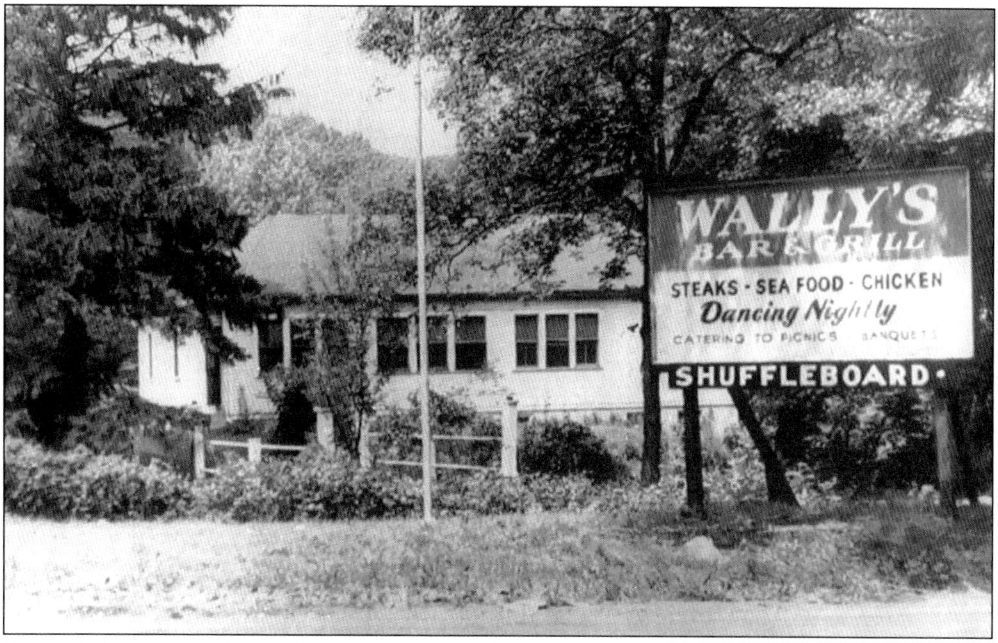

WALLY'S BAR AND GRILL. This restaurant and picnic grove at 154 Bonnie Burn Road has had many owners over the years. In the 1800s, it was a stopover for picnics and lunch, a favorite spot of wealthy New Yorkers who summered here. Early on, it was known as Winter Grove; later, it was known as Wally's, owned by Wally Heinzer, and then Stony Brook Inn. Today, it is the Colorado Café.

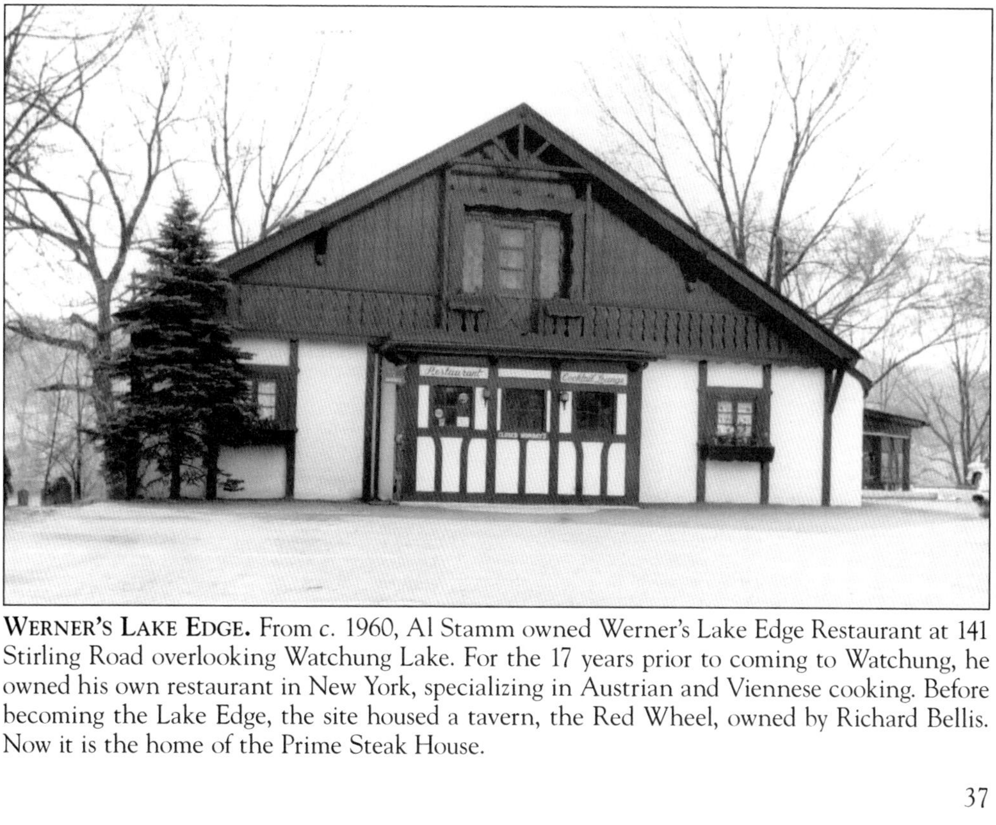

WERNER'S LAKE EDGE. From *c.* 1960, Al Stamm owned Werner's Lake Edge Restaurant at 141 Stirling Road overlooking Watchung Lake. For the 17 years prior to coming to Watchung, he owned his own restaurant in New York, specializing in Austrian and Viennese cooking. Before becoming the Lake Edge, the site housed a tavern, the Red Wheel, owned by Richard Bellis. Now it is the home of the Prime Steak House.

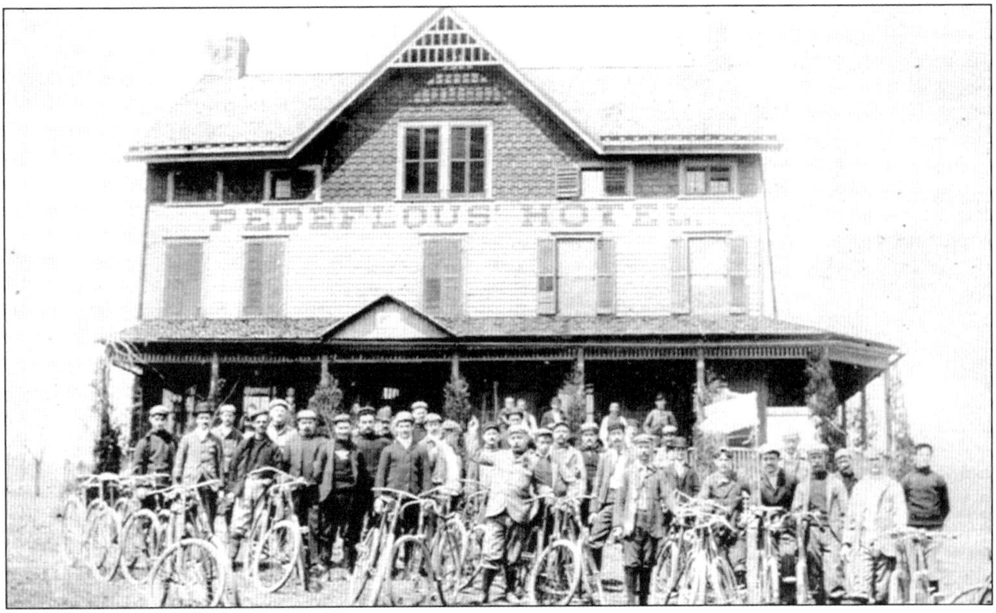

THE PEDEFLOUS HOTEL AND RESTAURANT. In 1888, Henry Pedeflous, a chef at a New York hotel, bought this building and turned it into a hotel and restaurant. Pedeflous had a mushroom farm, and his restaurant was famous for its steak and mushroom dinners. This photograph, taken in 1910, shows members of a cycling club stopping at the restaurant. Celebrities, including Laurel and Hardy, Mae West, and boxer Jack Dempsey, also used to stop at the hotel.

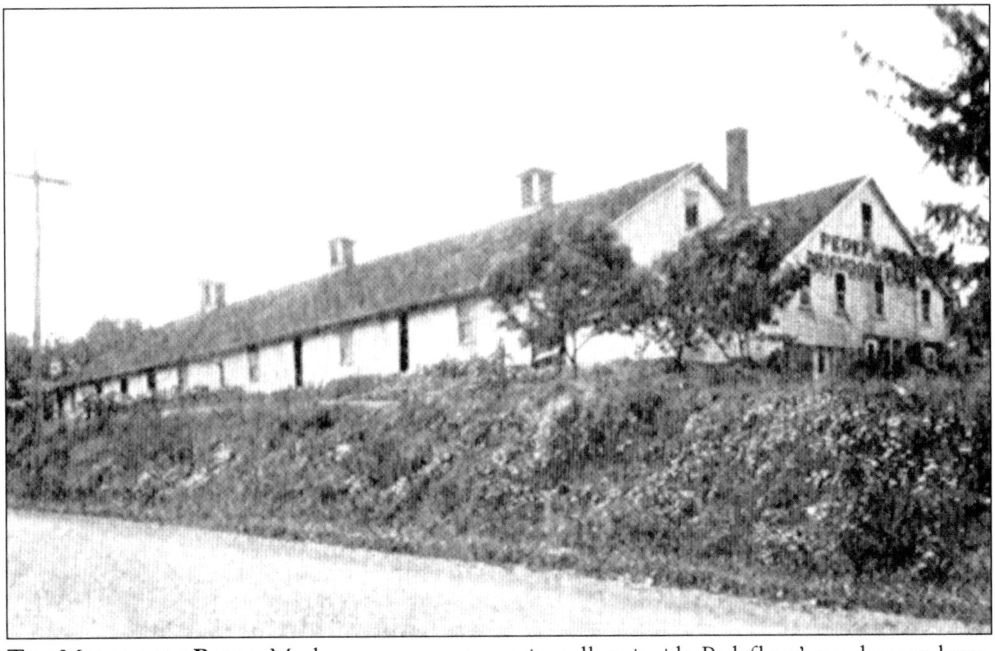

THE MUSHROOM BARN. Mushrooms were grown in cellars inside Pedeflous's mushroom barn, where the air was very humid. The mushroom barn ran parallel to Mountain Boulevard, just west of the restaurant. A 1930s brochure for the Pedeflous Mushroom Farm commented about the mushroom: "Man hath found true nourishment for body and mind—sweet repose and tranquility—in these luscious, captivating, quick-growing edibles."

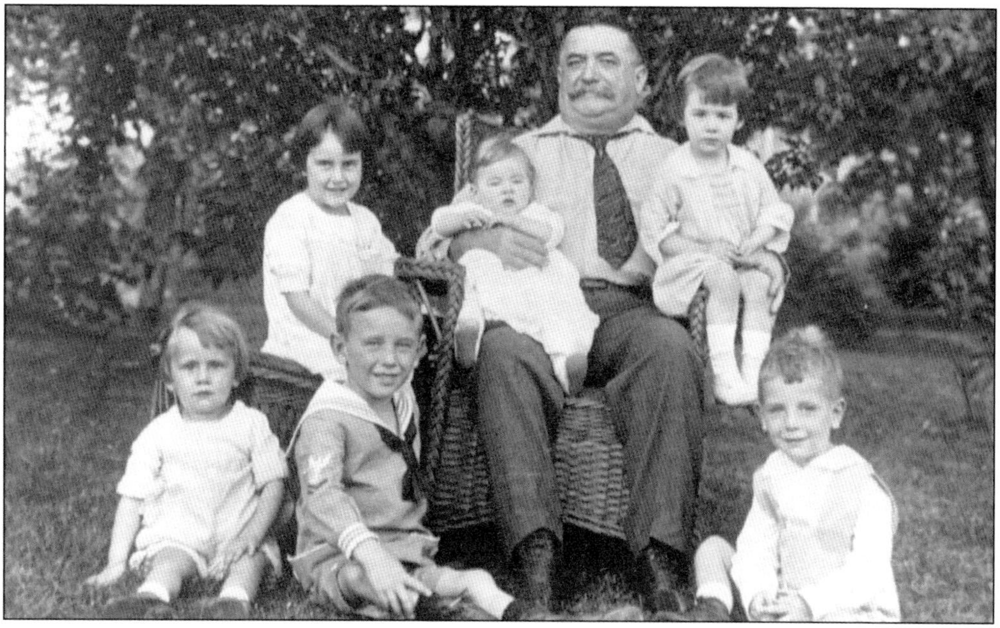

THE PEDEFLOUS FAMILY. Shown in the early 1900s is Henry Pedeflous with his grandchildren: Marie Louise, Jean, and Sally Pedeflous; John and Anna Vossler; and Eddie White. Henry had two daughters and a son, John, who took over the business when his parents died.

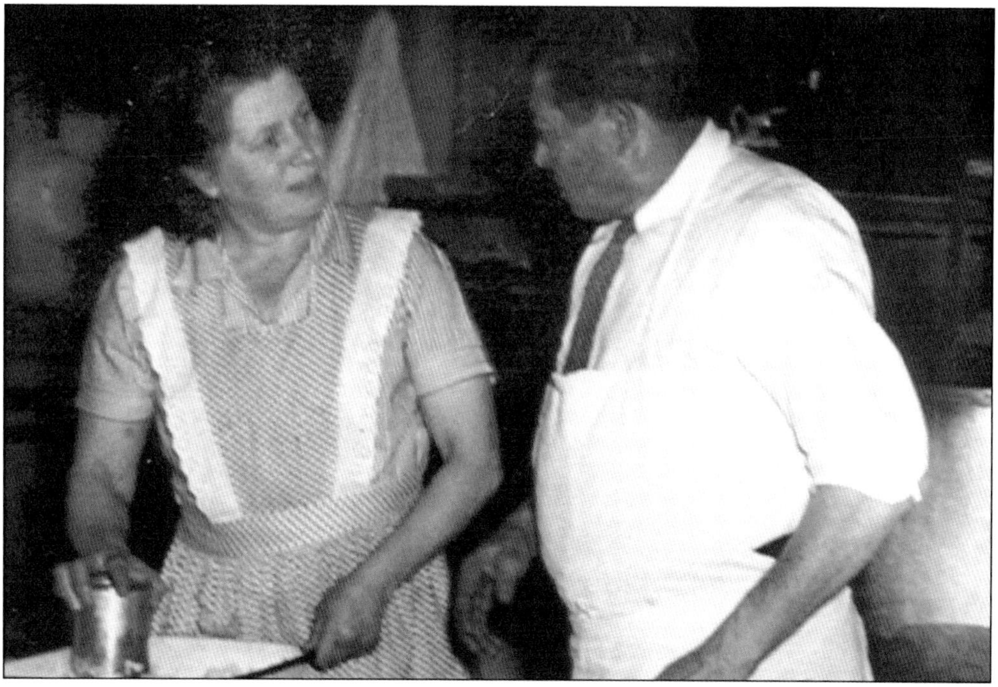

THE GHIDELLAS. Peter and Josephine Ghidella are shown in the late 1930s in the Pedeflous kitchen, making hashed browns. In the early 1930s, Ghidella bought the restaurant from Sadie Pedeflous, widow of John Pedeflous, and owned it until 1948. In 1970, the restaurant was bought by the Hagan family. Jack O'Connor became the general manager, and, as his family was known for a butcher shop they had in Plainfield, the restaurant was named O'Connor's.

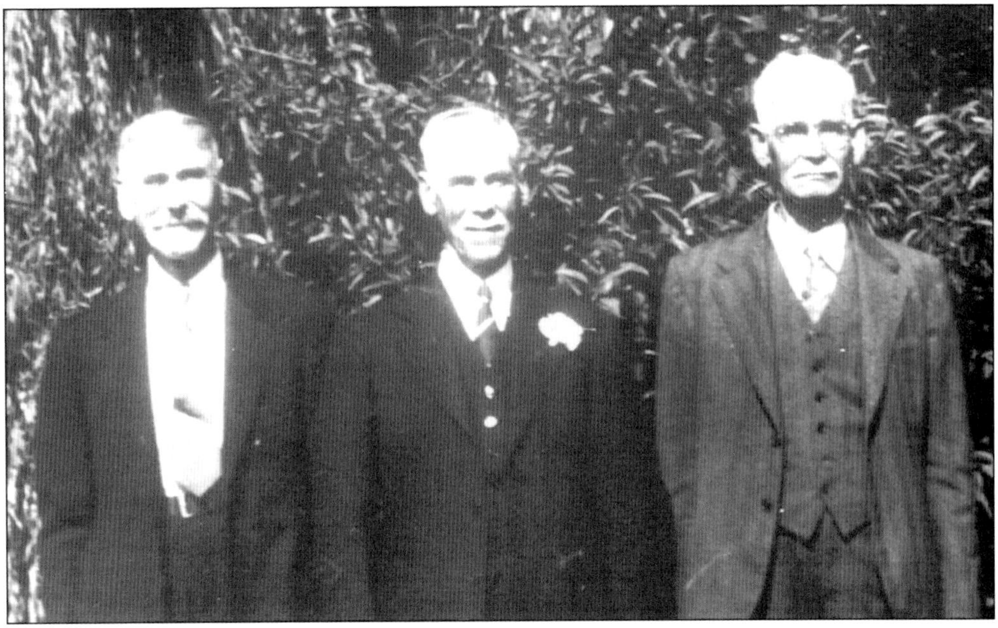

The Winans Brothers. George, Alfred, and Silas Winans are shown here in 1940. Their father, Isaac, bought property at the top of what is now Winans Lane c. 1859. Silas, who went into the kindling wood business with John Mobus, had a sawmill there. In January 1907, Mobus bought Winans's share of the business, and a 1908 map shows John Mobus' Kindling Wood Factory on Mountain Boulevard across from Watchung Lake.

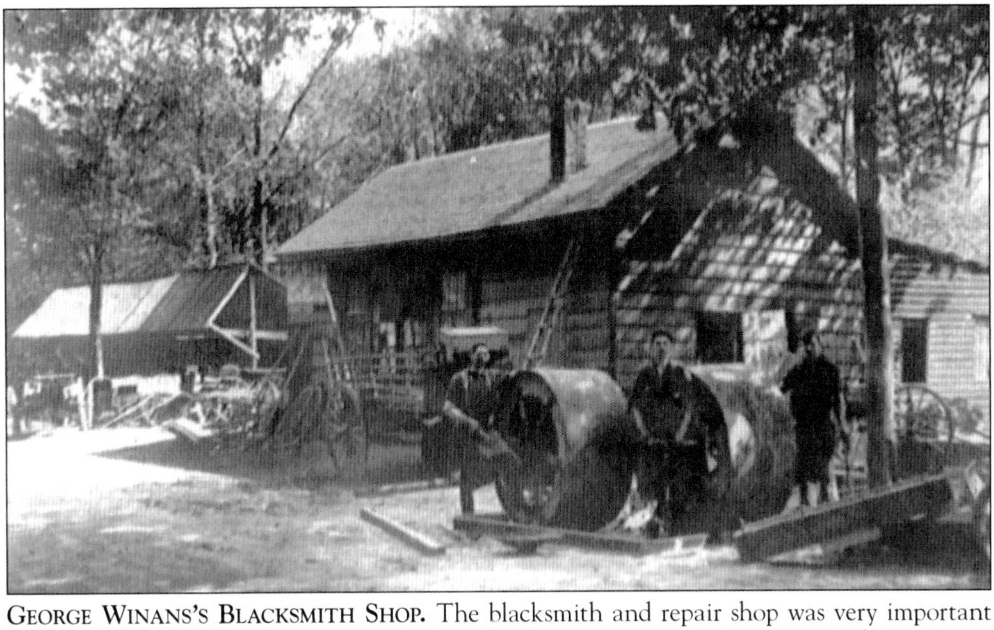

George Winans's Blacksmith Shop. The blacksmith and repair shop was very important to early communities. One such shop, operated by George Winans c. 1882, stood near Stony Brook at the junction of Somerset Street and Watchung Avenue. Winans supplied farmers with various farm implements and tools, all made in his shop. A flood destroyed Winans's blacksmith shop c. 1885. Later, Winans and his partners had a larger shop near Somerset Street and Johnston Drive.

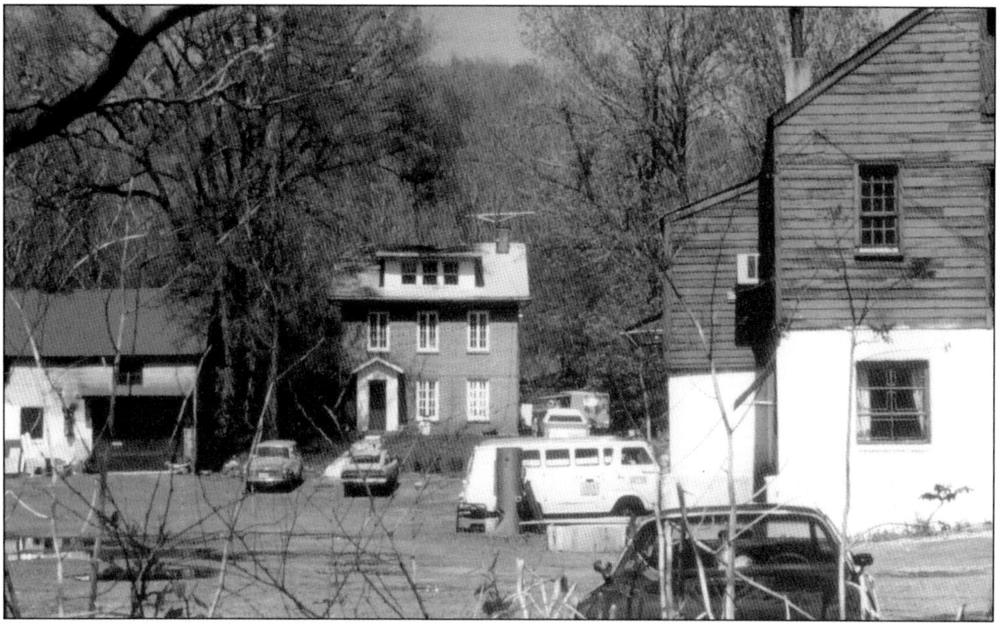

The Hat Factory. Brook Mill, the hatter's fur-manufacturing establishment of Harper, Hollingsworth, and Darby established in 1869, was situated at 33 Bonnie Burn Road near Scotch Plains. The fur was brought from New York to the mill where hats were fashioned and then shipped back to the city for sale. The site dates back to 1724 as a gristmill of Elijah Stites. It also served as a powder mill, as housing for troops in the Revolutionary War, and as a sawmill and a flour mill before becoming a fur mill.

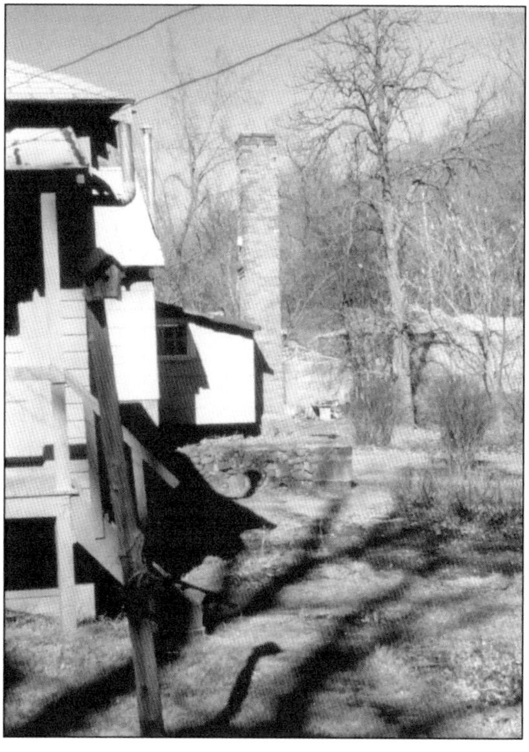

Mooney's Millwright Shop. This shop, located on New Providence Road, dates back to the mid-1800s and is shown on the 1873 map of Washingtonville. John Mooney, a blacksmith by trade, used knowledge learned in Ireland. His son, Charles Mooney, was also a millwright. The power to drive the millwright equipment was provided by a steam engine that was housed in a lean-to on the south side of the stream.

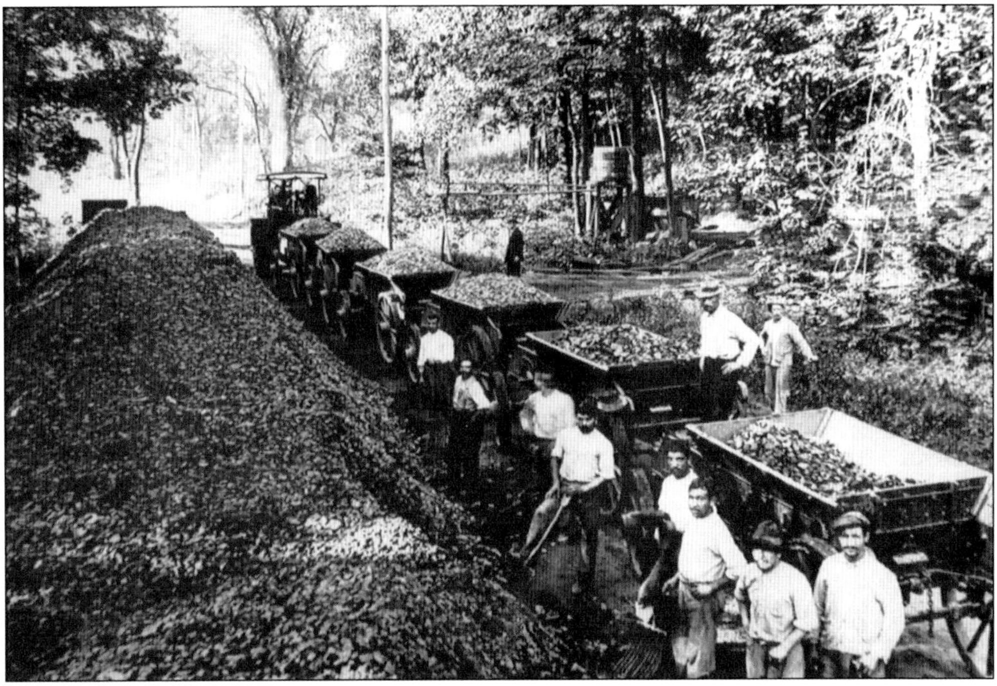

FANWOOD CRUSHED STONE. This 1910 photograph shows men loading stones at the Fanwood Crushed Stone Company. All the stone from the quarry is traprock. It is crushed into different sizes for use in the building of roads, bridges, and highways and for the production of asphalt and concrete. The quarry is still in operation as Weldon Quarry at the intersection of Bonnie Burn and New Providence Roads.

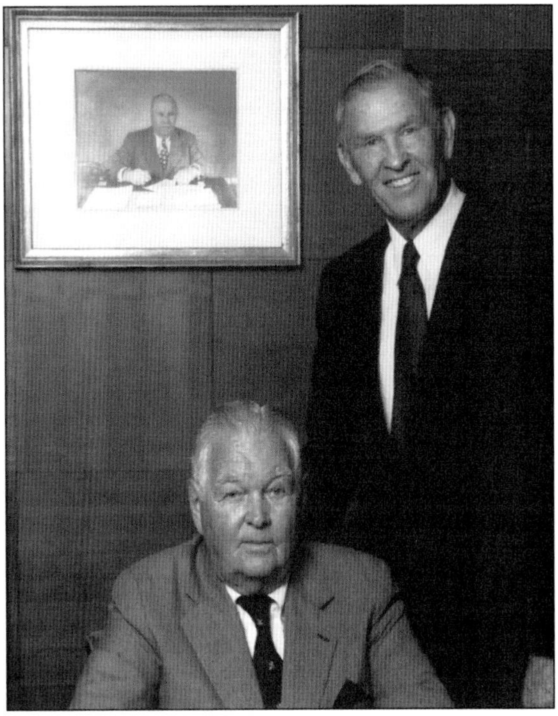

THE WELDON FAMILY. The Fanwood Crushed Stone Company was started by William H. Weldon, who came from Rahway. Shown here are his grandsons Robert F. Weldon (left) and Norbert Weldon—two brothers who ran the company from the 1950s through the 1980s. Shown in the background photograph is their father.

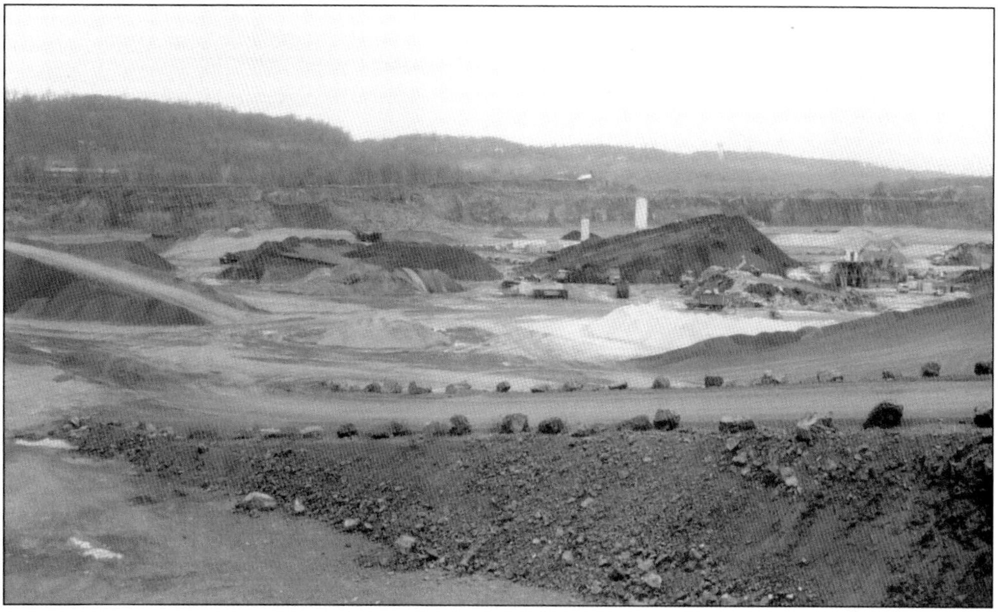

THE WELDON QUARRY. This quarry has produced more than 50 million tons of stone during its lifetime. Stone from the quarry has been used for Newark Airport, Interstate Route 78, the Meadowlands Complex, and the renovation of the Statue of Liberty. In 1901, stone was priced at 95¢ per ton delivered, while, in 2001, the price is set at $10.50 per ton delivered.

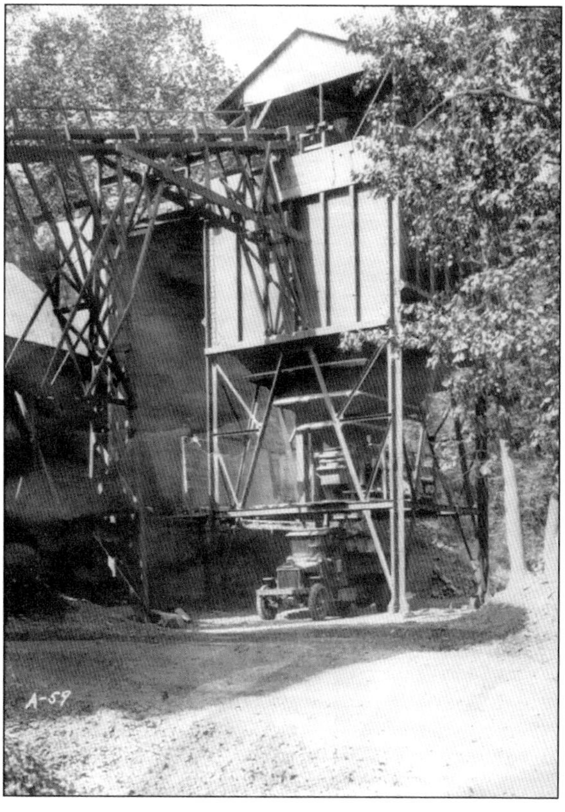

BATCHING STONES. This equipment for batching stones into trucks was shipped to the Fanwood Crushed Stone Company in 1929. Trucks drove under the bins to be loaded with stone by gravity. Today, many residents recognize the familiar orange and green Weldon cement mixers carrying cement from the supply yard at the quarry.

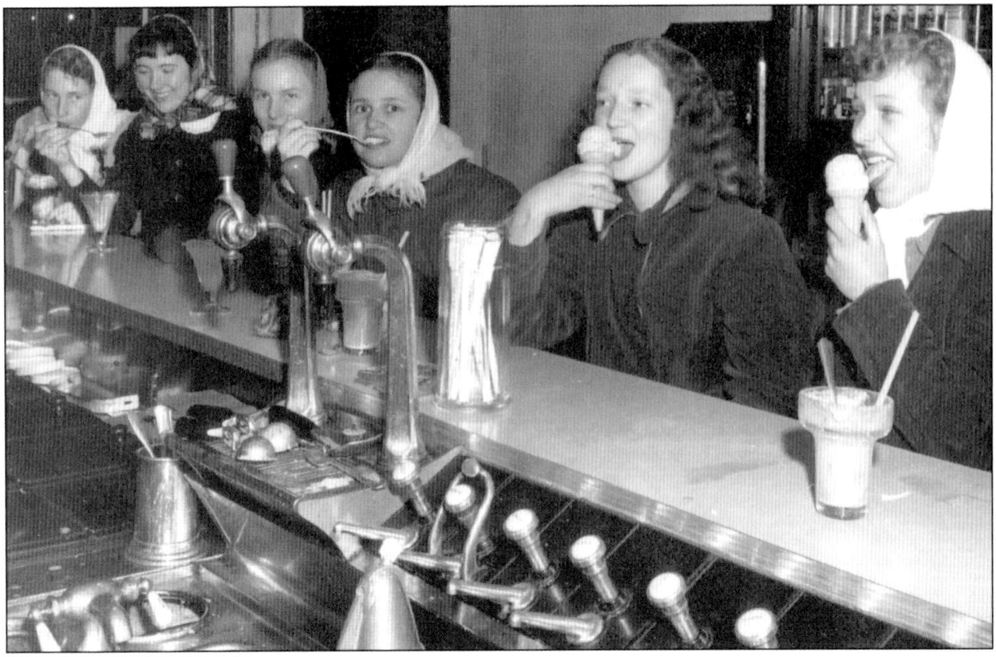

THE WATCHUNG PHARMACY. Girls enjoying ice cream at the soda fountain of the Watchung Pharmacy are, from left to right, Betty Jean Greves, Jane Abel, Barbara Barrett, Betsy Barrett, Midge Burrison, and Nina Goralczyk. Frank Castronovo opened the Watchung Pharmacy, originally located at 985 Somerset Street, in 1939.

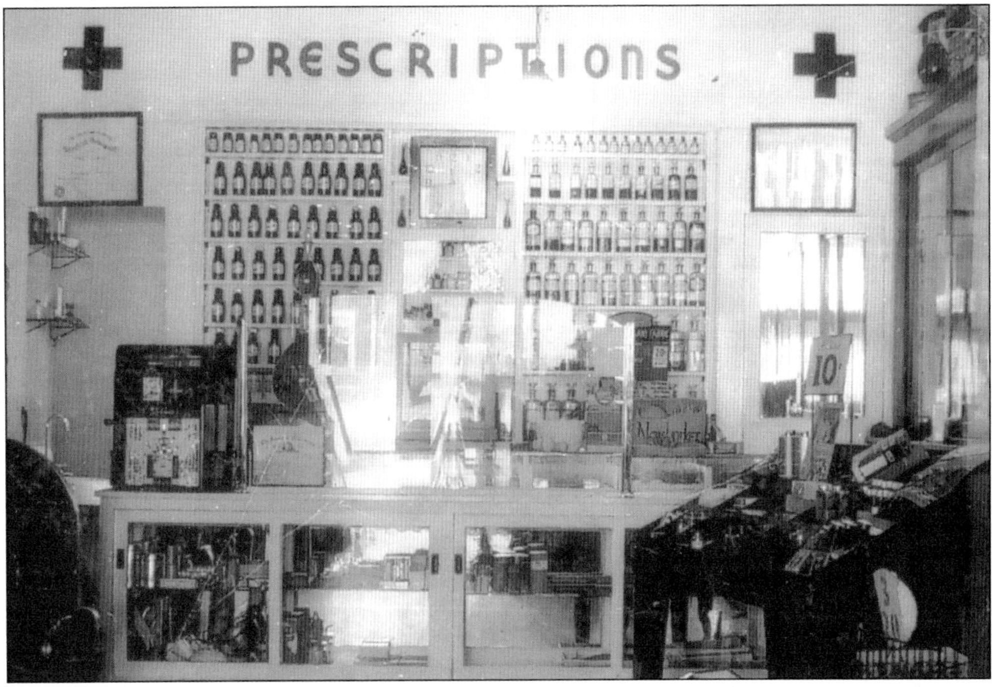

PRESCRIPTIONS. Herbal medicine and homeopathy were popular in the 1940s, just as they are today. Frank Castronovo's son Tom Castronovo and grandson Steve Castronovo continue the family tradition by owning and operating the Edgewood Pharmacy in Warren.

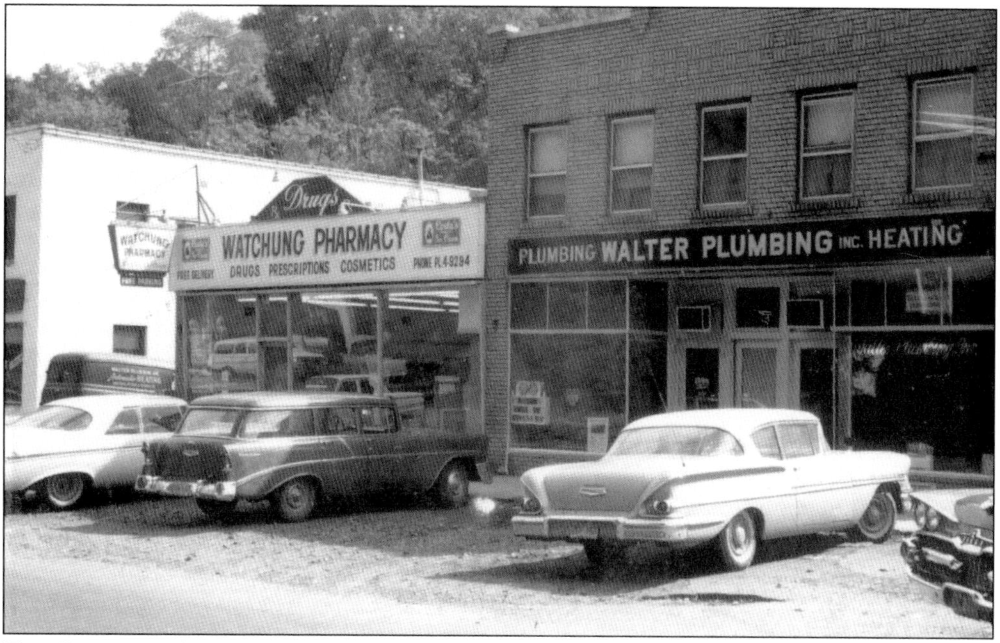

THE SOMERSET STREET LOCATION. The Watchung Pharmacy is shown here at 979 Somerset Street, next to Walter Plumbing. Under ownership by Jack Manhardt and Bob Aznar, it moved to the Watchung Triangle. During the 1990s, the store at the Triangle was sold to Eckerd and then closed when a larger store opened on Route 22.

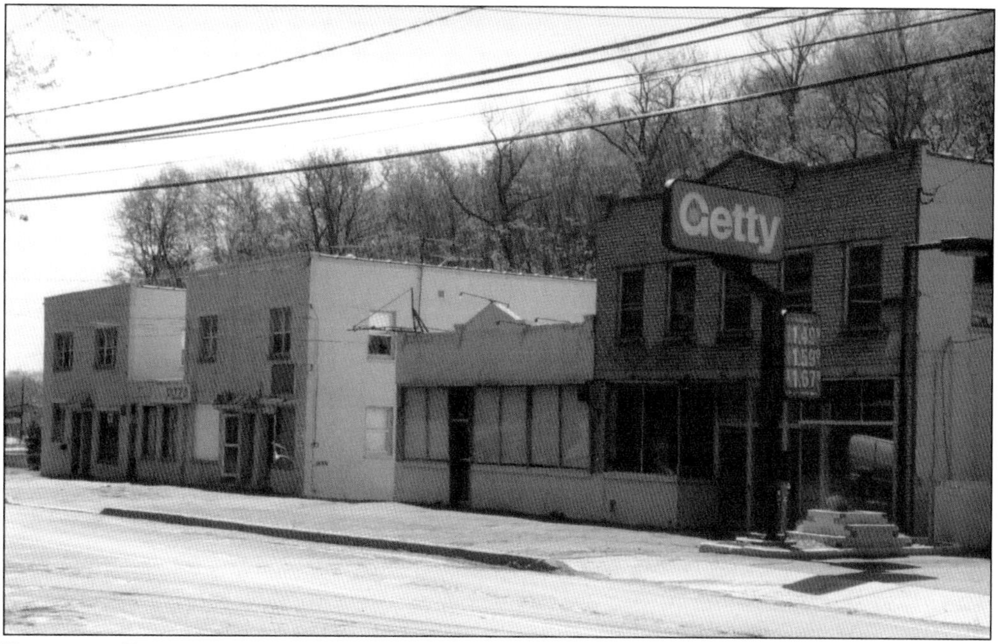

DESERTED BUILDINGS ON SOMERSET STREET. These two-story brick buildings date back to the 1920s and symbolize an era when much of Watchung's commerce was conducted along Somerset Street instead of Route 22. In 2001, the last business in these buildings, Roma Pizza, closed, and the borough purchased the tract with the intention of razing the buildings. A pair of similar buildings were destroyed in the 1973 flood and converted into open space.

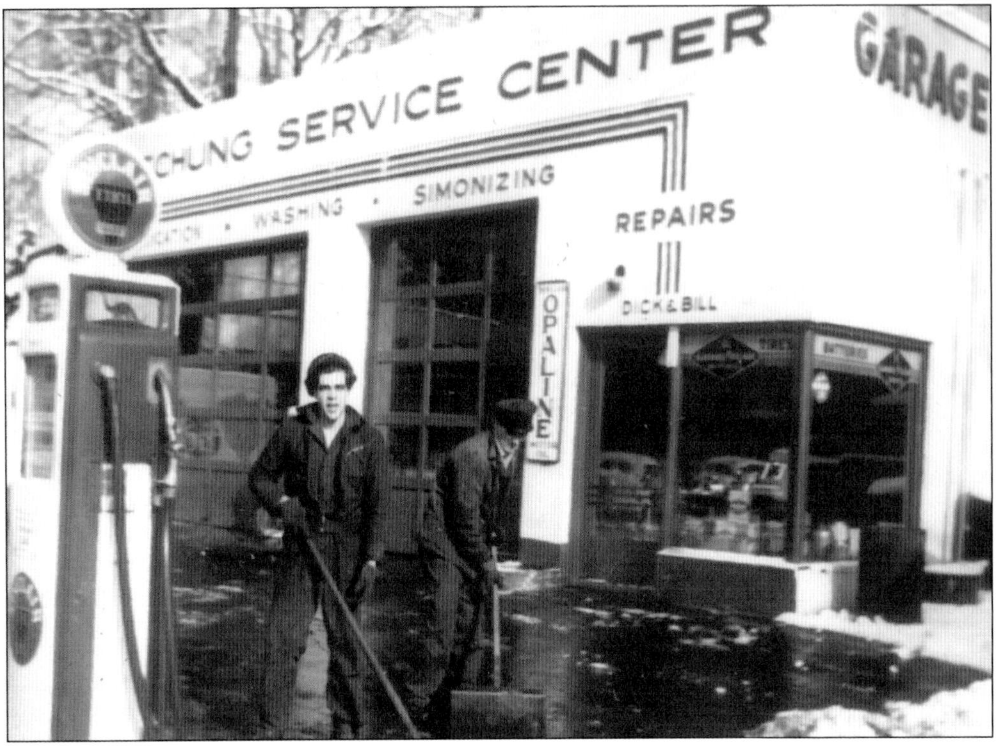

THE WATCHUNG SERVICE CENTER. The Watchung Service Center was located on the east side of Somerset Street, where the office building of James Richardson is currently located. The station was owned by Eddie Snoden and later by Dick Armstrong and Bill Kime, shown here.

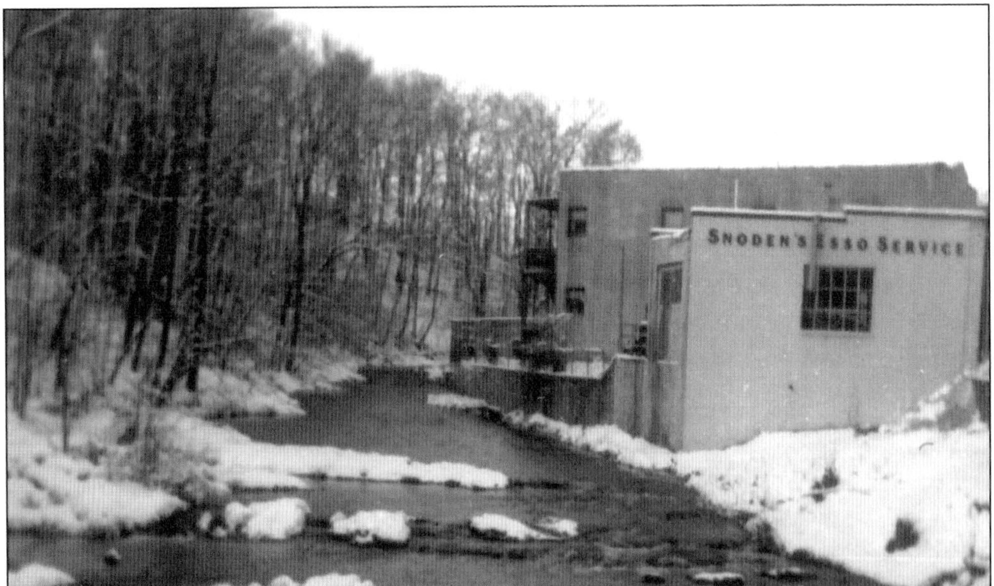

THE SNODEN BROTHERS SERVICE STATION. The Sinclair gas station was located on the west side of Somerset Street, opposite the Watchung Service Center. It was also owned by Eddie Snoden and later by Dick Armstrong and Bill Kime.

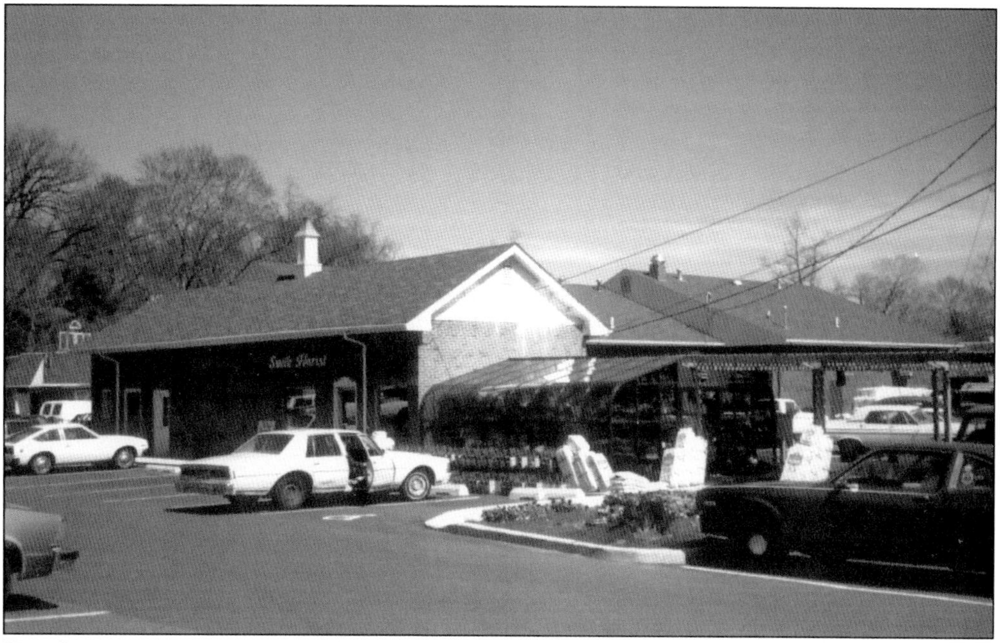

THE SMITH FLORAL SHOP. Established in 1865, the greenhouses and grounds near the junction of Somerset Street and Watchung Avenue were bought by the Smith family *c.* 1900. Plants and cut flowers were grown in the greenhouses year round, while a large variety of dahlias, in which the Smiths specialized, were grown in flower beds. The Smith Floral Shop, which was located at the Watchung Triangle, is no longer in business.

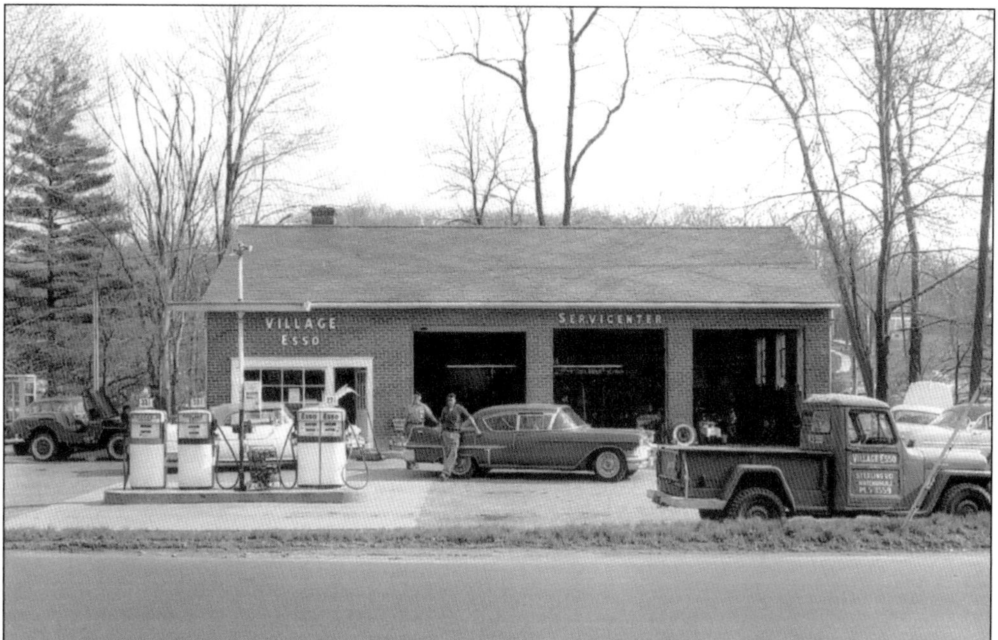

THE VILLAGE ESSO. This Esso station, located on the Watchung Circle, was owned by John Laing. For the last 27 years, the station has been operated as an Amoco station. Anthony J. Torr has owned and operated it for 23 of those years.

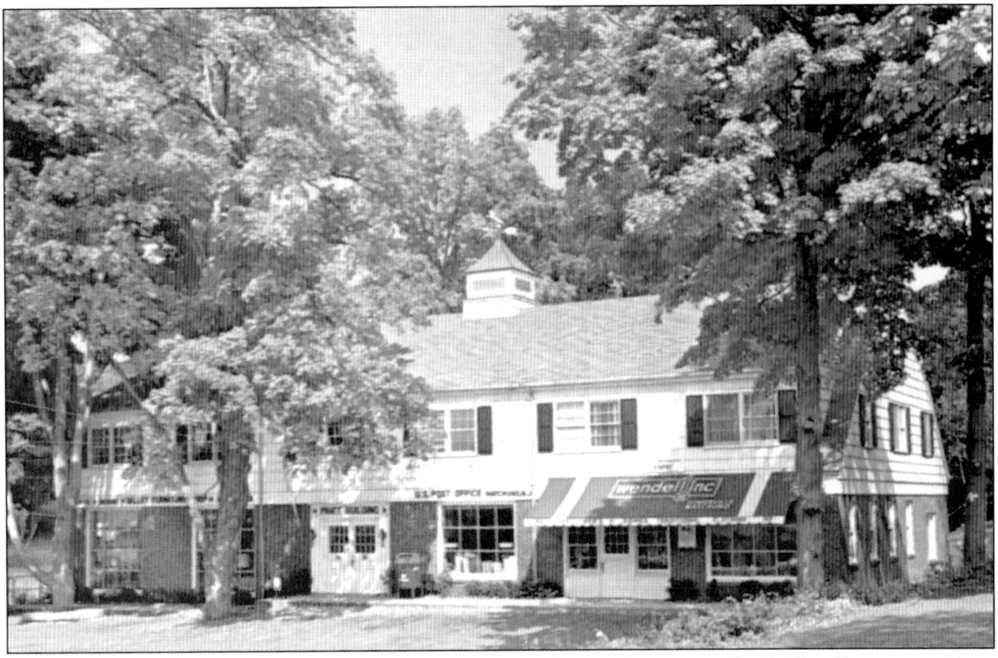

THE VALLEY FURNITURE SHOP. Established in 1947 by Harlan Pratt, the Valley Furniture Shop (located on the Watchung Circle) was originally housed in the old Spencer home. After a few years, Pratt replaced the old house with the Pratt Building, which was home to the Watchung post office, the Wendellinc Shop for "Gentlemen's and Dames' Traditional Clothing," and a dental office, in addition to the Valley Furniture Shop. After the building was sold in 1974 to the Kipe family, Valley Furniture was expanded to the entire building.

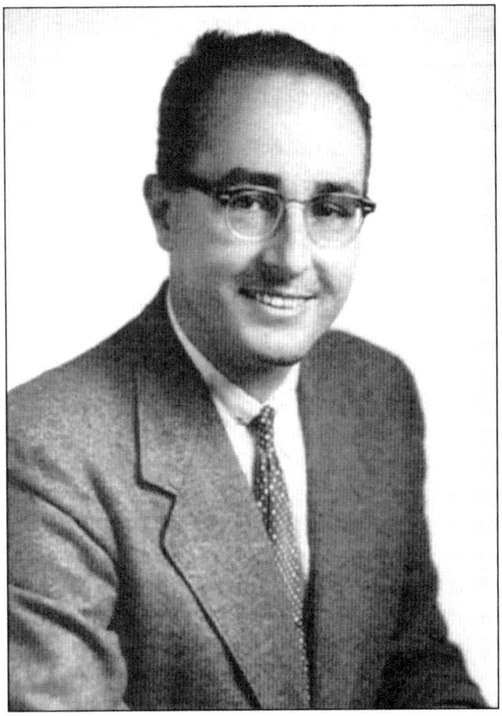

HARLAN PRATT. Born in East Orange, Harlan Pratt established the well-known Valley Furniture Shop, initially buying and selling antiques, as well as building cabinets and repairing furniture. He improved the area by building the Pratt Building and a warehouse, as well as a home on the hill behind the furniture shop, which is now the Watchung Public Library.

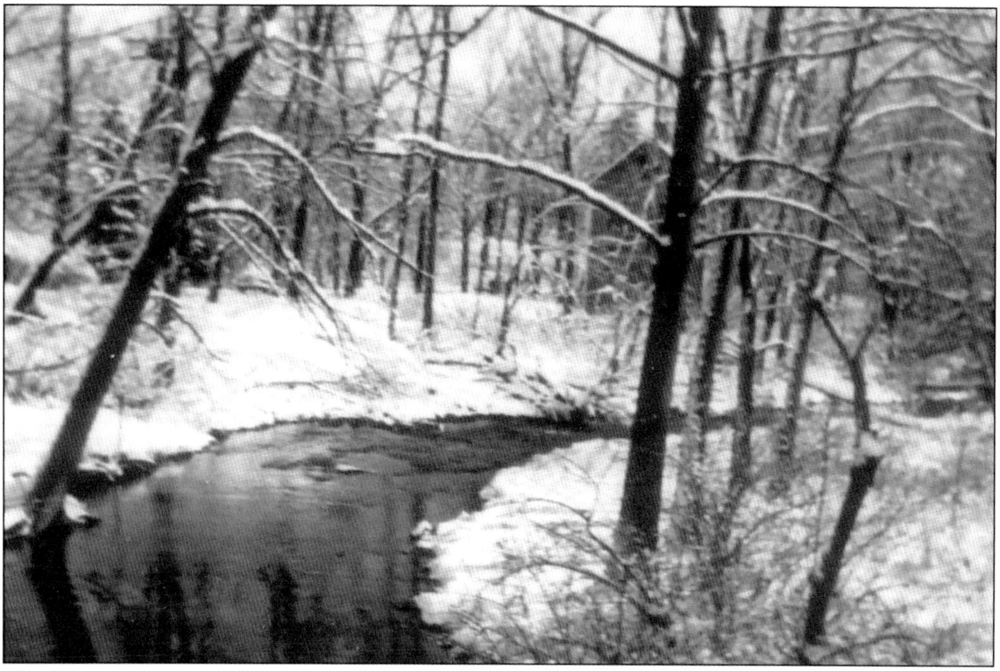

THE GUINARD GLASS FACTORY. This winter scene along a branch of Stony Brook faces eastward toward Watchung Center. The building just visible in the background was the Guinard Glass Factory, located at 555 Stirling Road on today's Watchung Circle.

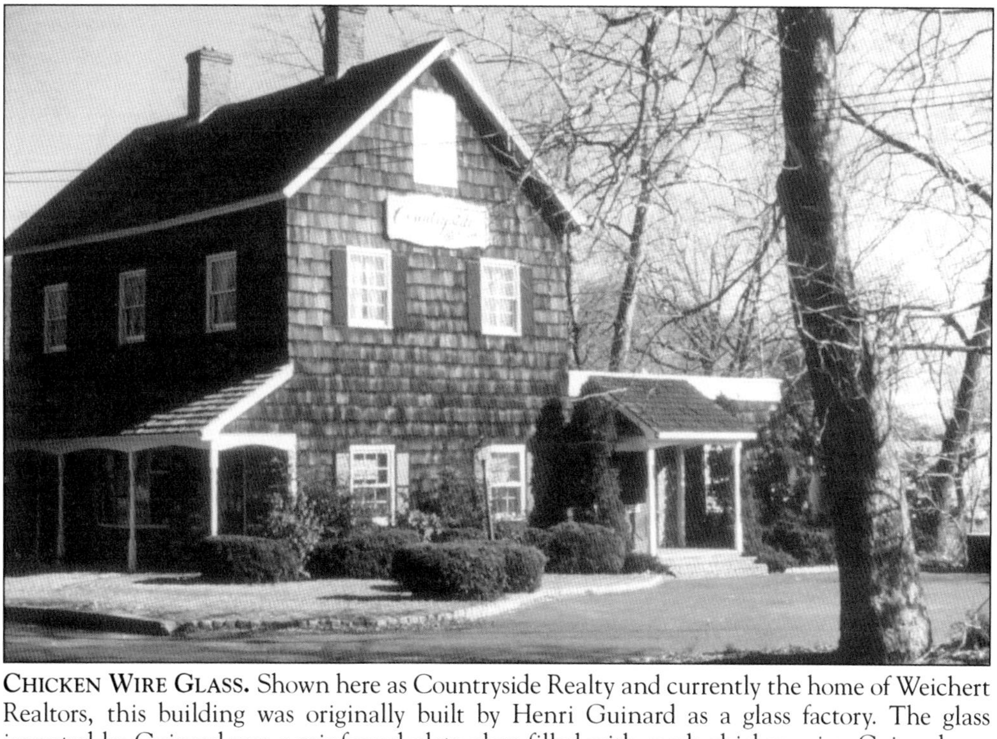

CHICKEN WIRE GLASS. Shown here as Countryside Realty and currently the home of Weichert Realtors, this building was originally built by Henri Guinard as a glass factory. The glass invented by Guinard was a reinforced plate glass filled with mesh chicken wire. Guinard was thought to be the first man to drive a car made in France through the streets of New York.

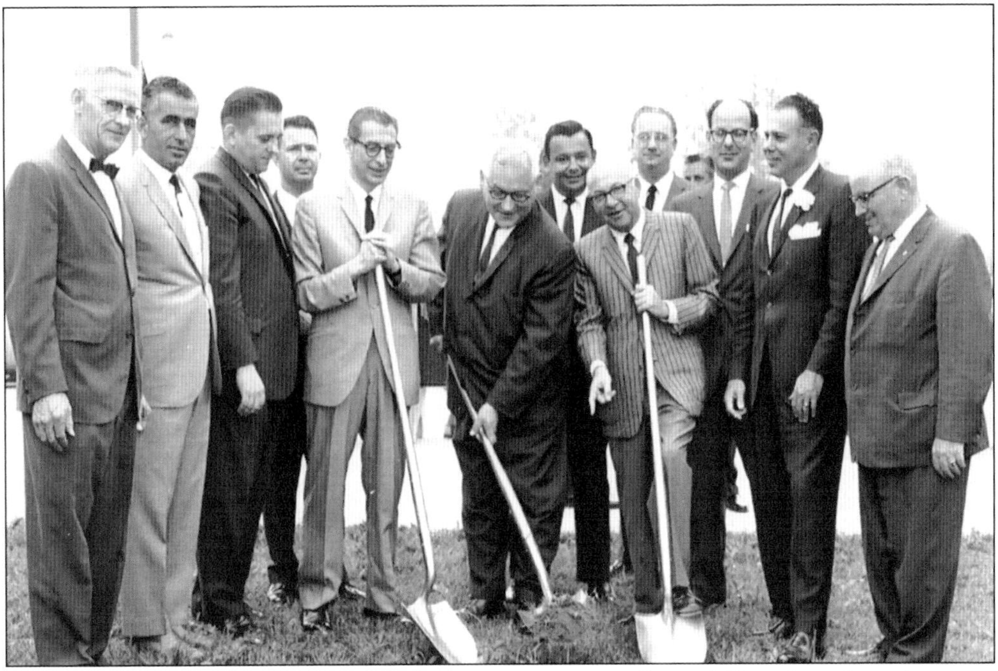

THE BLUE STAR MOVIE THEATER GROUNDBREAKING. One of New Jersey's early major shopping centers was the Blue Star Shopping Center on Route 22 in Watchung, which opened in 1959. Mayor Kenneth Schmidt is shown in the middle with a shovel on August 22, 1963, at the groundbreaking ceremonies for the addition of a 1,250-seat movie theater, the first indoor theater to be built in the area in 30 years.

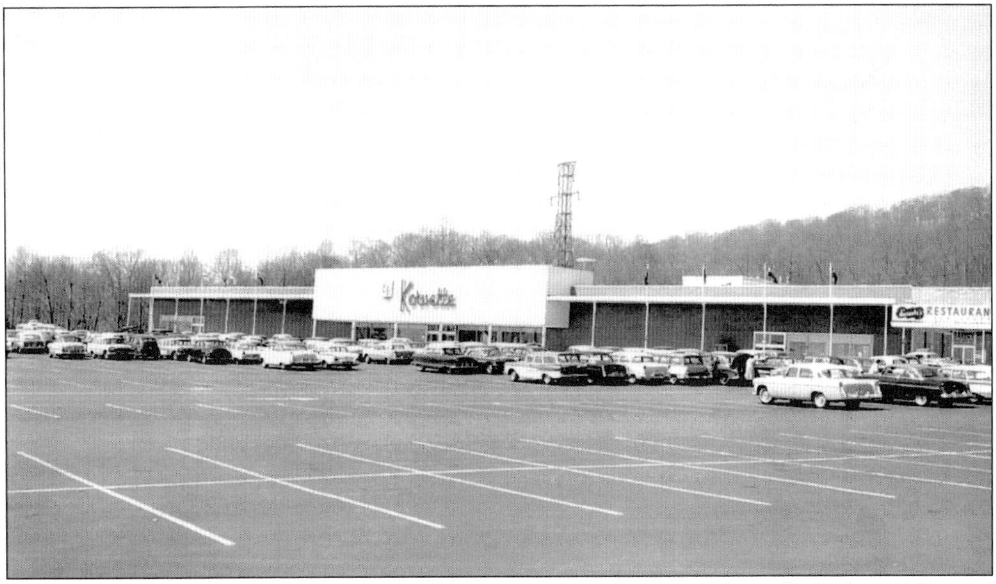

E.J. KORVETTE. The business zone along U.S. Highway 22 developed through the late 1950s and the 1960s. Shown in 1960, E.J. Korvette's located in the Blue Star Shopping Center advertised in the local newspaper, the *Watchung Whispering Leaves,* that it was "America's 12th Largest Department Store." Other establishments located at the time in the shopping center were Star Bowling, Kirch Furniture, Sav-On Drugs, and Durante's Restaurant and Soda Shoppe.

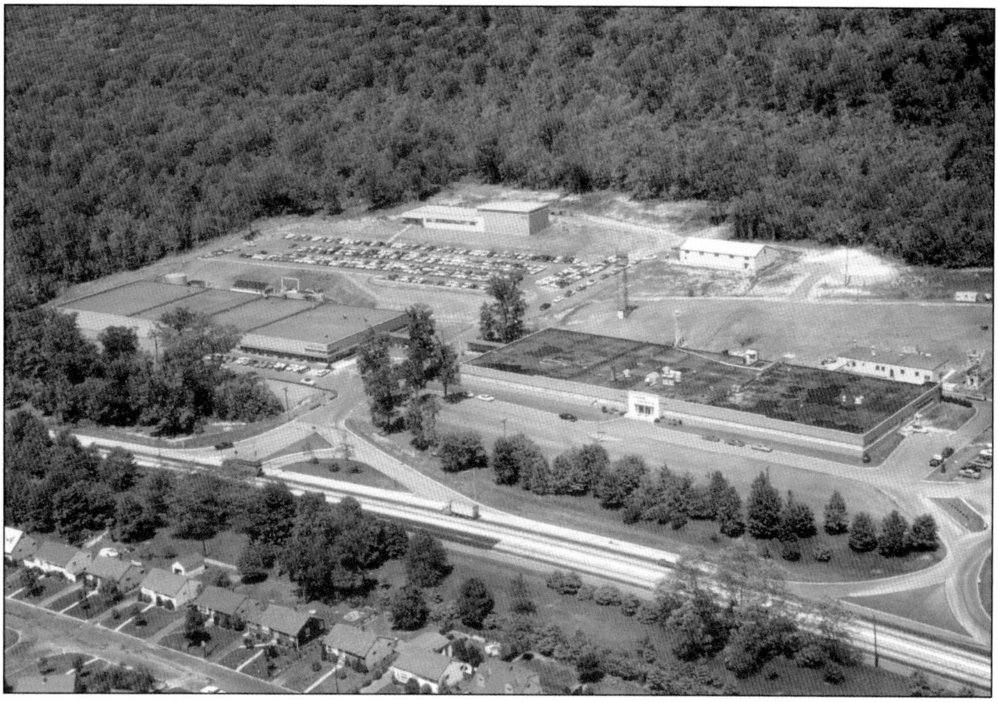

LOCKHEED. With the postwar years of the 1950s and 1960s, the population explosion was felt in Watchung. Among the numerous industries and businesses that located in Watchung along Route 22 was Lockheed Electronics in 1957. Today, the site is being developed as Watchung Square, a shopping mall of approximately 750,000 square feet.

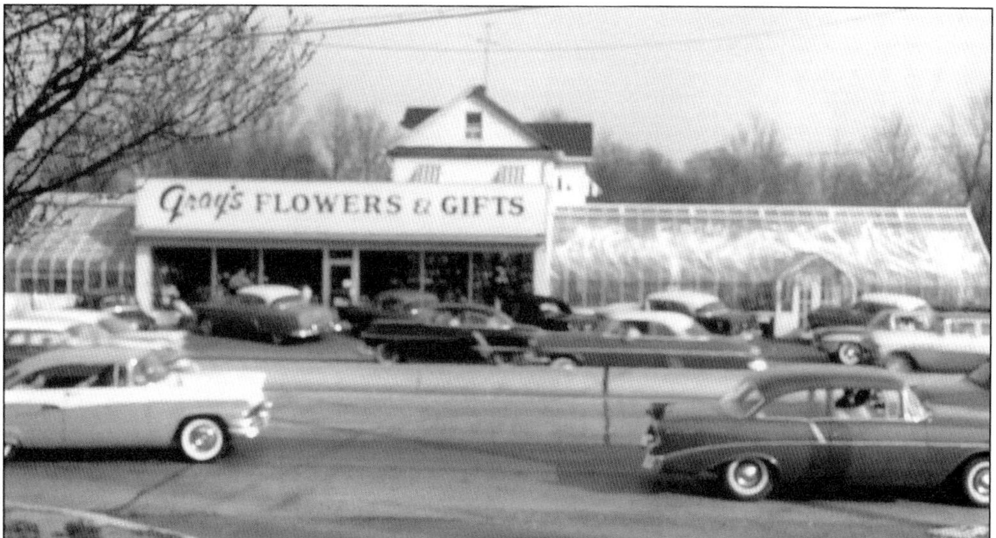

GRAY'S FLORIST. Born in Plainfield, Lewis "Luke" Gray came to Watchung in 1920. After leaving a brokerage firm, he started to truck farm in the area of the Pedeflous Hotel and Restaurant and then on Route 29 (later renamed Route 22). He subsequently went into the florist business, which still flourishes today. He was elected mayor in 1950, serving until 1960.

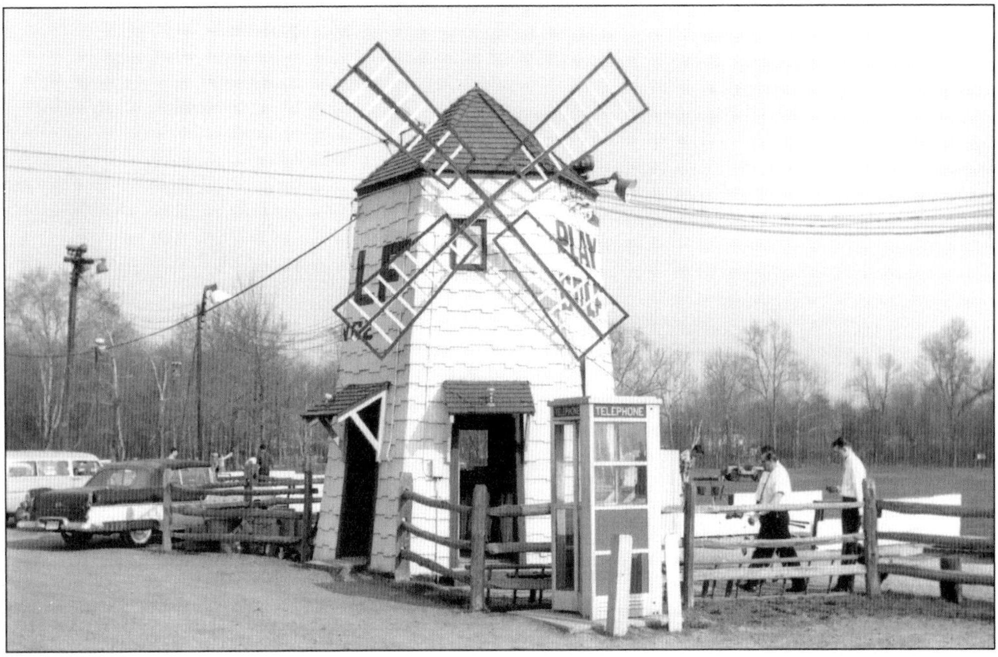

WINDMILL GOLF. Located at Terrill Road and Route 22, Windmill Golf offered a driving range and putting course. In 1960, Windmill advertised, "You Lace 'Em—We Chase 'Em." The land was rented from the Sisters of Mercy at Mount St. Mary's Academy and was later sold to Sears, now located at this site.

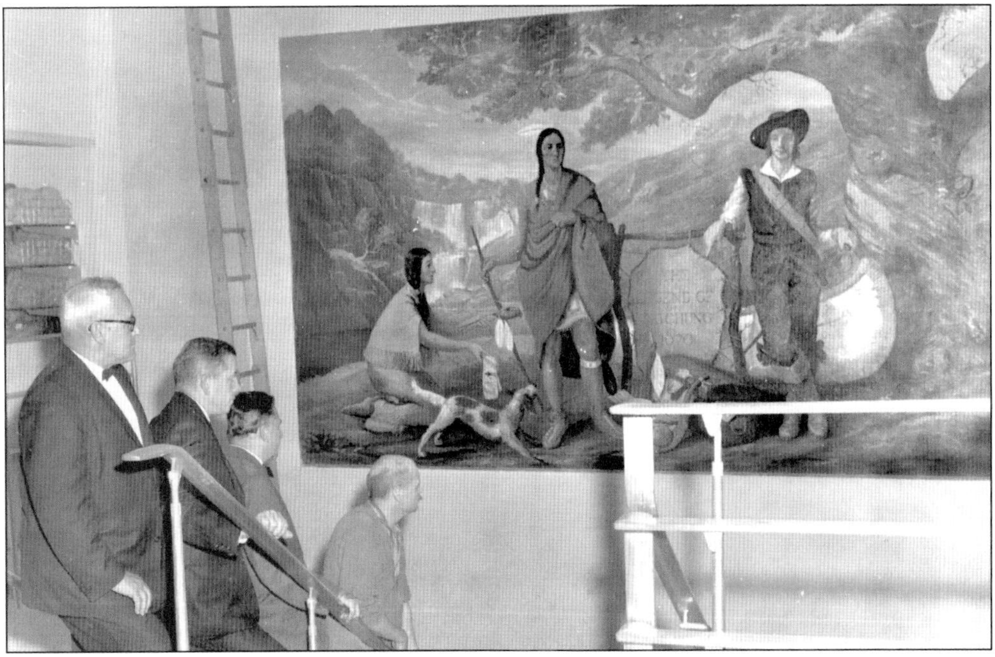

SEARS AND THE LEGEND. Sears opened on Route 22 in 1965. Mayor Kenneth Schmidt (left) is shown on the steps inside Sears looking at a mural that depicts the *Indian Legend of Watchung*. A plaque on the wall tells the story of Captain Michaelson, Princess Wetumpka, and Chief One Feather.

Three

Borough Services

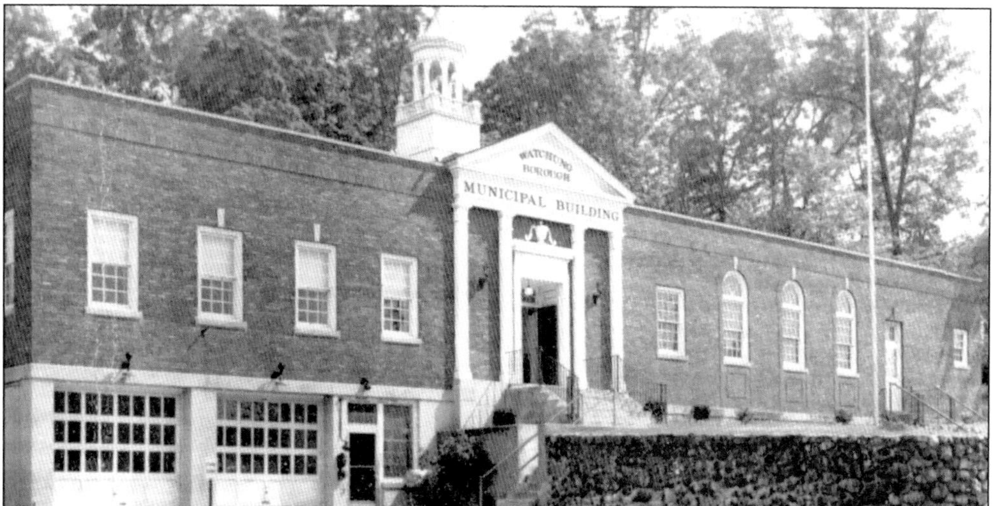

The Municipal Building. In 1929, the Old Mill was razed, and, on the site, the municipal building of the Borough of Watchung was erected. The stone wall in front of the building is from the original gristmill and contains the words "VanDoren 1823." In 1930, the borough hall also served as the firehouse. The building was renovated in 1976 and in 2001.

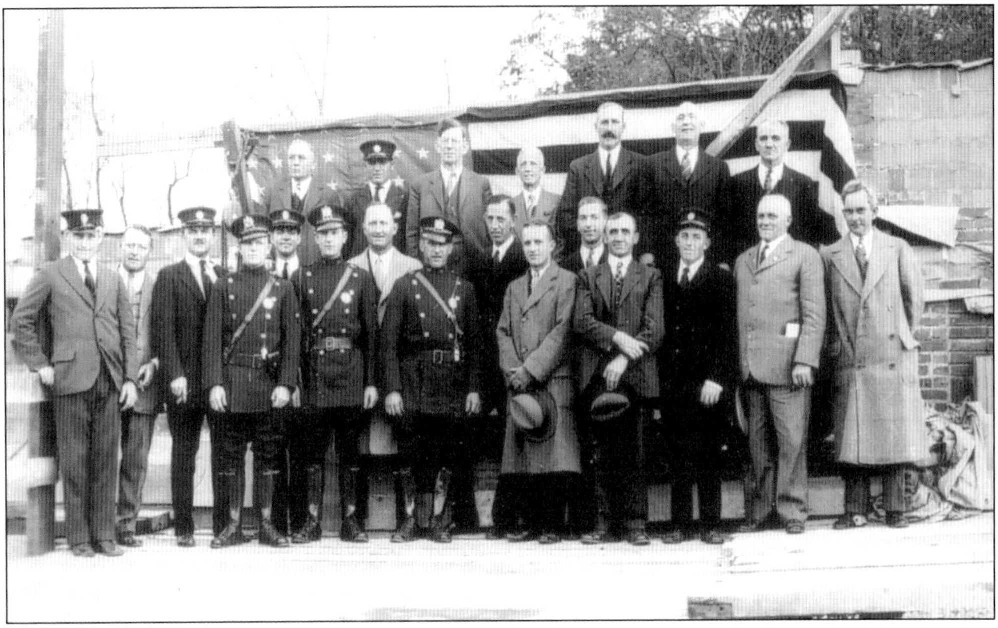

LAYING THE CORNERSTONE. The cornerstone for the new borough hall was laid in October 1929 with impressive ceremonies. Officials in attendance are shown, from left to right, as follows: (front row) Edgar Titus, Ed Schmeyer, Charles Schulick, Fred Greves Sr., Emile Perret, Everett Marsh, Guy A. Rendall, Chief Al Schmeyer, Mayor Edwin Corey, Robert Lohr, Councilman Douglas W. Demler, collector John Mobus, Elston Wakefield, George A. Schmidt, and Police Chief Richard Bellis; (back row) Francis Bodin, Dave Mobus, Edward Canning, William Patte, Charles Meyers, William Titus, and Clerk George Mobus.

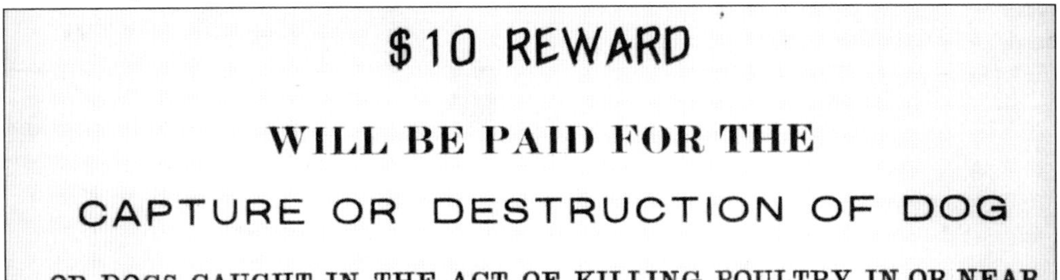

$10 REWARD

WILL BE PAID FOR THE

CAPTURE OR DESTRUCTION OF DOG

OR DOGS CAUGHT IN THE ACT OF KILLING POULTRY IN OR NEAR

WATCHUNG. PROOF REQUIRED!

By order of THE TOWNSHIP COMMITTEE.

Watchung, N. J., February 10, 1916.

George Mobus
Township Clerk

REWARD. George Mobus was the first town clerk for the Borough of Watchung. Before the borough was incorporated, he served as township clerk for North Plainfield Township, as shown in this 1916 proclamation concerning dogs and poultry. In 1915, the newspaper reported that in order to preserve game and prevent forest fires, hunting was being prohibited by nearly all the owners of property on the First and Second Mountains.

MAYOR MACDONALD. Popularly known as "Harry," Henry Baldwin MacDonald was Watchung's first mayor, serving from 1926 to 1928. Beginning in 1887, MacDonald worked for the Plainfield Savings Bank. Although he started out sweeping floors, he later became the bank's president.

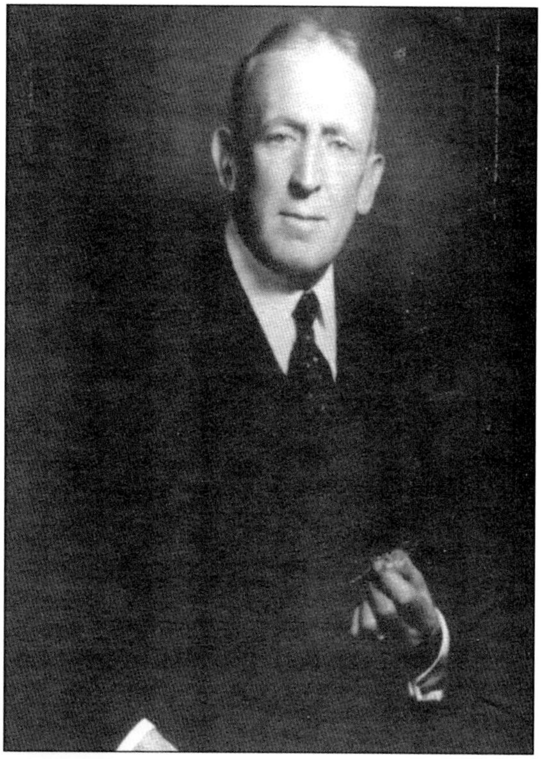

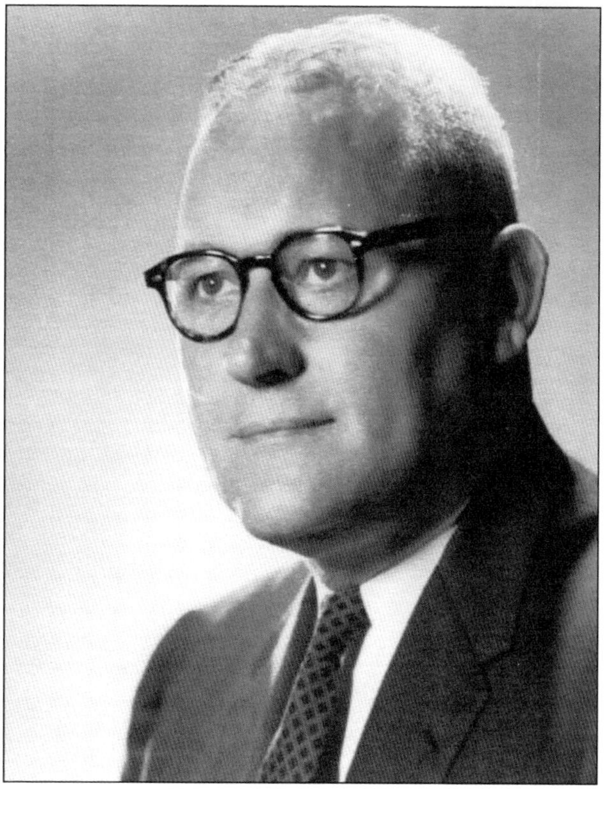

MAYOR SCHMIDT. Kenneth Schmidt, a lifelong resident of Watchung, was mayor for 31 years, beginning in 1961. His long list of civic services included the Watchung Borough Council, the Watchung Planning Board, the Rotary Club, the Somerset Republican Committee, the Watchung fire department, and the Boy Scout Troop 32 Committee. He died in 1992 at the age of 83.

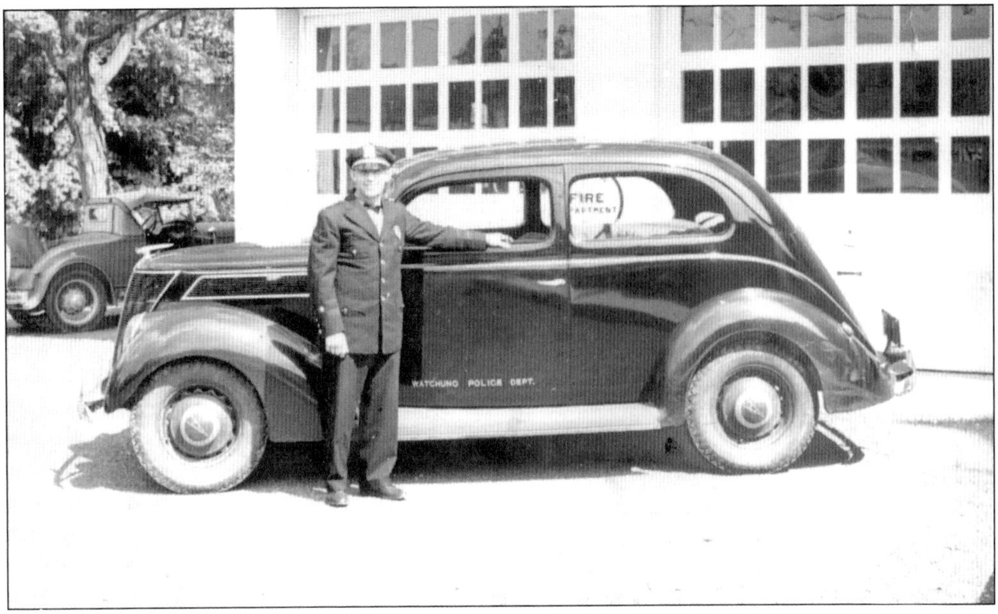

CHIEF NUNN. The Watchung Police Department was created under Ordinance No. 1 in December 1926. It was not until 1935 that Watchung had two paid police officers, Al Schmeyer, who was a sergeant, and Elmer Nunn, who was a patrolman. In 1937, Nunn was appointed chief at an increase in salary to $1,200 per year. Chief Nunn is shown in 1937 by a Watchung Police Department car (notice the lettering on the car door).

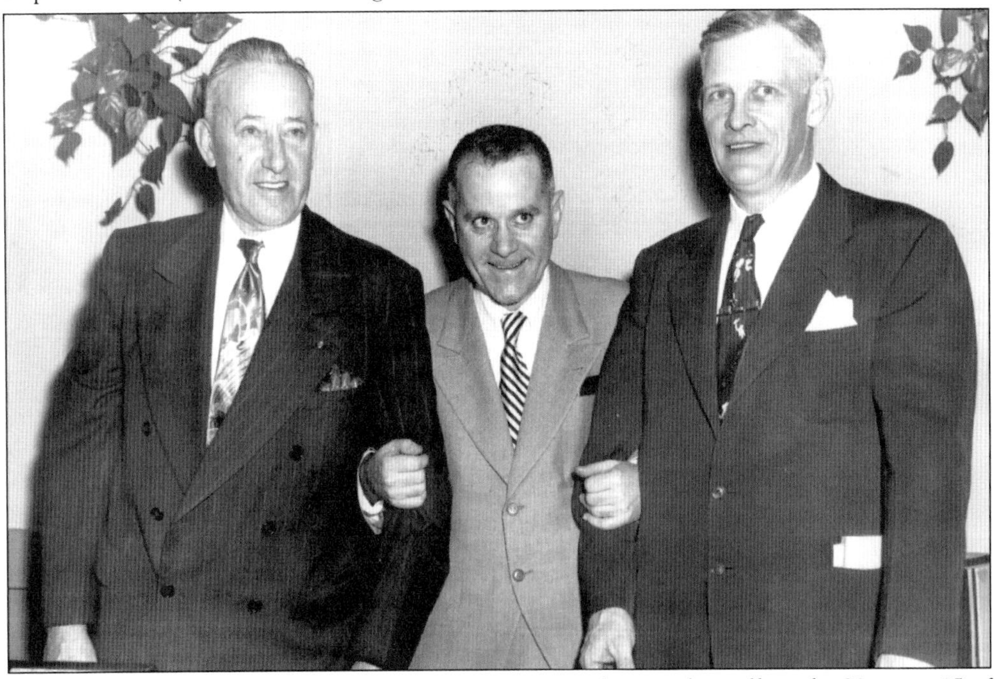

CHIEF BARRETT. Ralph Barrett, born in Bayonne, served as a police officer for 30 years, 15 of those as chief. Shown, from left to right, are retiring Chief Al Schmeyer, an unidentified man, and Chief Barrett in 1952 at the time of his promotion. Chief Barrett was instrumental in forming the Somerset County Police Chiefs Association and was its president in 1962.

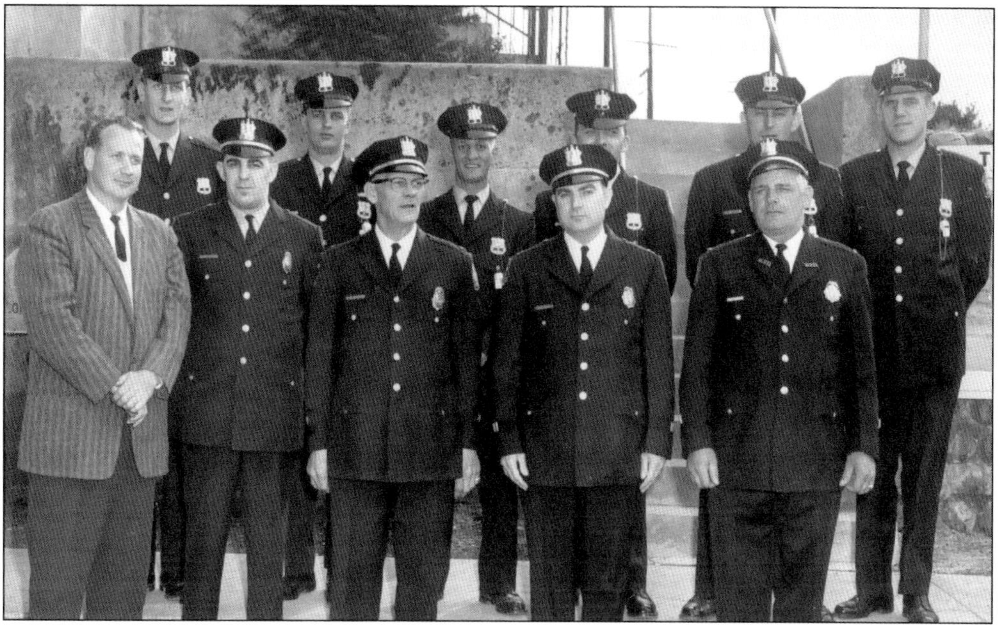

THE 1965 POLICE FORCE. Members of the Watchung Police Department in 1965 are shown, from left to right, as follows: (front row) councilman Bob Finney (police commissioner), Henry Scotti, Chief Ralph Barrett, Frank Wright (who became chief in 1968 after Barrett), and Donald Laing (who became chief in 1976 after Wright); (back row) Ron Unkert, Robert Bradley, Ron Zambetti, John Frank, Eberhard Schmiede, and George King (who became chief in 1984). In 2001, there are 27 officers on the force.

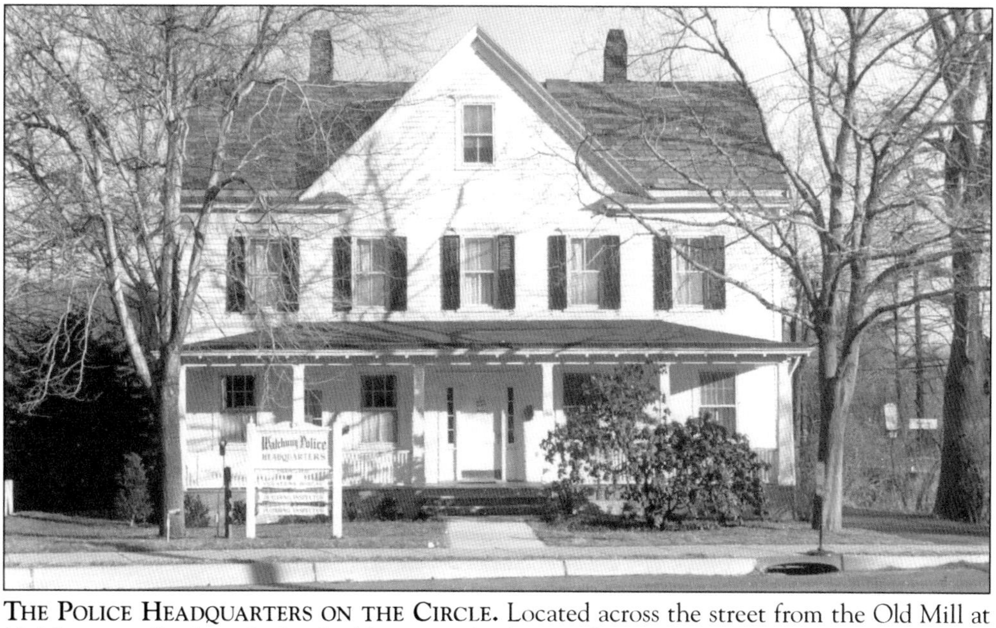

THE POLICE HEADQUARTERS ON THE CIRCLE. Located across the street from the Old Mill at 10 Mountain Boulevard, this building was the home of Hippolyte Texier in the early 1900s. Before the police car got a radio, Mrs. Texier would take police calls and turn on the porch light to alert the patrolling policeman to stop by. In 1965, the police moved their operations to the Texier House.

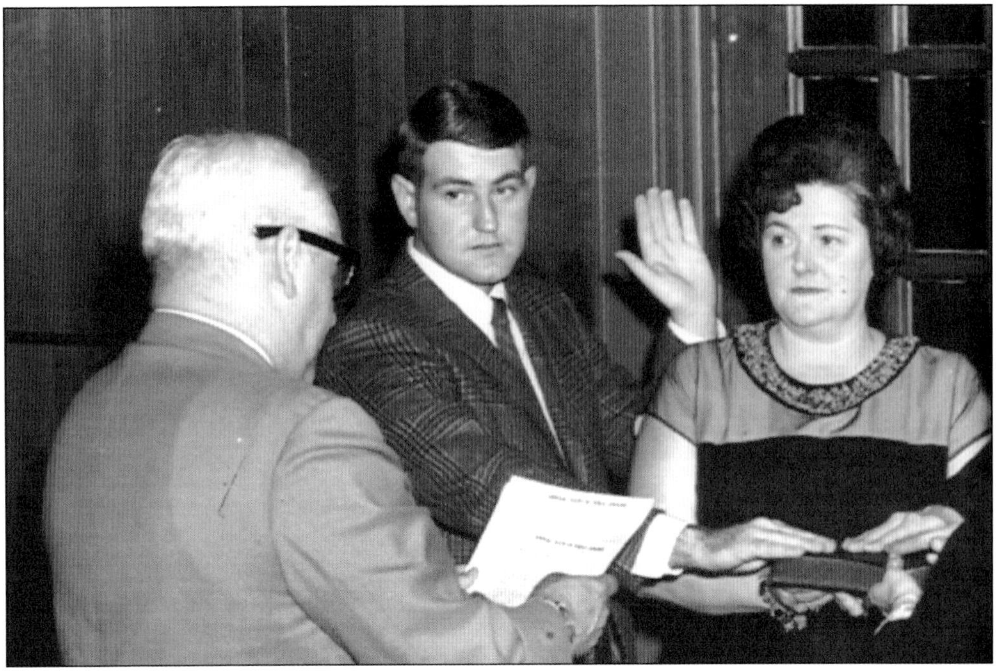

SWEARING IN. In February 1969, Mayor Kenneth Schmidt (left) is shown swearing in police officer Robert S. Reilly (center), along with Reilly's mother, Mary. Reilly became police chief in 1997 and plans to retire at the end of 2001.

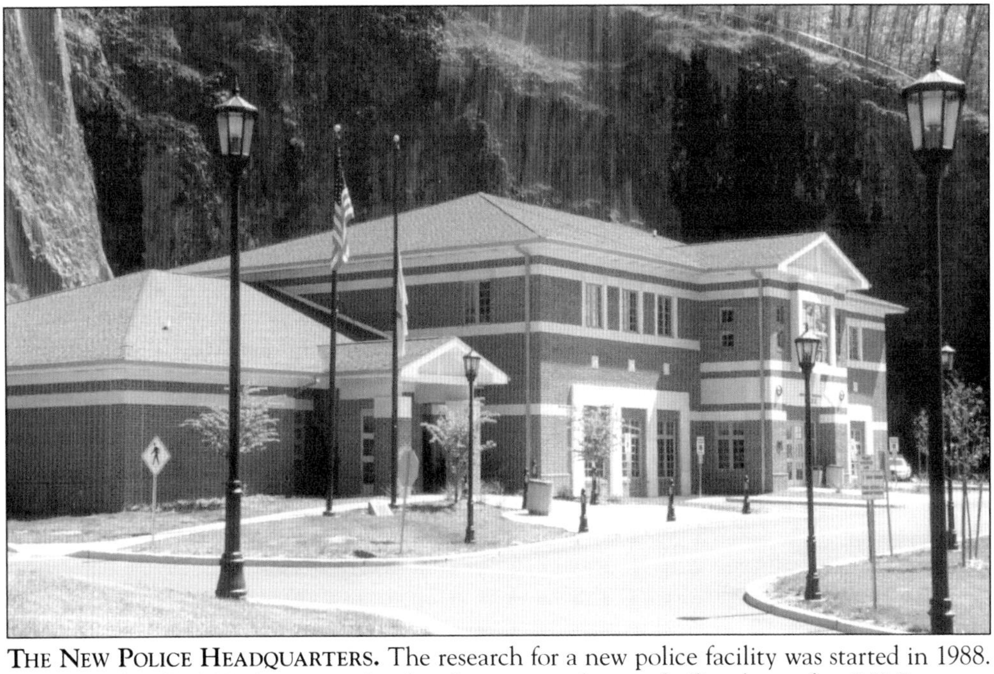

THE NEW POLICE HEADQUARTERS. The research for a new police facility was started in 1988. On November 7, 1999, the new police headquarters and court facility, located at 840 Somerset Street at the former site of Wilson's Quarry, was dedicated in memory of Chief Richard Ryan. Ryan became chief of the Watchung Police Department in 1977, serving until 1984, when he died of a heart attack at age 39.

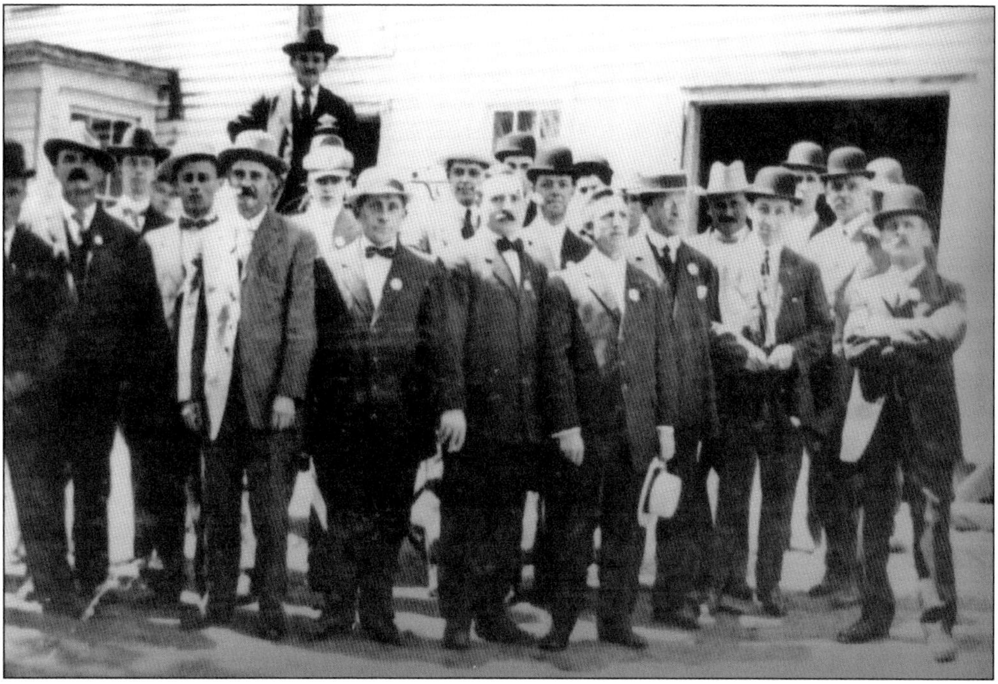

The 1910 Charter Members. On August 18, 1910, a group of men were gathered at what was later known as the Washington House. As a hotel employee tested a nearby hand fire extinguisher, William de La R. Anderson suggested that a fire company was sorely needed. His friends readily agreed, and a meeting was called to order by George Mobus, the township clerk. The Watchung Chemical Engine Company was formed, consisting of 35 charter members.

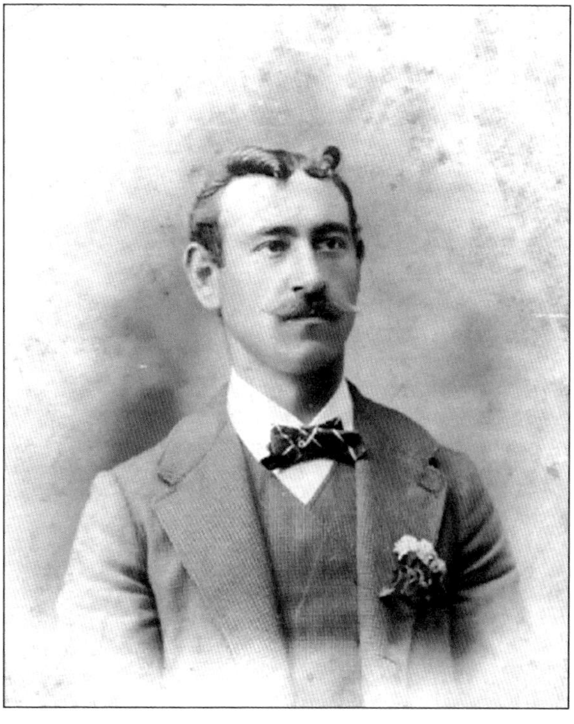

William Titus. William Titus was elected to be the first fire chief by the charter members, serving from 1910 to 1912. Temporary headquarters were established in Chief Titus's barn, but, four months later, Texier's Mill became permanent headquarters. His son Edgar Titus also served as fire chief, first in 1933 and again for a three-year period starting in 1949.

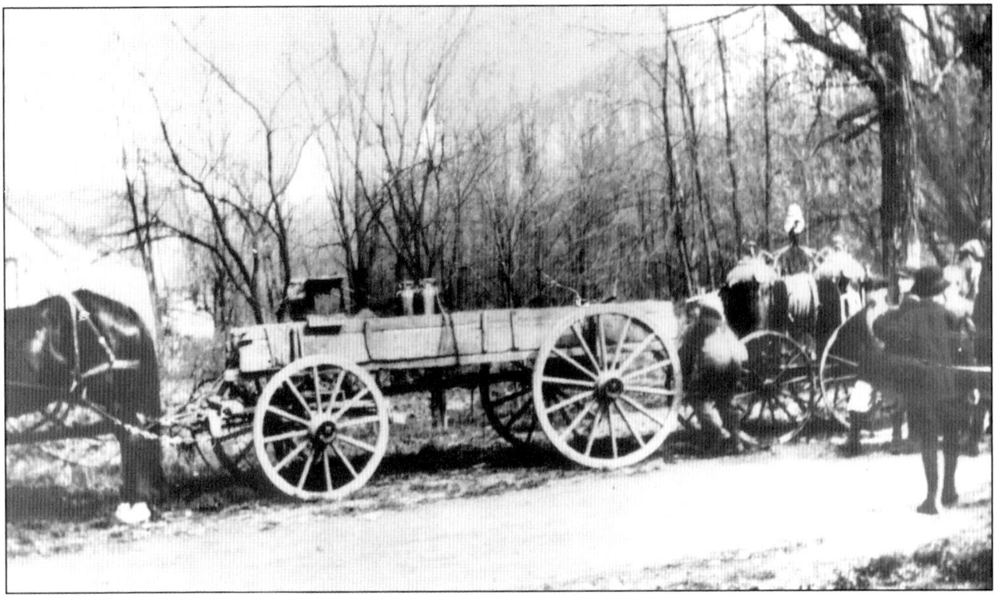

THE FIRST ENGINE. The company's first piece of equipment was a hand-drawn chemical engine purchased in September 1910 from the Township of Scotch Plains at a cost of $100. There was an auxiliary supply wagon towed behind the truck, and a fee of $2 was paid to anyone supplying a vehicle or horse to pull the equipment to a fire. In 1914, the hand-drawn engine was sold for $25 to the Quakertown Fire Company.

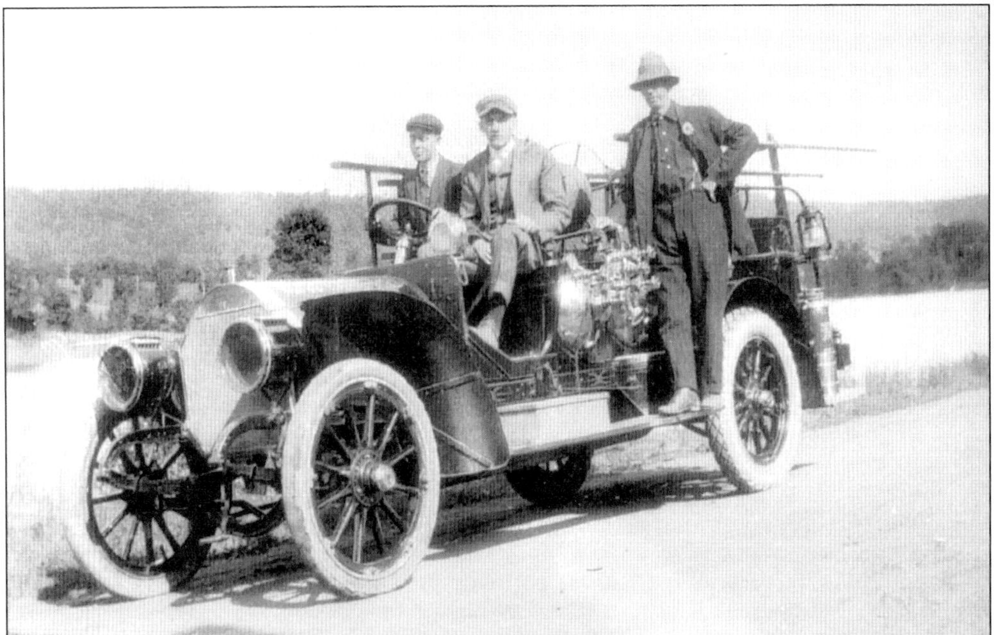

THE SECOND ENGINE. In 1914, a 1908 Locomobile purchased for $415 and equipped with chemical tanks was put into service. It was the first motor-driven fire equipment in an area where other departments still used horse-drawn trucks. The photograph shows, from left to right, Edward Marfinz Jr., Albert Perret Jr., and George Dunn answering a fire call c. 1914.

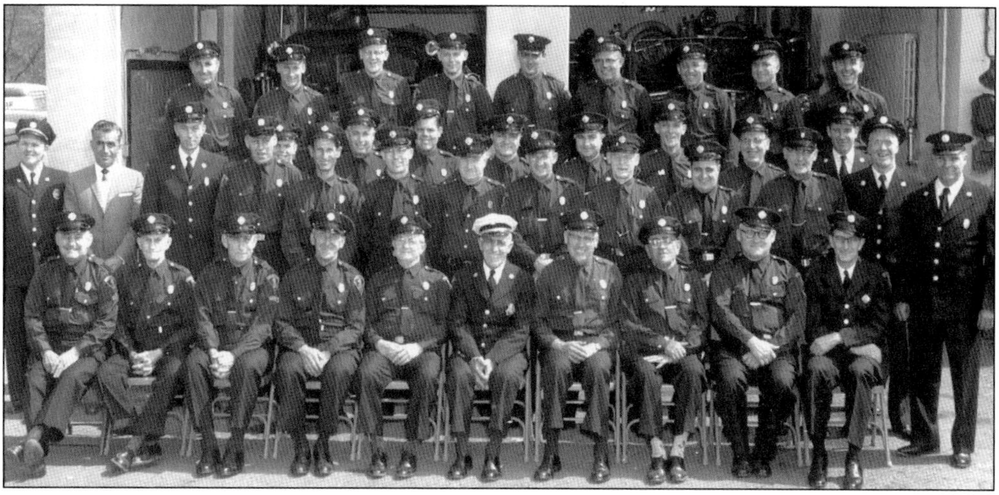

THE 1960 CHEMICAL ENGINE MEMBERS. Members of the all-volunteer Watchung Chemical Engine Company in 1960 are, from left to right, as follows: (first row) Edgar Titus, Everett Marsh, H. Rudy Steffens, Raymond Adams, Frederick Greves Sr., Chief Robert Taylor, Bertram Smith, Alfred Bennett, Kenneth D. Schmidt, and Roland Ost; (second row) Asst. Chief Frederick Greves Jr., fire commissioner Carl Santo, J. Robert Larson, James Miller, Theodore Shawiak, John Gausz, Ernest Jones, George Ammon, Edward Davis III, John Klein, William Matthews, David Chalker, and Raphael Roberts; (third row) Kenneth Nilsen, Neil Stanziola, A. Delunas, John Frank, Frank Wright, Richard Laing, James Keir, and Albert Perrotta; (fourth row) Carmen Riccardi, Robert Bittle, Edmund Sigmund, Steven Zarhardt, Richard Lange, L. Delunas, William Melnick, James Murray, and John Blackadar.

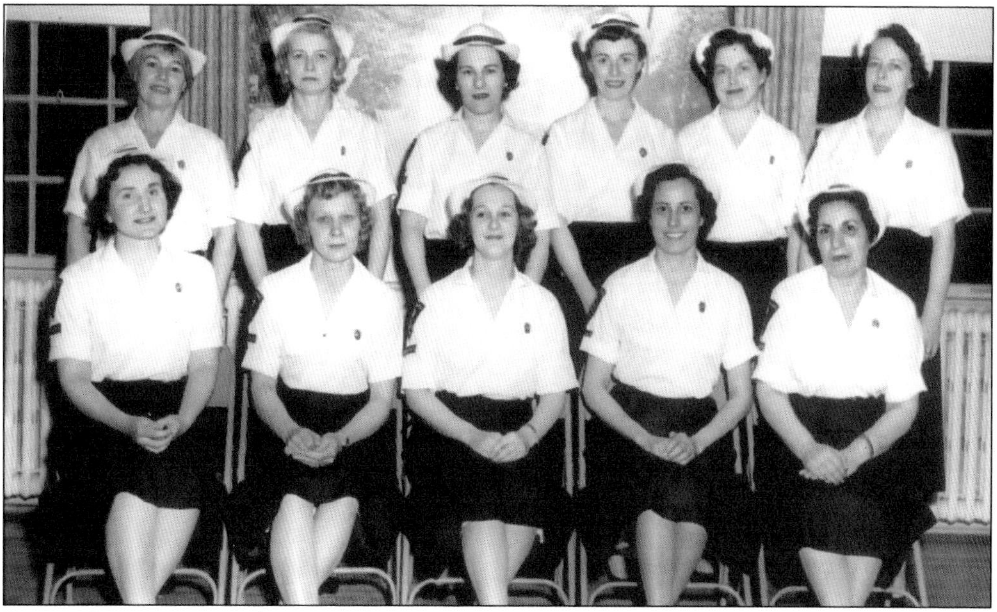

RADIO OPERATORS. Volunteer radio operators of the Watchung Chemical Engine Company in 1960 are, from left to right, as follows: (front row) Phyllis Blackadar, Vivian Dove, Shirlee Greves, Betty Laing, and Frances Ammon; (back row) leader Katherine Davis, Bette Feiring, Mary Krajewski, Evelyn Miller, Ann Larson, and Bette Laing. This was probably the first such group in the state.

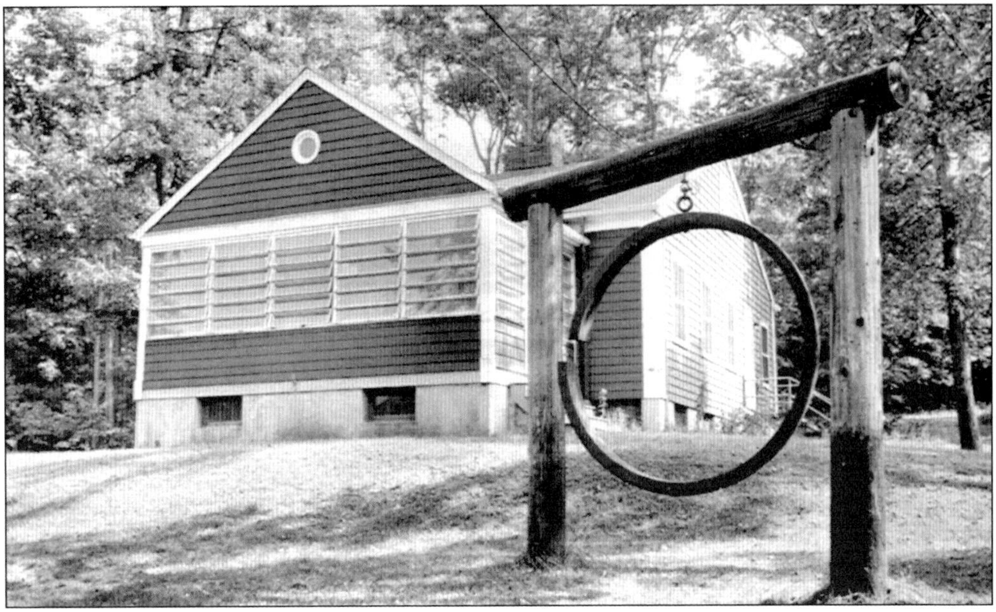

THE EXEMPT FIREMEN'S CLUB. The Watchung Exempt Firemen's Association was initially organized as the Association of Exempt Firemen of the Township of North Plainfield in 1921. A fireman is eligible to become an Exempt member by answering 60 percent or more of the fire calls during a seven-year period. The clubhouse, shown in 1960, was dedicated in 1942. The old locomotive tire in front of the building used to be struck by a sledgehammer as a fire alarm.

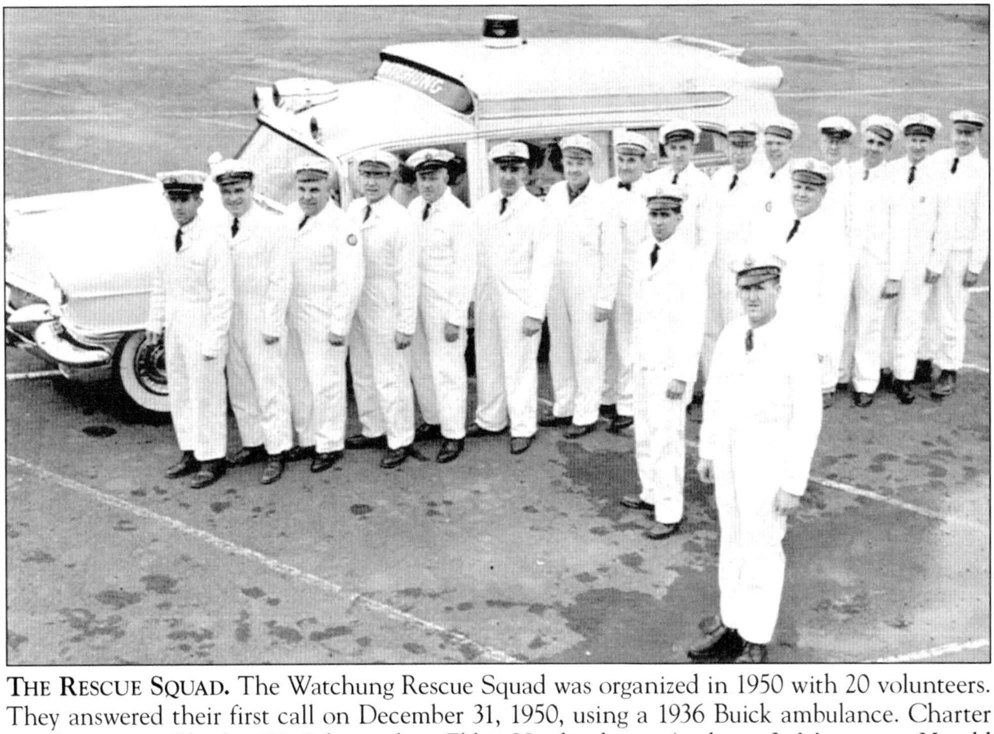

THE RESCUE SQUAD. The Watchung Rescue Squad was organized in 1950 with 20 volunteers. They answered their first call on December 31, 1950, using a 1936 Buick ambulance. Charter members were Charles W. Schumacher, Ebbit Hardingham, Anthony J. Manziano, Harold Powell, William Kime, Harold D. Gehling, George Pepe, Frank Wright, and Harold Scribner.

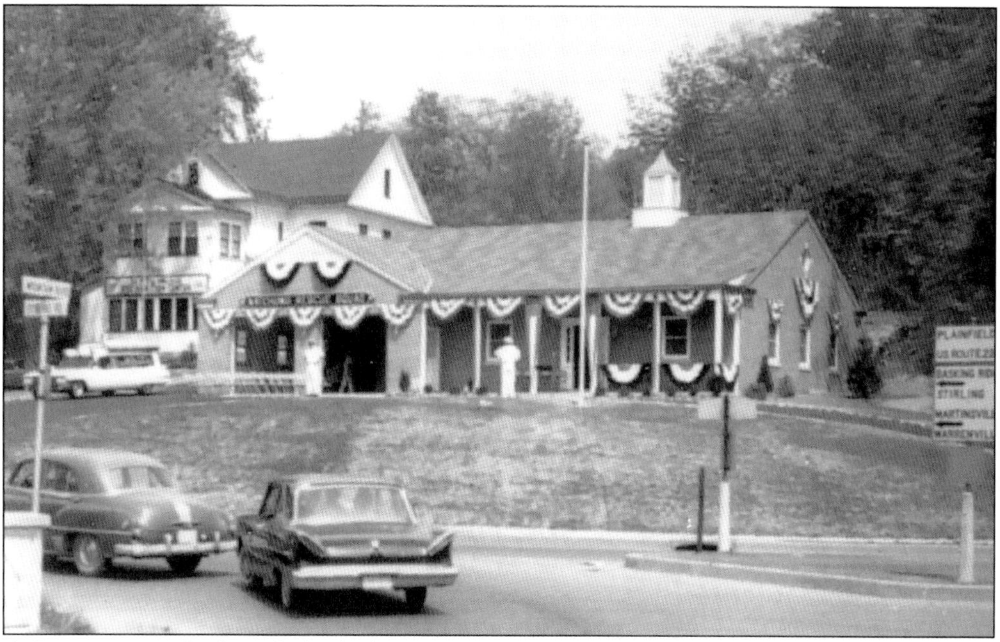

A DEDICATION. Built with funds donated by residents, the Watchung Rescue Squad building on the Watchung Circle was dedicated on May 16, 1965. The Girl Scouts of Cadette Troop 474 of Valley View School formed an honor guard. Squad president Jack Pardue introduced the speakers, including Mayor Ken Schmidt.

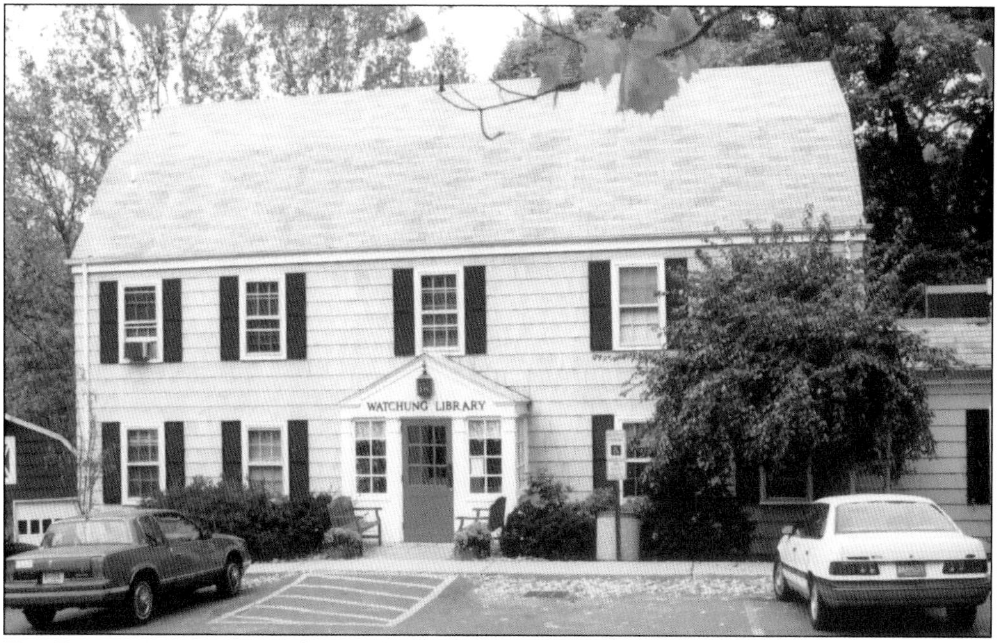

THE PUBLIC LIBRARY. Watchung's first public library was housed in French's General Store on Somerset Street. Later, it was located in the old schoolhouse, now the Watchung Arts Center. It then moved to this building at 30 Valley Road, which Harlan Pratt built *c.* 1950 as a home for his family. In 2001, Watchung is facing a decision whether to expand the current facility or build a new library to meet the need for additional space.

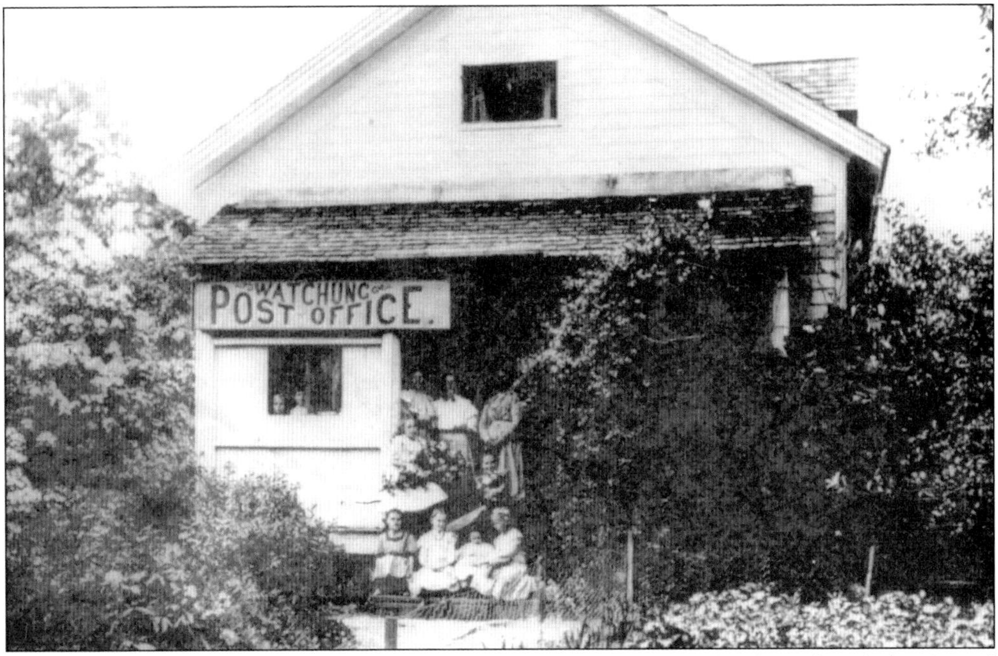

The Post Office. A former schoolhouse, this building was bought by the Schmidt family and moved to the site where the Schmidt Professional Building now stands at 60 Stirling Road on the Watchung Circle. The building was the home of George Schmidt, father of Mayor Ken Schmidt, and the post office was installed in the Schmidt home in 1898. George Schmidt was postmaster and his wife was assistant postmaster over a period of 20 years.

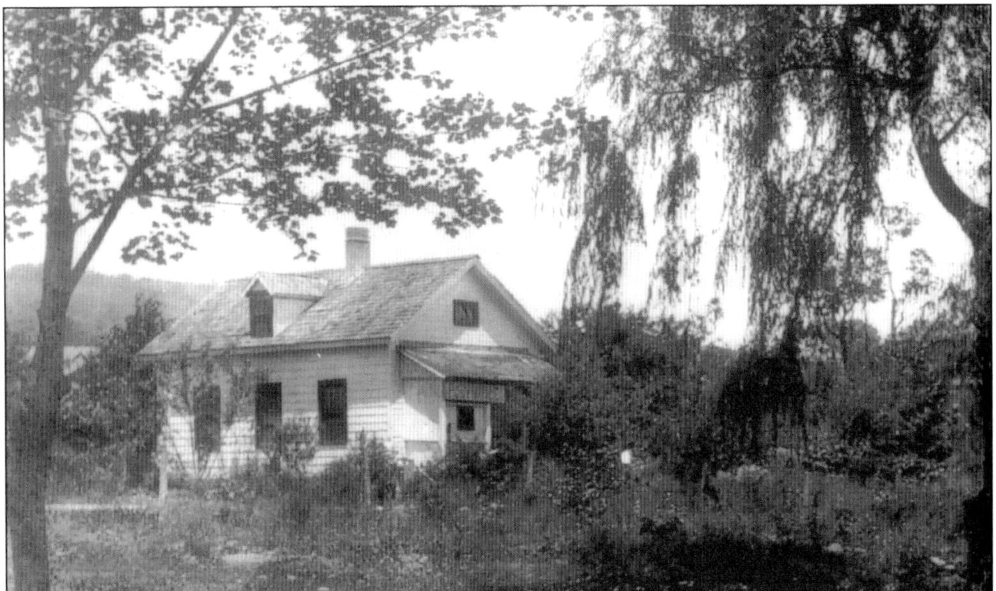

A Distant View of the Post Office. This photograph shows how rural Watchung Center was in the early part of the century. A new Watchung post office opened for service on August 21, 2000. Effective July 1, 2000, the U.S. Postal Service approved a new zip code for Watchung after many requests over 10 years.

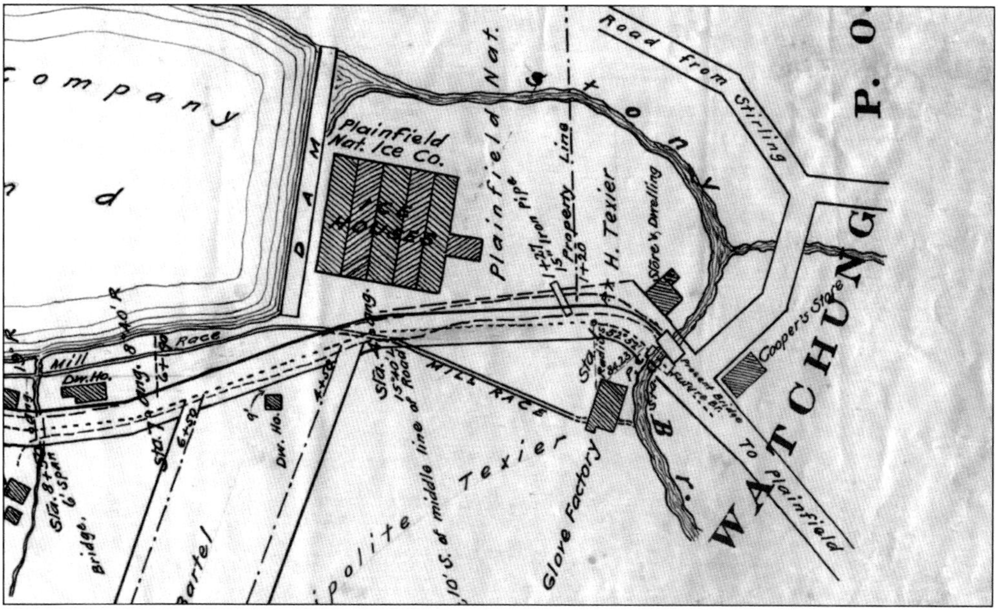

WATCHUNG CENTER. This section of a 1908 map from the Somerset County Engineering Department shows Watchung Center prior to creation of the traffic circle. Well-known landmarks shown here are the Plainfield Natural Ice Company icehouse, Texier's glove factory, Texier's home, and the general store (at this time Cooper's Store).

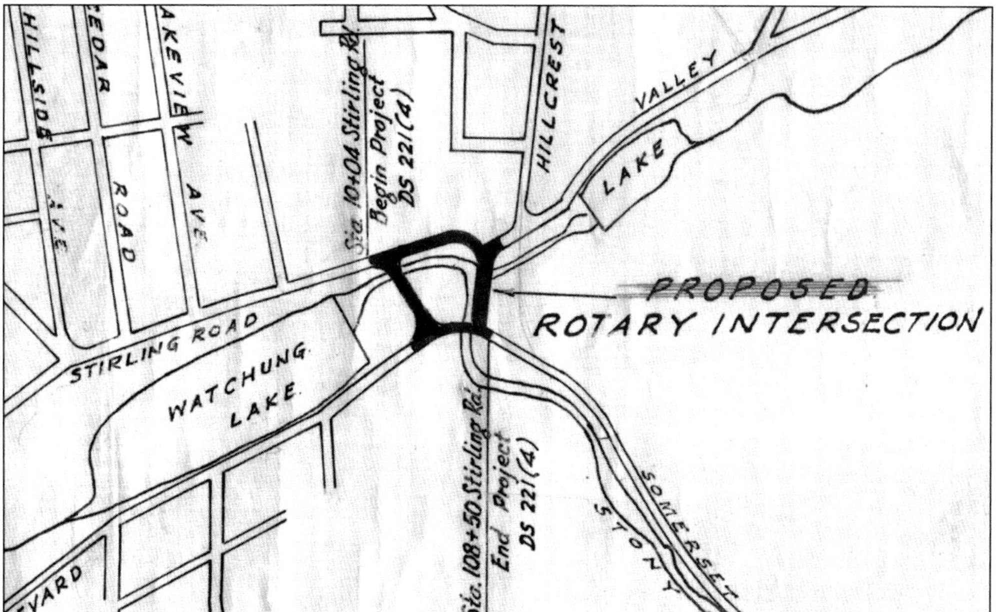

WATCHUNG CIRCLE. This 1956 Somerset County Engineering Department drawing shows the proposed "rotary intersection." In 1953, Police Chief Ralph Barrett met with state and local officials to request aid to eliminate the hazardous corner at Watchung Center by building a traffic circle and widening Somerset Street to a four-lane highway. To back his case, Chief Barrett cited that 12,374 cars passed through the intersection on July 19, 1953, as recorded by a traffic survey machine.

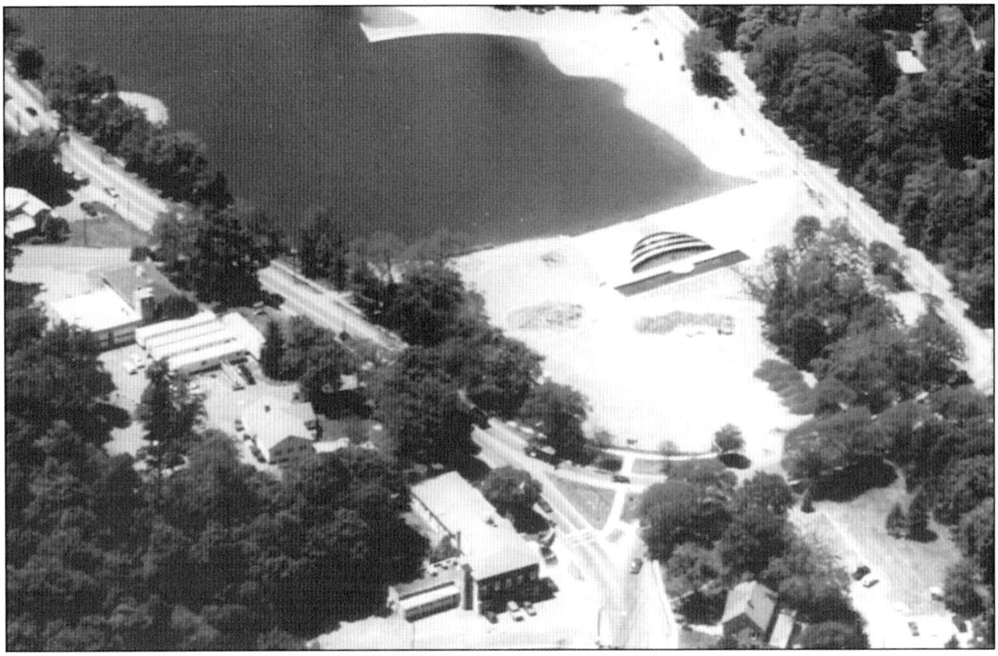

THE 1999 WATCHUNG CIRCLE. Efforts to improve the center of Watchung continued in the 1990s. The site of the old icehouse, which had been a dirt parking lot for many years after the icehouse was razed, has been turned into a village green. The borough hall (which replaced the glove factory), the Texier House (now used for borough offices), and a new spillway that replaced the 1894 dam are visible in this aerial view.

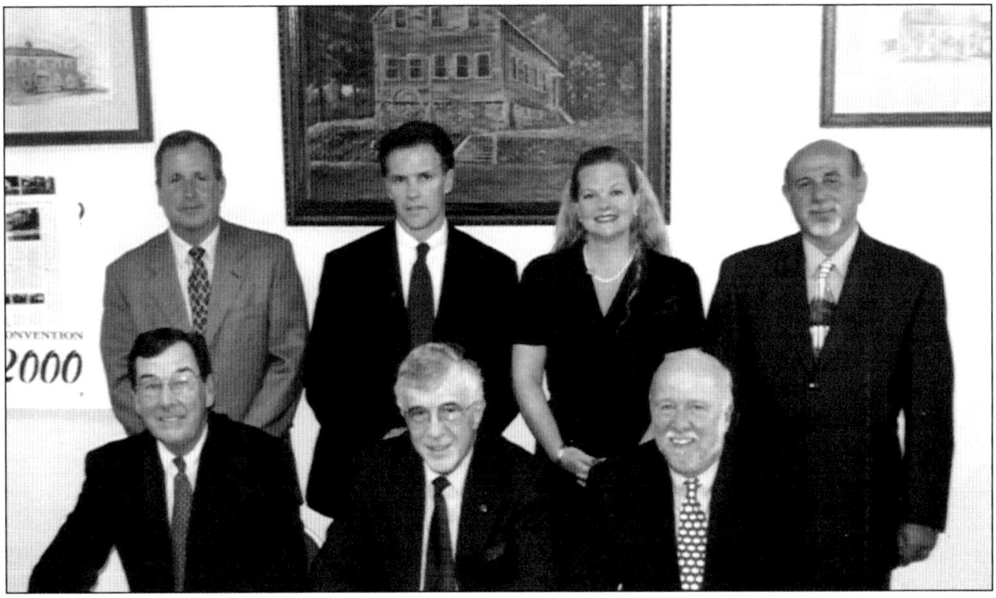

THE MAYOR AND COUNCIL. A borough form of government is made up of a mayor and six councilmembers. They are nonsalaried positions, with the qualifications being residence in Watchung and registration as a voter. The 2001 officials are, from left to right, as follows: (front row) council president Albert Ellis, Mayor Anthony Addario, and Bruce McCumber; (back row) Wayne Otto, Stephen Black, Catherine Ilchert, and Tom Franklin.

Four

Residences

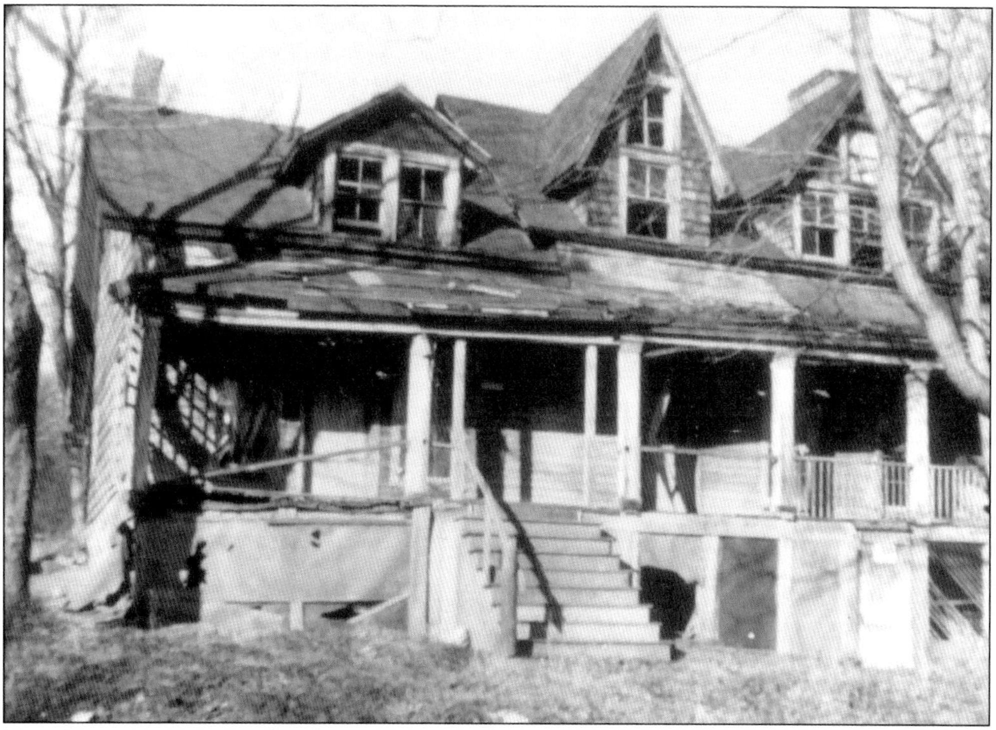

The Spencer Home. This homestead, owned by the Spencer family and later by Henry Guinard, stood where the medical building stands today at 40 Stirling Road. In the 1880s, this house was popular because it had a large so-called "ballroom" where square dances and masquerade parties were held. People would walk for miles by lantern light to these affairs, many times in costume.

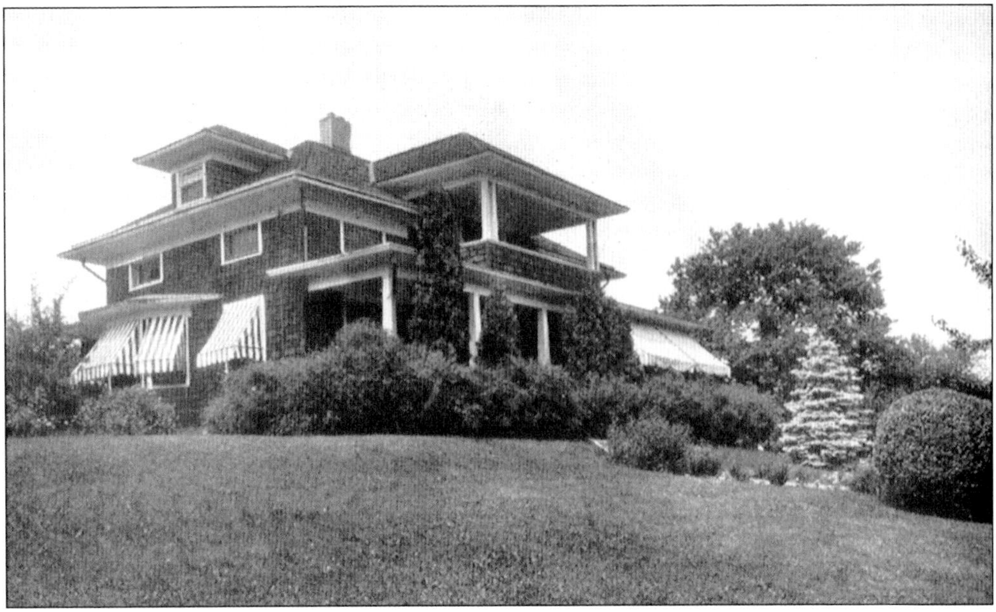

93 VALLEY ROAD. Shown around the time it was built in 1920, this house was home to Mayor Harry MacDonald and Jeanette MacDonald. Mrs. MacDonald, born in 1879 in Plainfield, was one of the founders of the Watchung Parent-Teachers Association (PTA) and served as its first vice president. During both world wars, she was an organizer and volunteer in the Watchung Red Cross. She died at the age of 99.

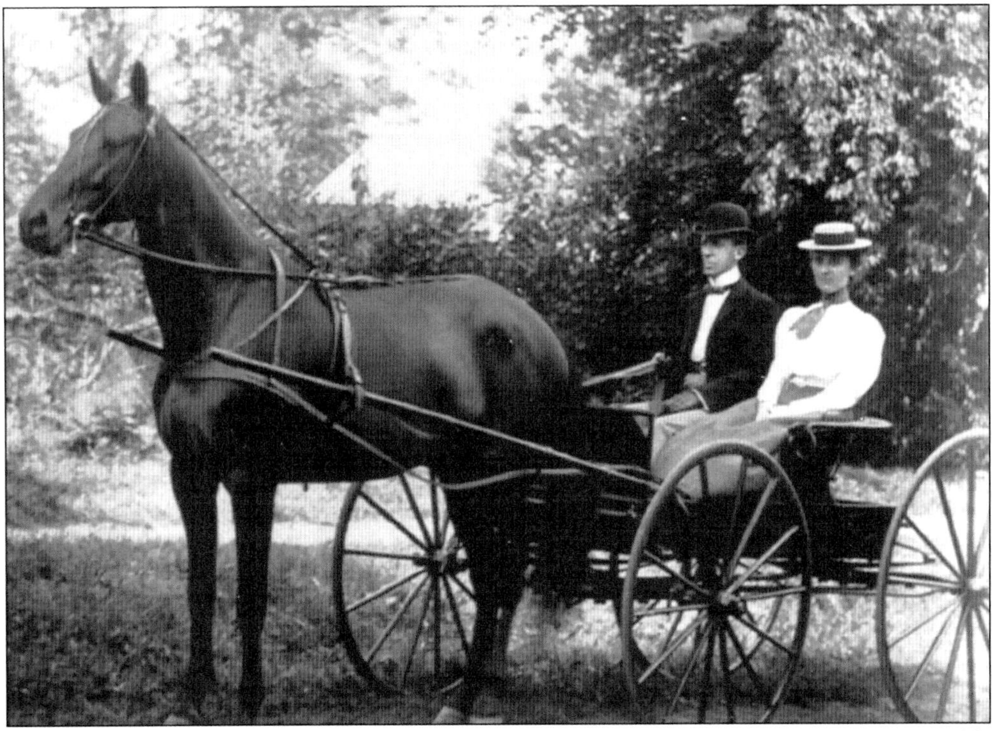

A BUGGY RIDE. Mr. and Mrs. Harry MacDonald are shown in the early 1900s. MacDonald's ancestors dated back to 17th-century settlers. He was born in 1870 and lived to the age of 91.

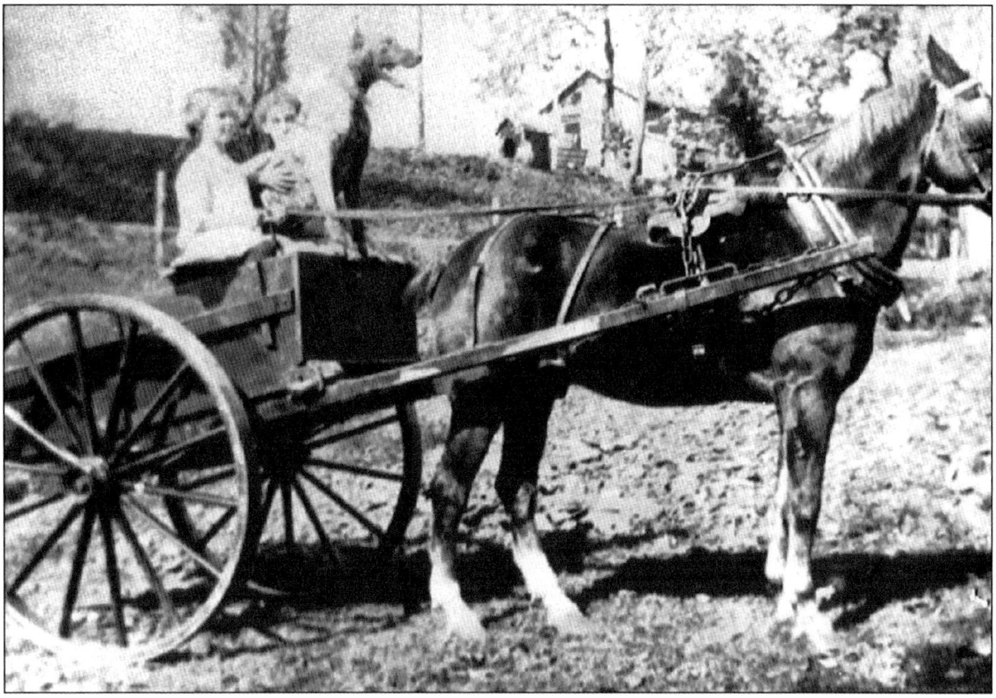

EXCAVATING A POND. Helen MacDonald (Eaton) and cousin Margaret Demler are shown *c.* 1913 helping to excavate for the MacDonald pond at property on Valley Road. The horse was thought to be named Gwendolen.

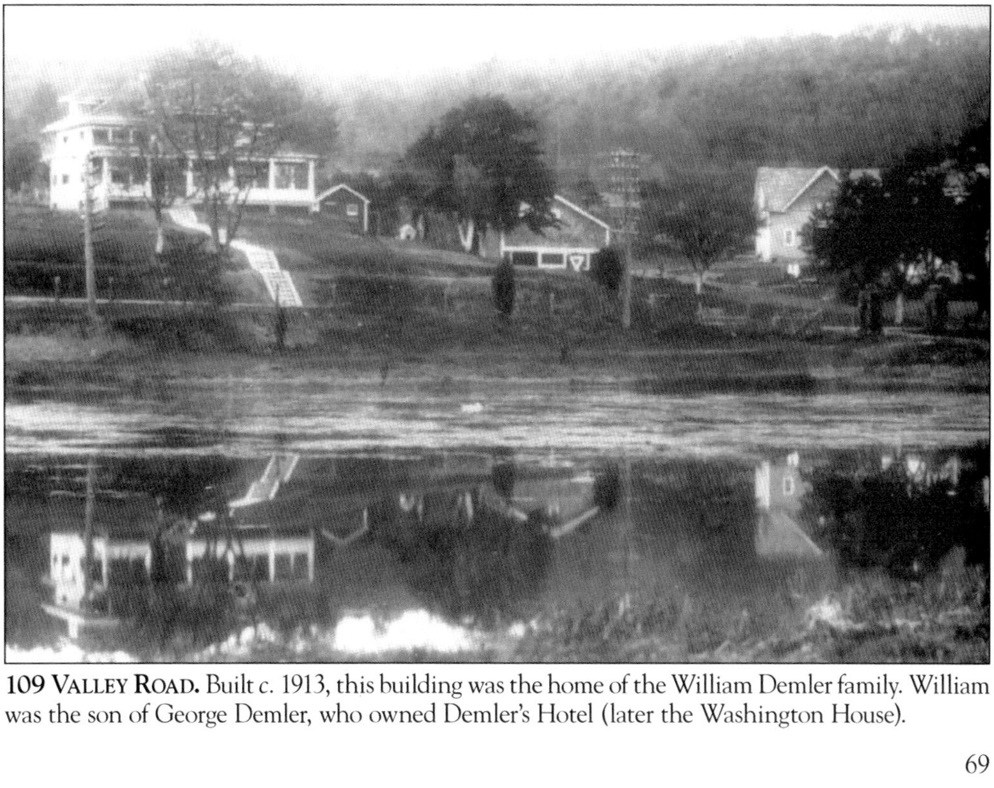

109 VALLEY ROAD. Built *c.* 1913, this building was the home of the William Demler family. William was the son of George Demler, who owned Demler's Hotel (later the Washington House).

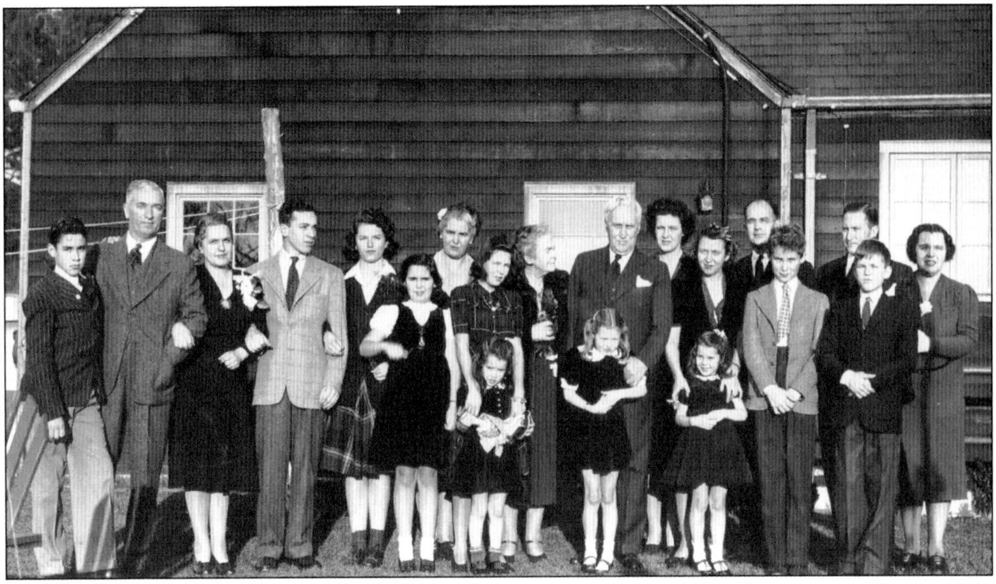

The Eaton Family. Dr. Charles Aubrey Eaton, a resident of Watchung, served as a U.S. congressman for 28 years. Eaton and his wife, Mary, are shown here with their extended family in 1941. They are, from left to right, Charles Eaton III, Douglas Demler, Margaret Eaton Demler, Douglas Demler Jr., Mary Evelyn Demler, Ann Corey, Frances Winifred Eaton Corey, Winifred Wilma Corey behind Nina Sabilla His, Mary Eaton, Hester Hyde, Charles Eaton, Star Eaton Hyde Stoneham, Helen MacDonald Eaton and daughter Janice, Charles Eaton II, Macdonald Eaton, George His, Noel His, and Mary Eaton His.

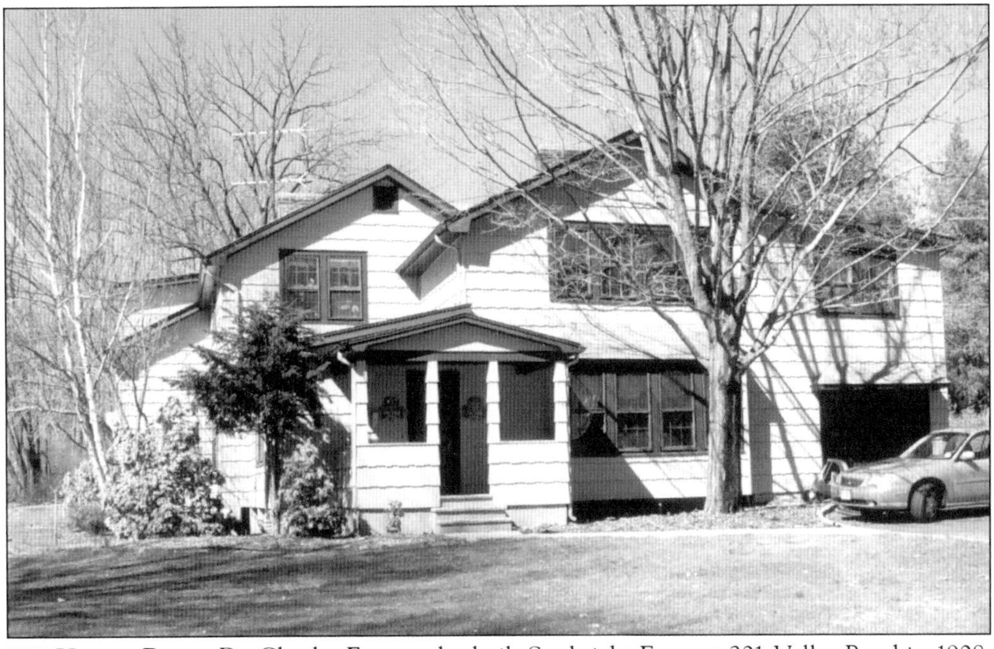

201 Valley Road. Dr. Charles Eaton, who built Sunbright Farm at 201 Valley Road in 1908, often entertained foreign dignitaries at his home. Born in Nova Scotia in 1868, Dr. Eaton was a clergyman, author, editor, farmer, and statesman. While a minister in Massachusetts, he married Mary Winifred Parlin in 1895.

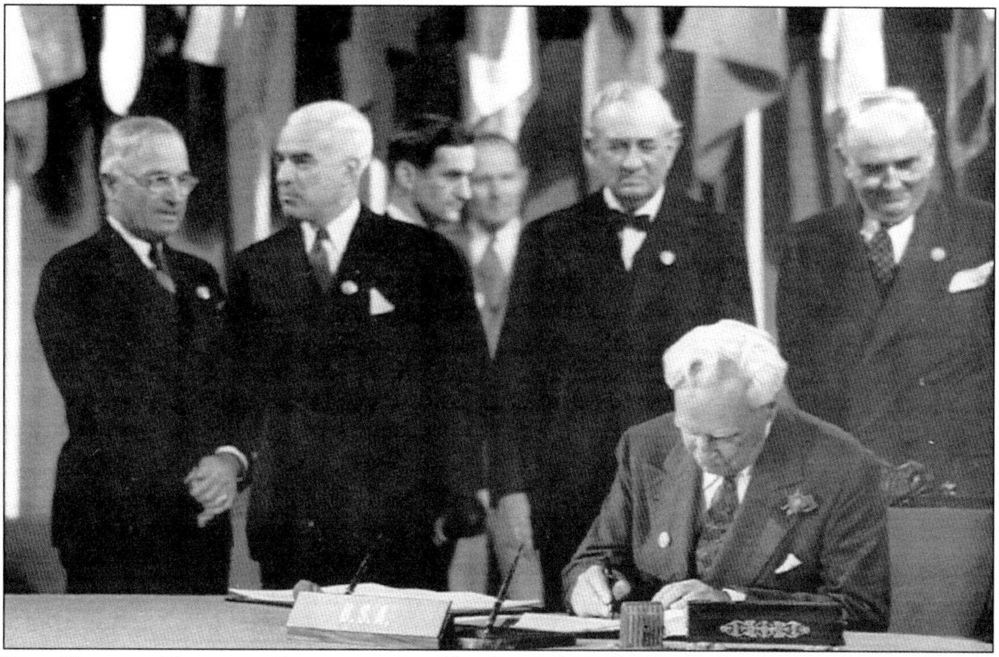

THE UNITED NATIONS CHARTER. Dr. Charles Aubrey Eaton is shown signing the United Nations Charter on behalf of the United States on June 25, 1945, in San Francisco. Standing behind Dr. Eaton are, from left to right, Pres. Harry S. Truman, Secretary of State Edward R. Stettinius Jr., Sen. Tom Connally, and Sen. Arthur H. Vandenberg. Dr. Eaton was appointed a delegate to the United Nations Charter Conference by Pres. Franklin D. Roosevelt.

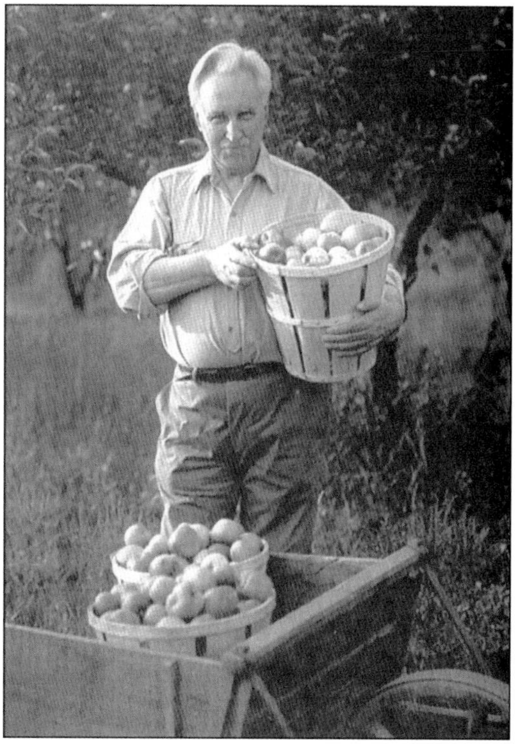

PICKING APPLES. Dr. Eaton is picking apples at Sunbright Farm, his home on Valley Road. His granddaughter Hester Hyde recalled, "Whenever Grandfather came home to Watchung from Washington, the first thing he did was to sit down at the big kitchen table and have a piece of apple pie with cheddar cheese."

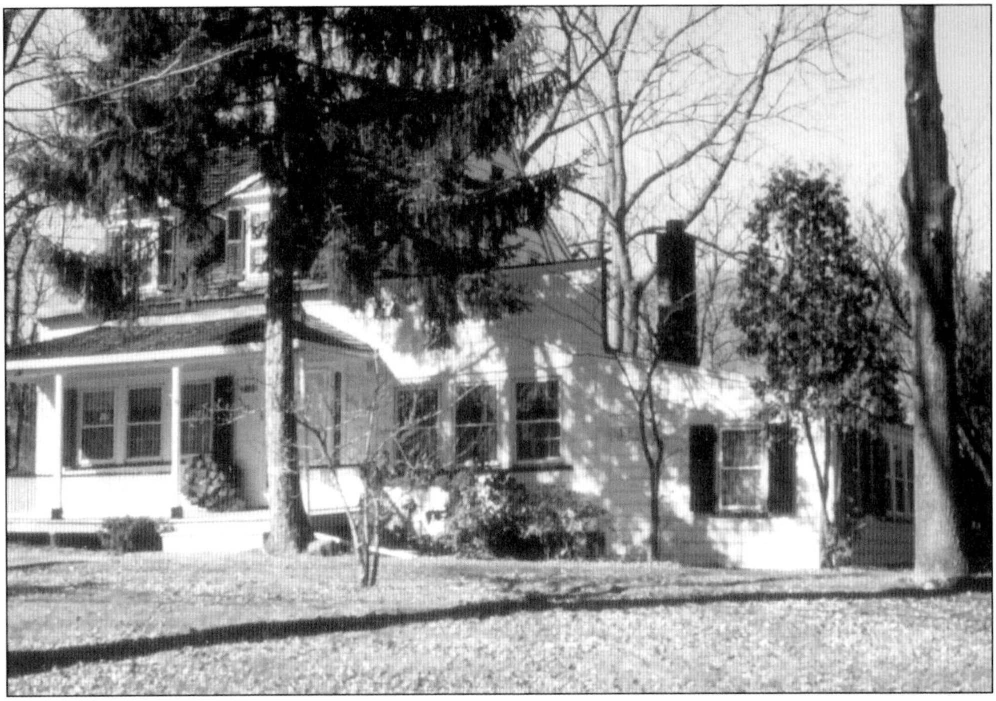

253 VALLEY ROAD. Built in 1740 by the same family as the historic Drake House in Plainfield, the original building was one room with a loft above. Edward Drake came from Piscataway and settled in Washington Valley. His descendants included Jeremiah, Andrew, Noah, Ezra, Jonathan, Humphrey, Martin, Randolph, Edward, William, and Nathaniel Drake.

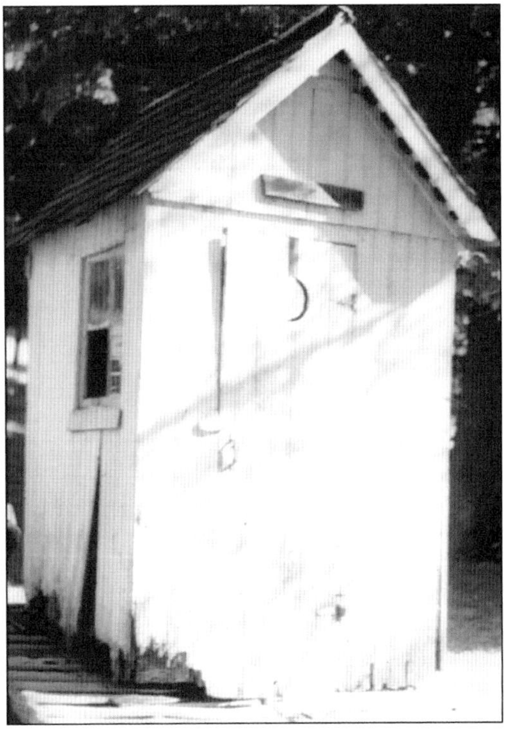

THE PIERINI OUTHOUSE. This outhouse, probably built c. 1900, was originally owned by the Pierini family, who had a home on Mountain Boulevard built c. 1840. Former resident Joe Ward replicated it with members of the Watchung Cub Scouts. The new outhouse is located behind the Texier House on the Watchung Circle.

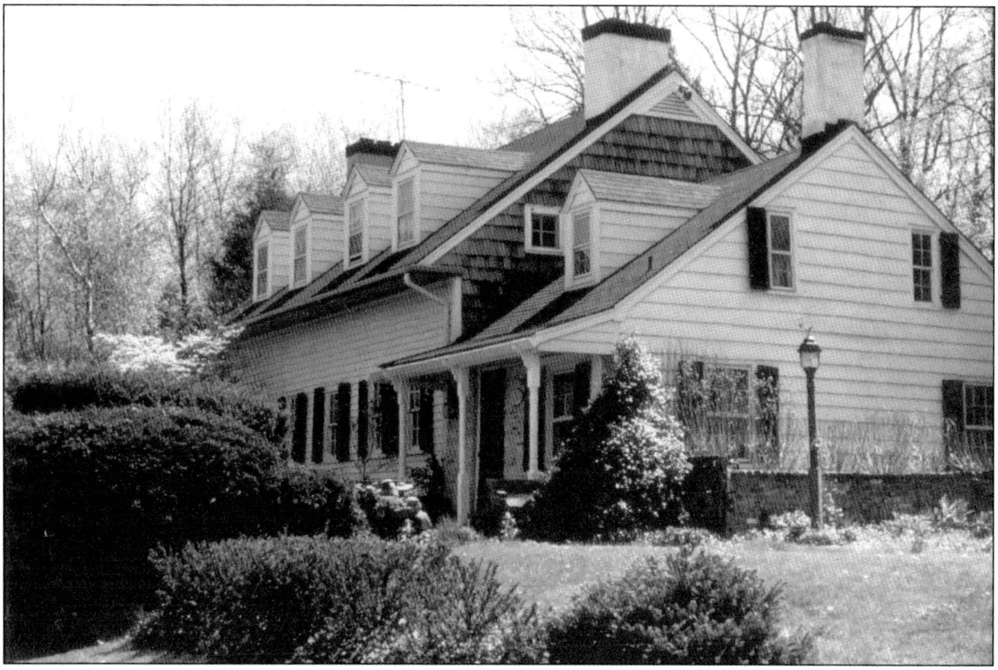

260 VALLEY DRIVE. Built by Aaron Allen before 1730, this house was put together with pegs instead of nails. The lean-to wing was added some years later, and the gabled wing was added c. 1850. In 1925, the house was moved by Louis Hyde from a place where another house now stands at 391 Valley Road.

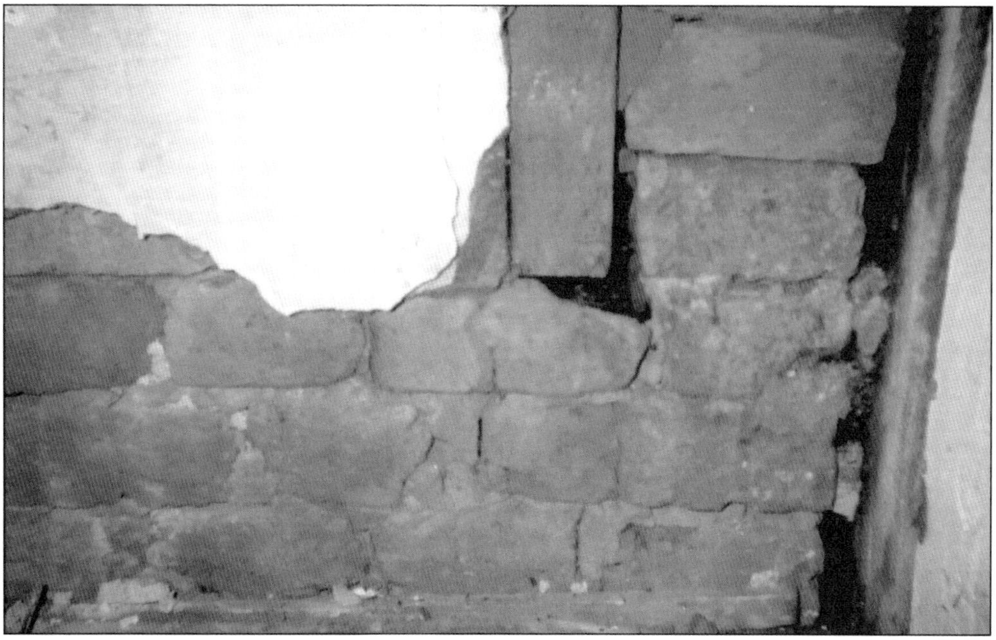

INSULATION. These handmade bricks, found in the walls of the Pierini home once located at 289 Mountain Boulevard, were once used as insulation in the walls. At 260 Valley Drive, all of the walls except for the gabled wing are brick-filled, the bricks being held together with mortar made of clay, lime, and goat hair.

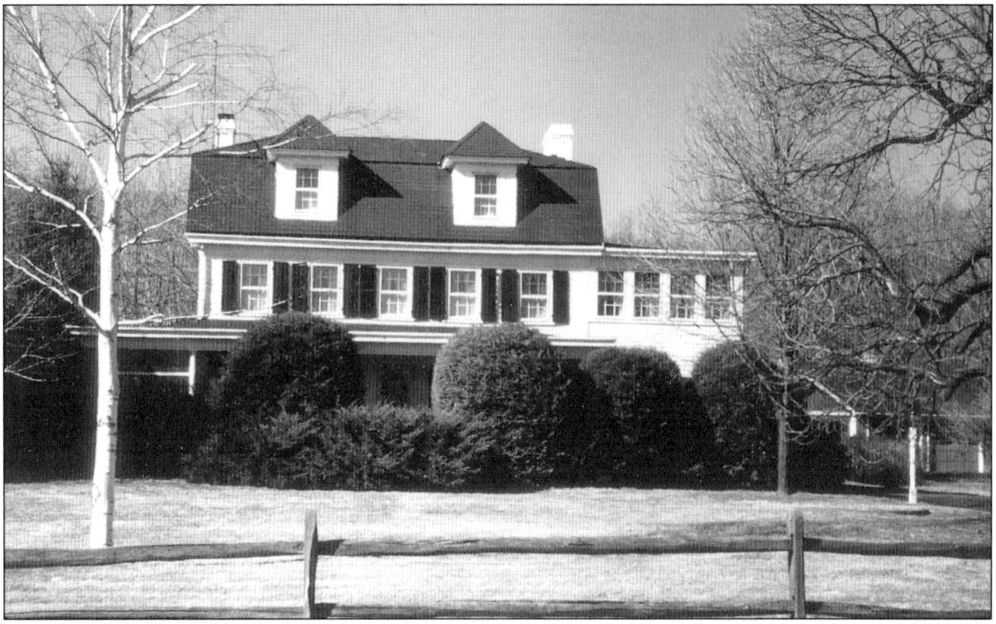

301 VALLEY ROAD. This house was built by Elias Allen in 1747. Although deeds were destroyed when the Somerset County Court House was gutted by fire during the Revolutionary War, it is believed that the house was passed on to Elias's nephew Col. John Allen, who passed it on to his brother David when the colonel moved west in 1812.

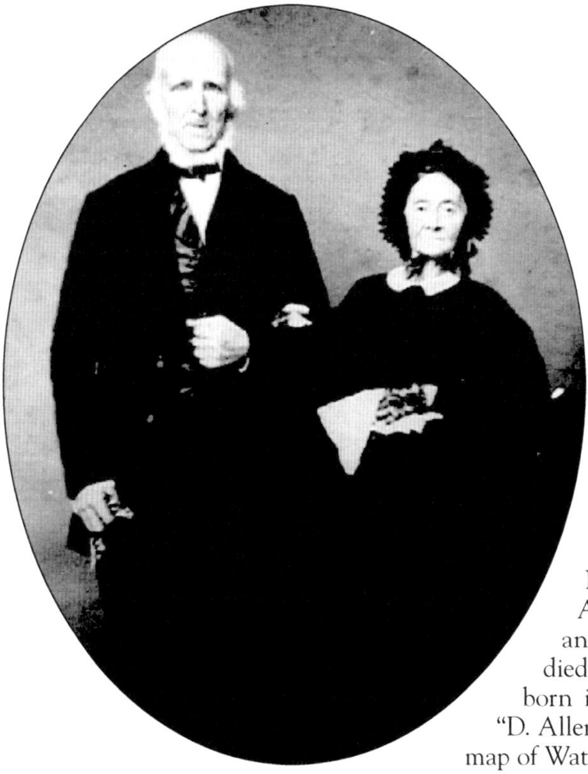

DAVID AND SUSAN ALLEN. David Allen Jr., the 11th son of David Allen and Mary Camp, was born in 1787 and died in 1871. His wife, Susan Townley, was born in 1792 and died in 1871. The name "D. Allen" appears on Valley Road on the 1850 map of Watchung.

Elias Allen. This Elias Allen was born in 1824 to David Allen Jr. and Susan Townley Allen and died in 1903. He married Elizabeth C. Spencer, daughter of James L. Spencer, in 1849. Elias Allen was the great-great-grandson of Joseph Allen Sr., one of the earliest-known settlers to this area, coming from England before 1740, and thought to have been born in 1671.

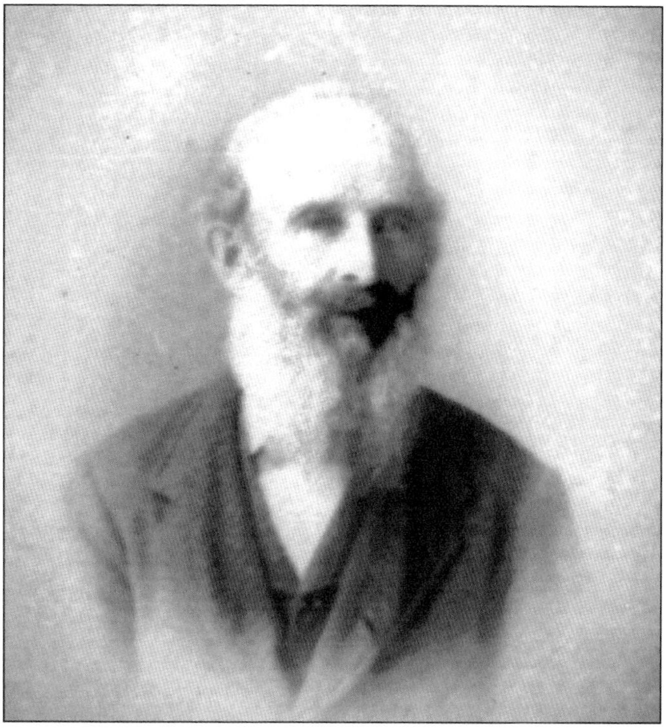

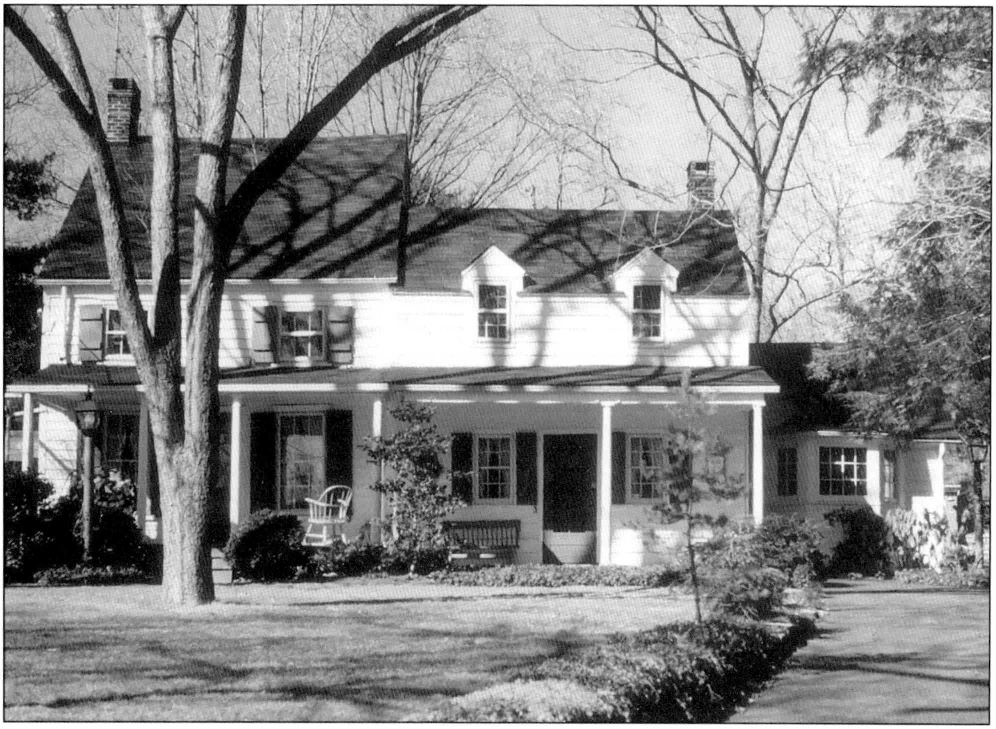

537 Valley Road. The oldest wing of this house, sometimes called the Gavett Farm House, was built c. 1770. The main part of the house was added about 20 years later. The house was moved in 1930 from a site just east of Cardinal Drive.

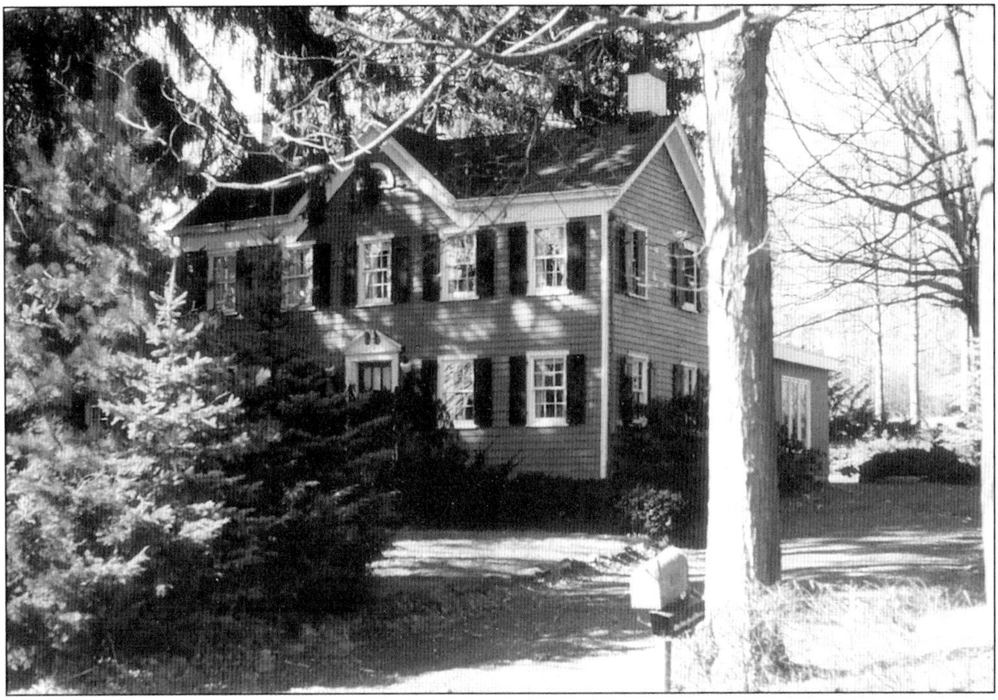

561 Valley Road. In 1850, the main body of this house was skillfully added to an original single room built *c.* 1780 to make the Alfred Moldenke house. This addition was done so carefully that the entire structure, referred to as Cottage Elsinore, appears to have been built at once. The Moldenkes lived here while Castle Elsinore was being constructed.

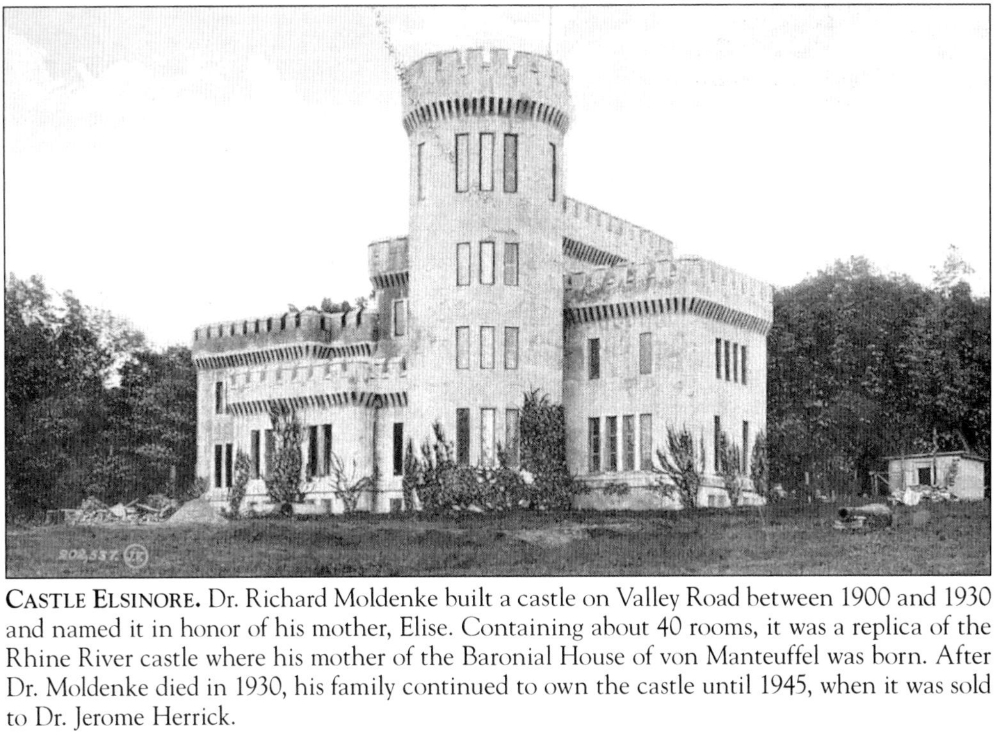

Castle Elsinore. Dr. Richard Moldenke built a castle on Valley Road between 1900 and 1930 and named it in honor of his mother, Elise. Containing about 40 rooms, it was a replica of the Rhine River castle where his mother of the Baronial House of von Manteuffel was born. After Dr. Moldenke died in 1930, his family continued to own the castle until 1945, when it was sold to Dr. Jerome Herrick.

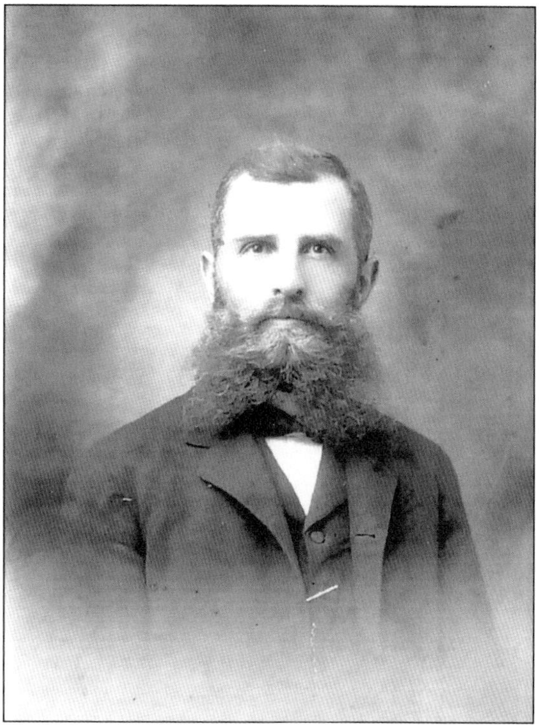

DR. RICHARD MOLDENKE. Educated at Columbia University, Dr. Richard Moldenke spent 10 years in Pittsburgh, where he made his reputation as an expert in metallurgy and in solving foundry problems. In 1900, he retired to Watchung, where, until his death in 1930, he acted as a metallurgical advisor to a number of iron and steel plants here and abroad.

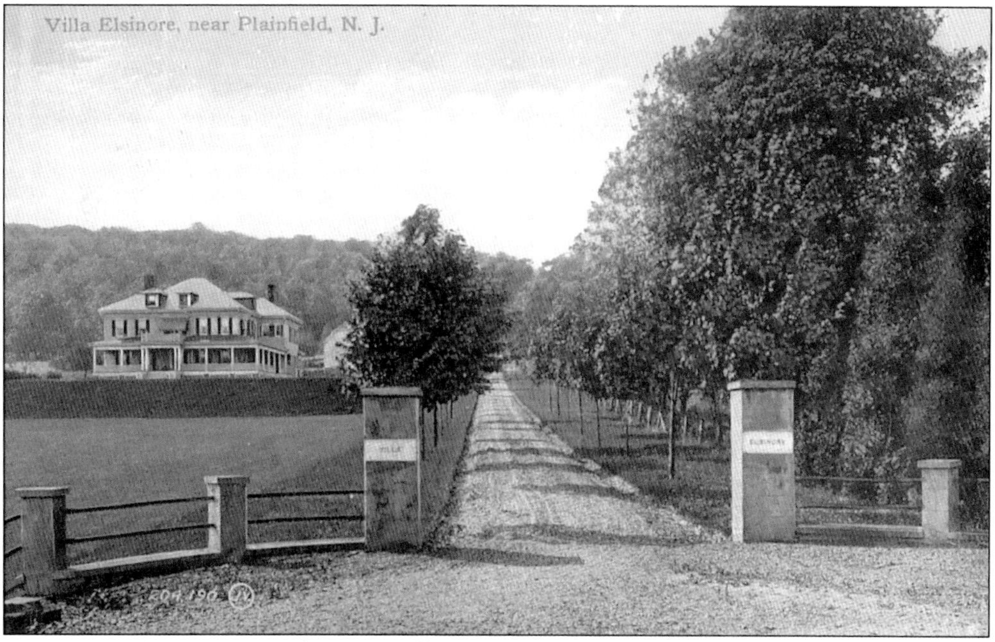

601 VALLEY ROAD. Located across Valley Road from the place where Castle Elsinore stood, this house was the home of Charles Moldenke, brother of Richard. It housed Charles's printing press and bindery used for his Eygptological works, as well as his son's *Flora of the Watchung Mountains*. Known as Villa Elsinore, the house was originally built *c.* 1706, with additions in the 1800s.

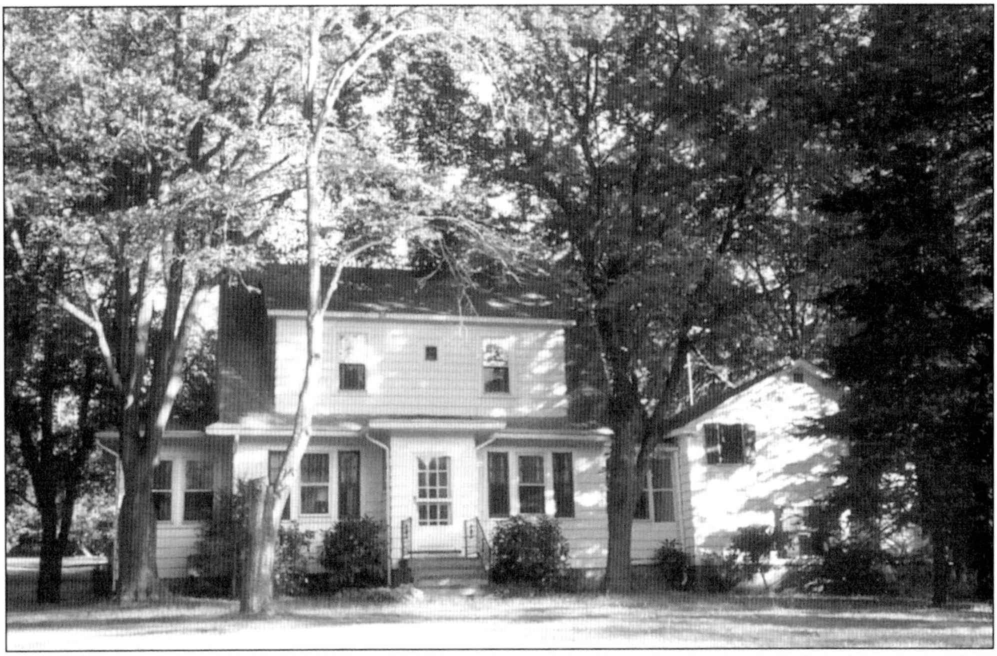

780 VALLEY ROAD. Shown in 1993, this house was the home of Harry and Mildred Wolford for more than 50 years. In the 1960s, the Wolfords sold 15 of their 25 acres to be used for a new school, Bayberry. In 1996, the house, barn, pool, and outbuildings were razed, and the lot was subdivided into six residential lots, served from an access road from Valley Road known as Wolford Court.

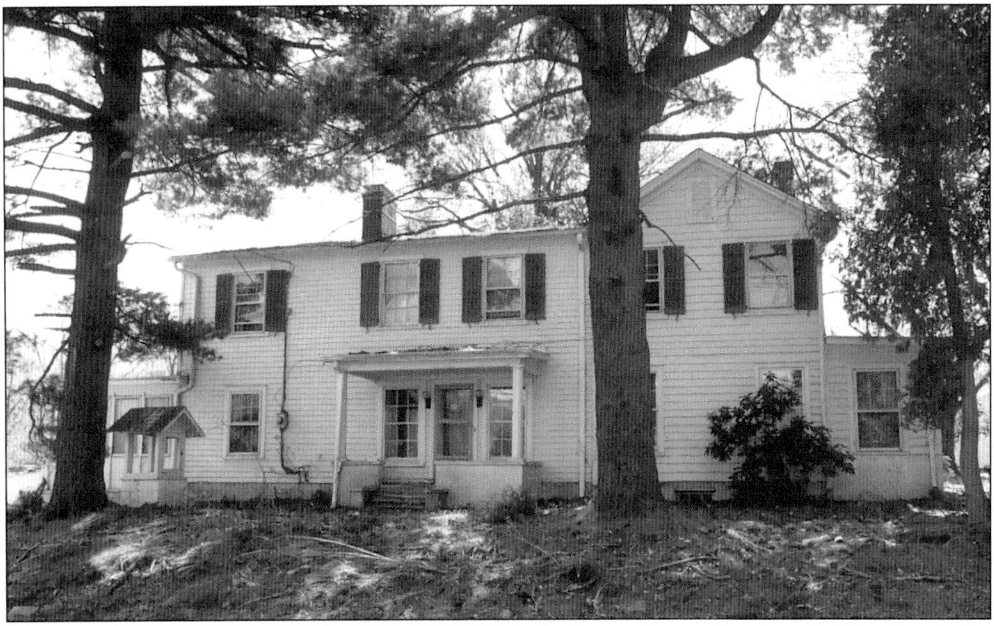

808 VALLEY ROAD. Thought to be the first house built on the south side of Valley Road, the center section constructed in 1732 was one room enclosed by stone-filled walls more than two feet thick. The south side was considered less desirable because it was on the shady side of the First Mountain. The present owners are building a Tudor-style castle behind this house.

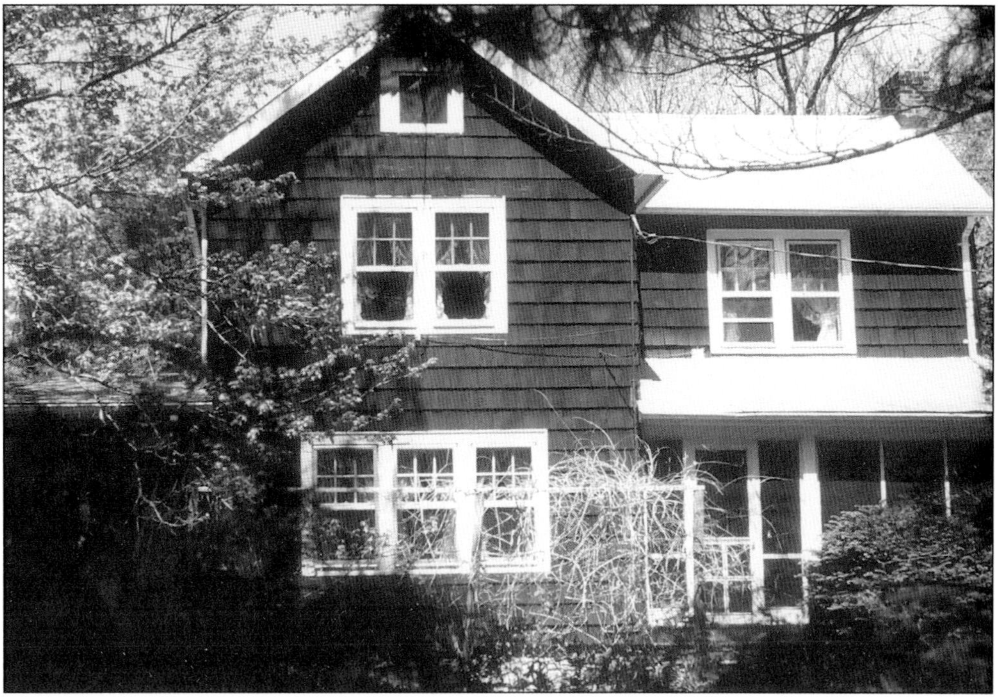

72 Stirling Road. This house, built *c.* 1930, was the home of Mayor Kenneth Schmidt. It sits on a hill just west of the site where his parents, George and Theresa Schmidt, lived.

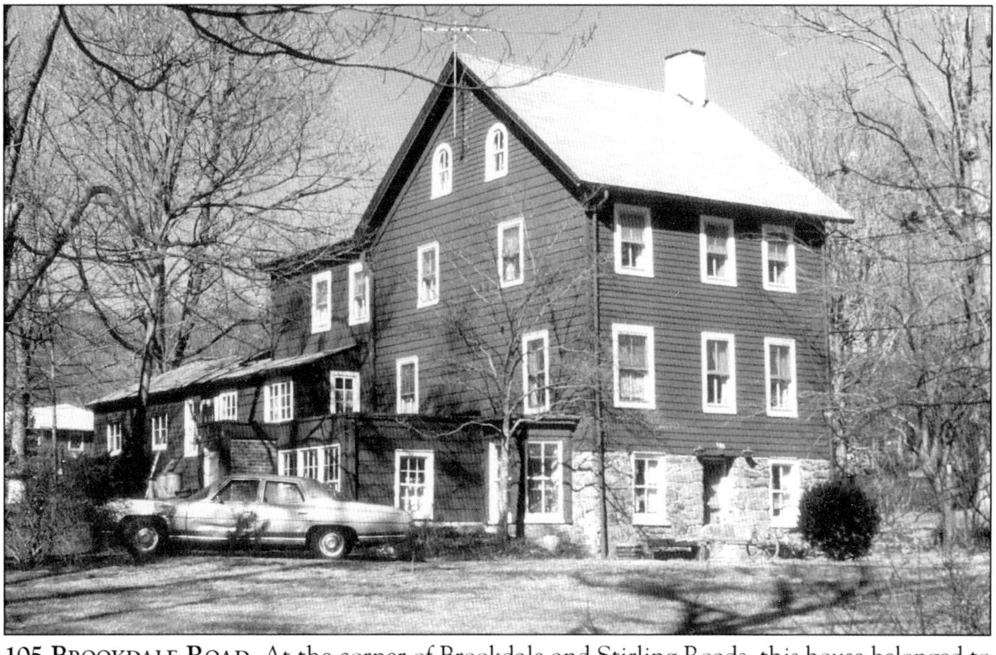

105 Brookdale Road. At the corner of Brookdale and Stirling Roads, this house belonged to Henry Doty in 1789 and remained in the Doty family until 1825. The house is often referred to as the Beeching House, due to the Beeching family having lived there from 1872 until 1944. Rumored to be Catterlin's Tavern, it was probably used as a stagecoach stop, as Stirling Road was part of the route to Morristown.

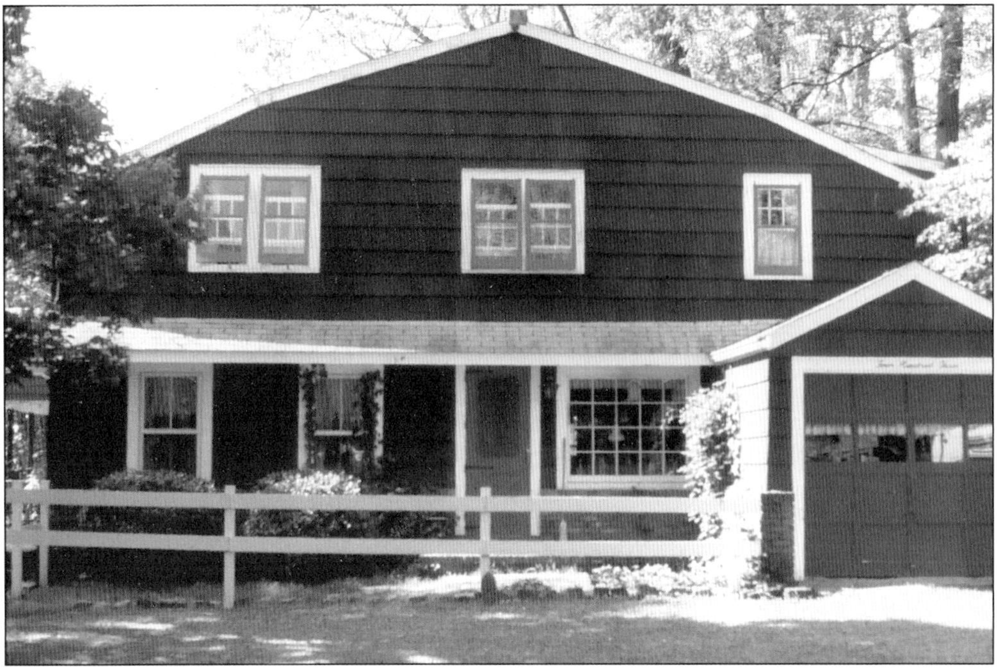

403 MOUNTAIN BOULEVARD. This house, which sits high on the First Mountain, was part of the Anderson estate. R.W. Anderson built it as a honeymoon home for his daughter in the late 1800s.

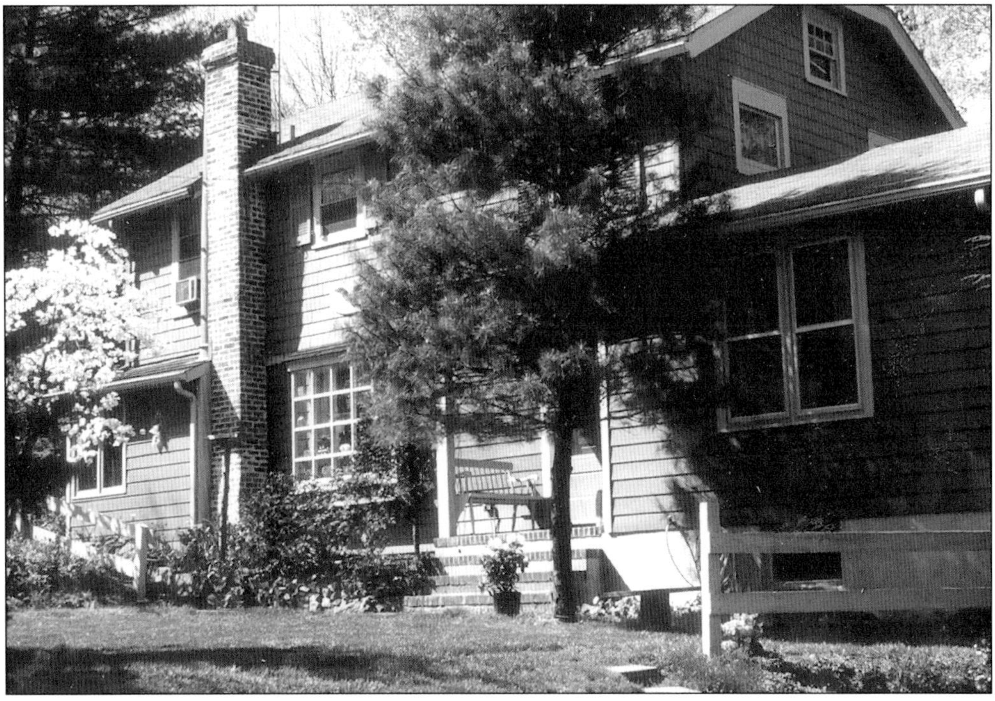

22 WINANS LANE. This was formerly a one-story summerhouse built before 1875. The foundation was built on bedrock with cellar gutters that allow heavy rains to flow in, through, and out the other end. Many owners have enlarged and restored the house and property.

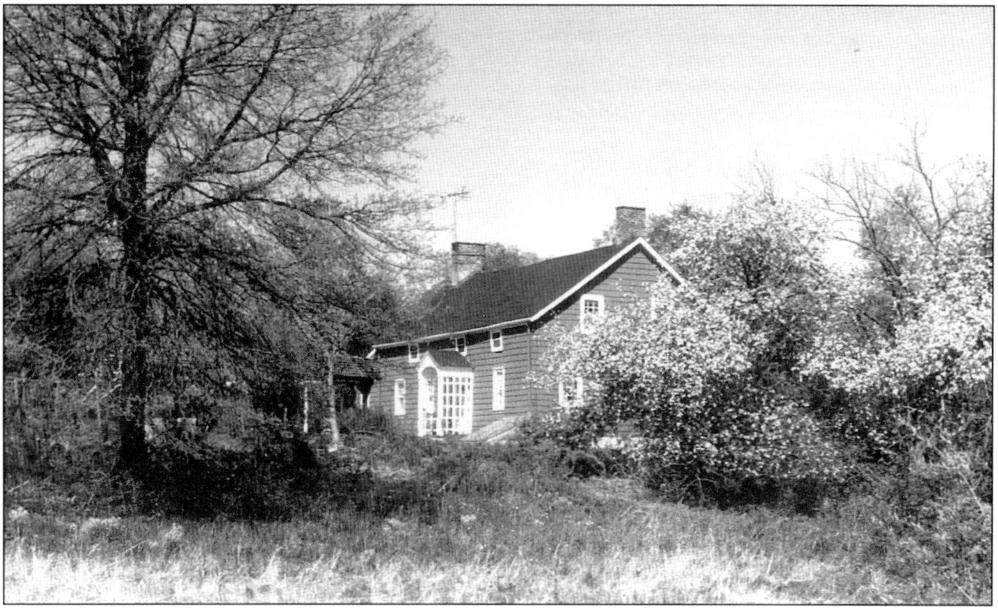

680 Mountain Boulevard. Known as the Santucci House and the Coon House, this dwelling was built *c.* 1732. Hippolyte Texier lived here during the late 1800s, before he built a home in Watchung Center. Texier started his glove manufacturing in the old barn on the property. The house retains many original features, including a fireplace with a bake oven to the side located in the living room.

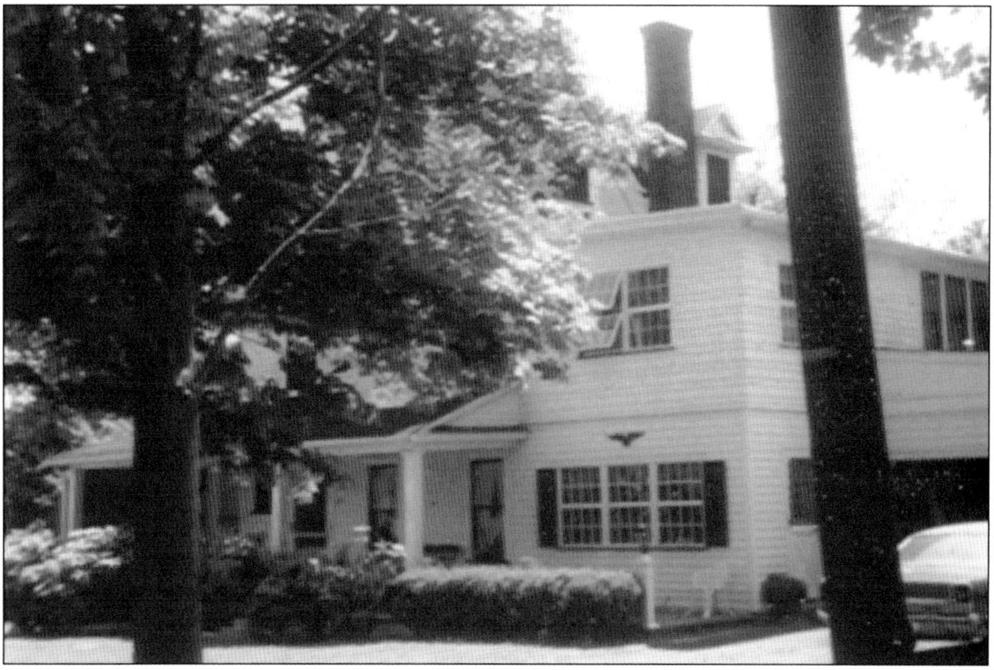

125 Washington Rock Road. The original section of this house is said to date from the 1700s. It is located on the road that leads to Washington Rock just outside Watchung's border. During the Revolutionary War, General Washington used this outlook to watch British activities on the plains below. It was also a popular tourist spot in the 19th century.

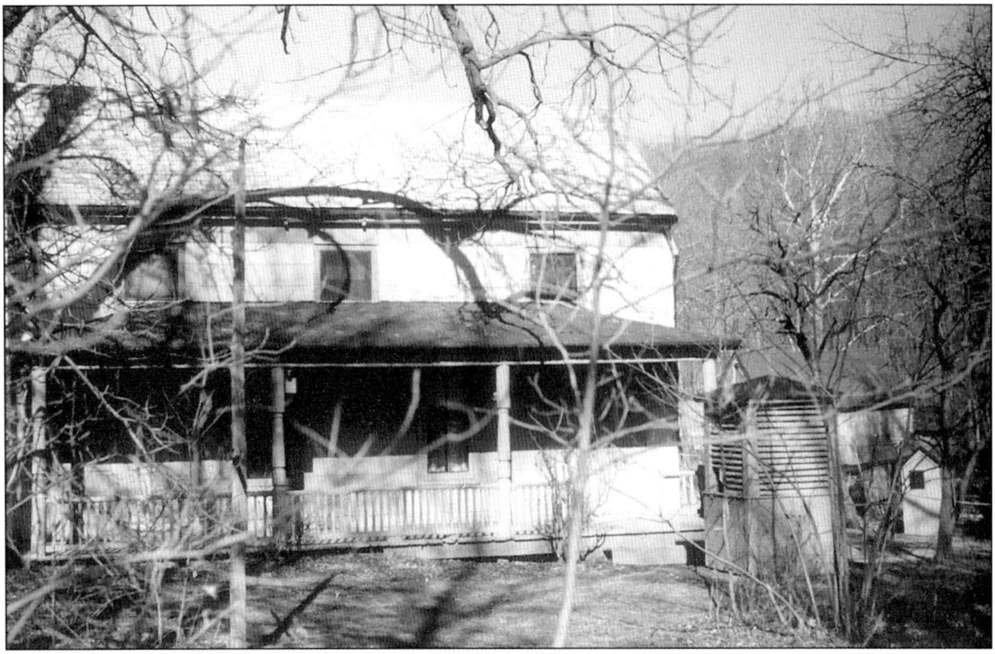

64 NEW PROVIDENCE ROAD. This house was moved to this location by John Mooney, who operated a millwright shop nearby. The deed for this property was dated April 1, 1849.

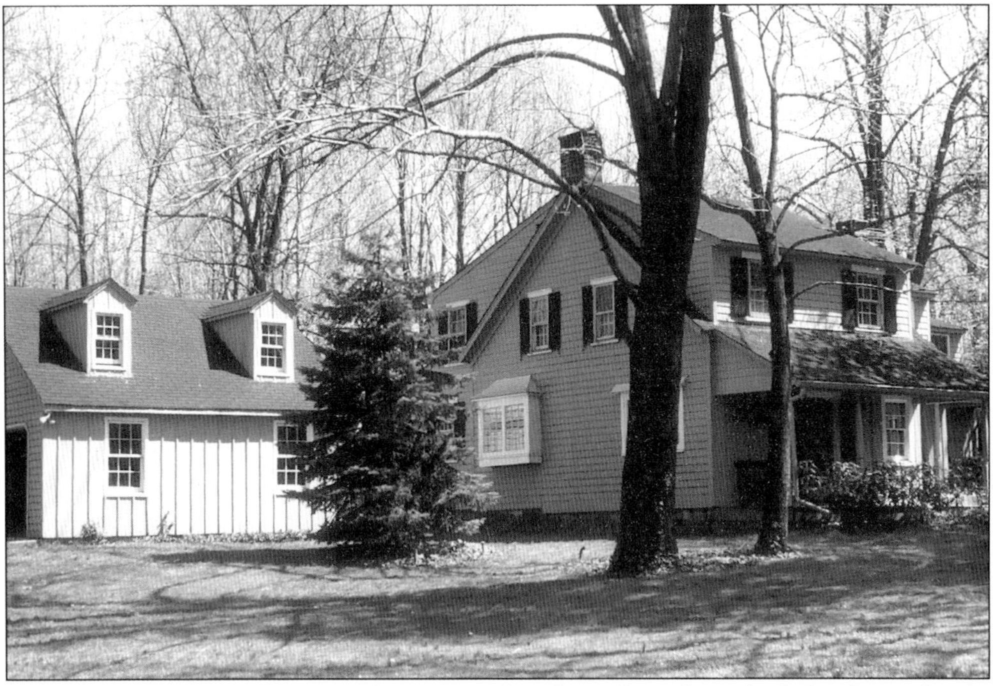

320 BONNIE BURN ROAD. This house was thought to have been built by the Willcocks (Wilcox) family before 1768. In 1768, Peter Willcocks willed his son John "home, lot, and 30 acres." In 1778, John Willcocks willed his son Daniel the "other half of my homestead, one half the grist mill, one fourth my sawmill, one half my quarry, one half my part of the mine." Daniel and Deborah Wilcox lived here until 1820.

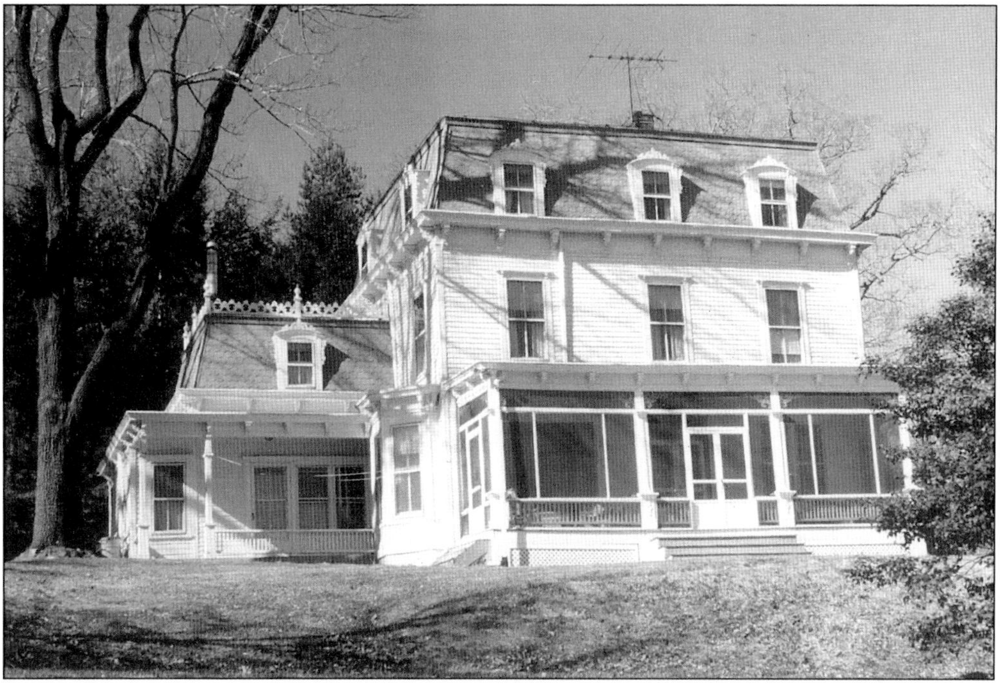

1370 Johnston Drive. John Spencer built this house in the late 19th century. Later, it was the home of the fur miller, Loftus Hollingsworth, whose mill was just south on Bonnie Burn Road. Before the Hollingsworth family moved to this "big house on the hill," they had the first cast-iron bathtub in the area.

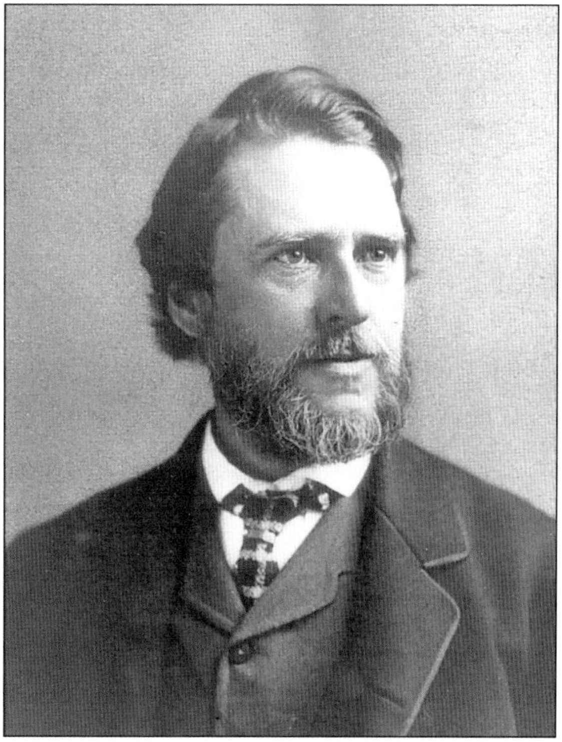

John Taylor Johnston. President of the Central Railroad of New Jersey, John Taylor Johnston purchased extensive landholdings up to the crest of the first Watchung ridge, where in 1876 he laid out a scenic roadway named in his honor. Dynamic and resourceful, Johnston was the first railroad president in America to put his trainmen in uniform, set up prizes for men who maintained their grounds well, and put a car on all trains for unescorted women.

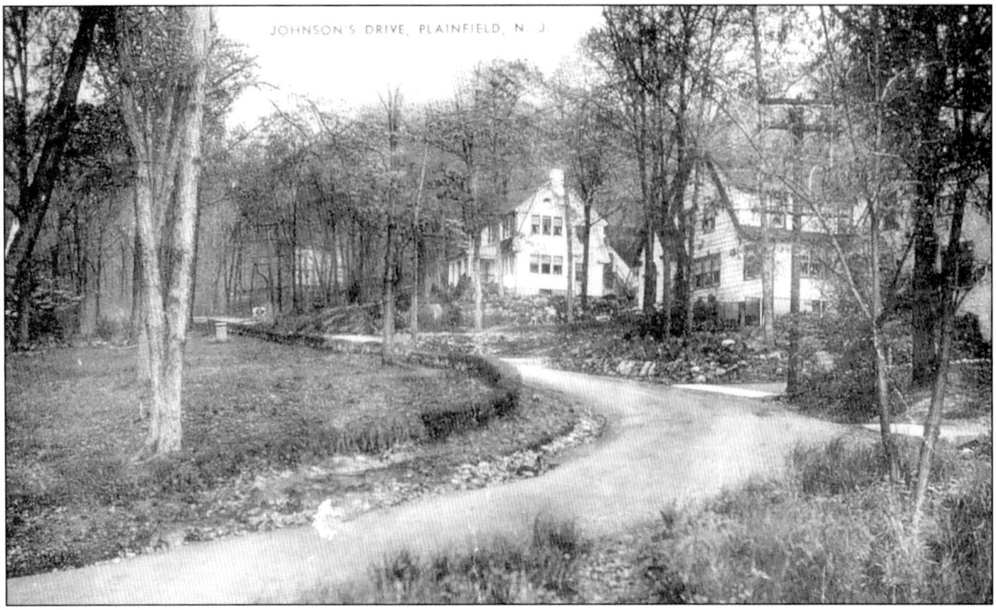

JOHNSTON DRIVE. Nine feet wide, three and a half miles long, and macadamized its entire length, Johnston Drive was the first hard-surface road of this extent in central New Jersey. The route was surveyed with difficulty through dense woods and undergrowth. Grading was begun on January 17, 1876, with 40 workmen on the job. The grade was so steep that 13 bumps were put in the roadway to prevent vehicles from rolling downhill and to provide a resting point for horses.

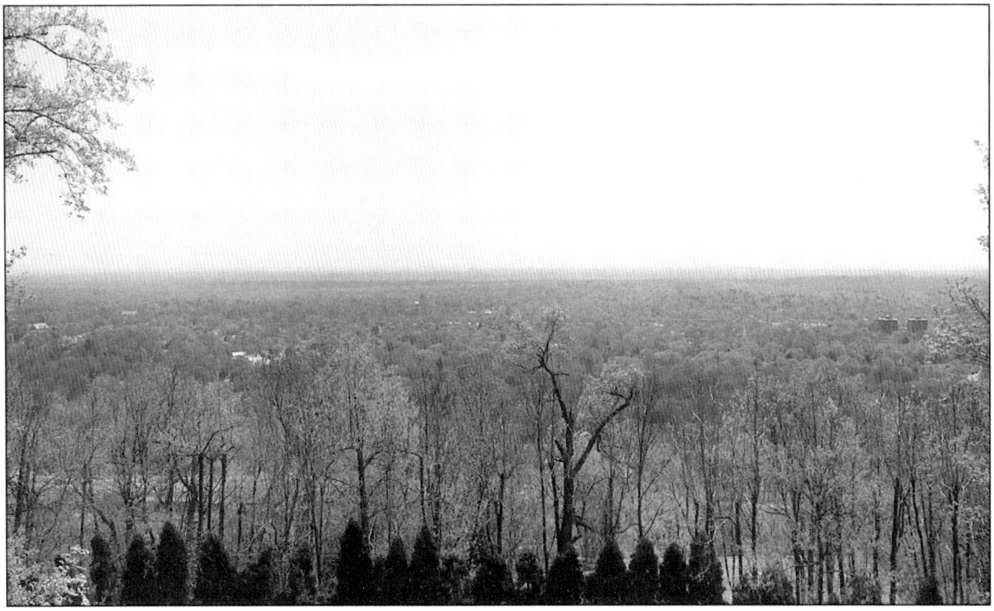

A PANORAMIC VIEW FROM JOHNSTON DRIVE. Marveling at the sweeping panorama spread out below, as many as 300 people would come by carriage from New Brunswick, Elizabeth, and New York on a Sunday afternoon to enjoy the fresh mountain air on Johnston Drive. The drive also became popular with bicyclists during the cycling craze of the 1880s and 1890s. Here, Louis Chevrolet tested his Frontenac Special, which he had built in a North Plainfield garage.

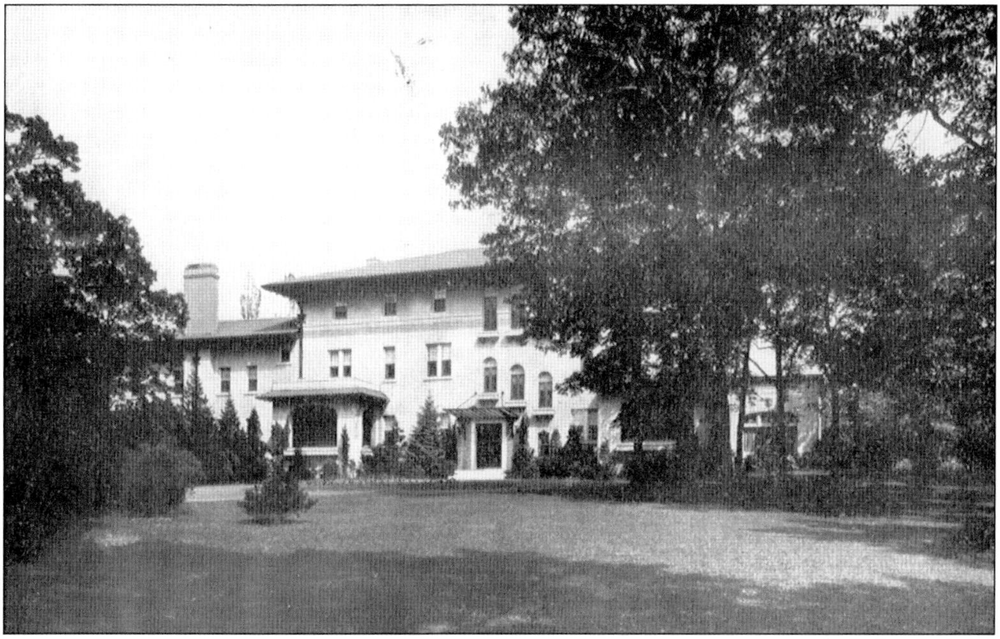

THE HYDE MANSION. Louis K. Hyde, son of Charles Hyde, then president of City National Bank, constructed a lavish mansion in 1911 at the top of the First Mountain on Johnston Drive. He spent $35,000 to build a private road, Mountain Drive, using crushed rock obtained from Wilson's Quarry. The Hyde mansion was converted to a nursing home before it was destroyed by fire.

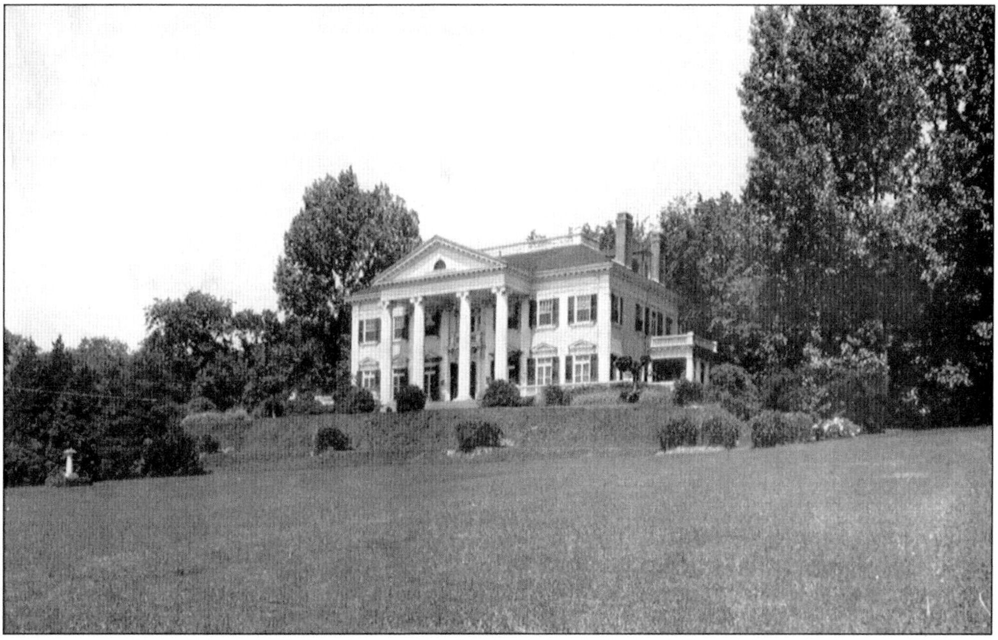

HYDEWOOD HALL. Just below Johnston Drive, Hyde built a magnificent home for one of his children. Nearby was the Hyde's private nine-hole golf course, which later became Hyde Park Golf Club. Regency Village now occupies the site of Hydewood Hall, which was gutted by fire in 1963.

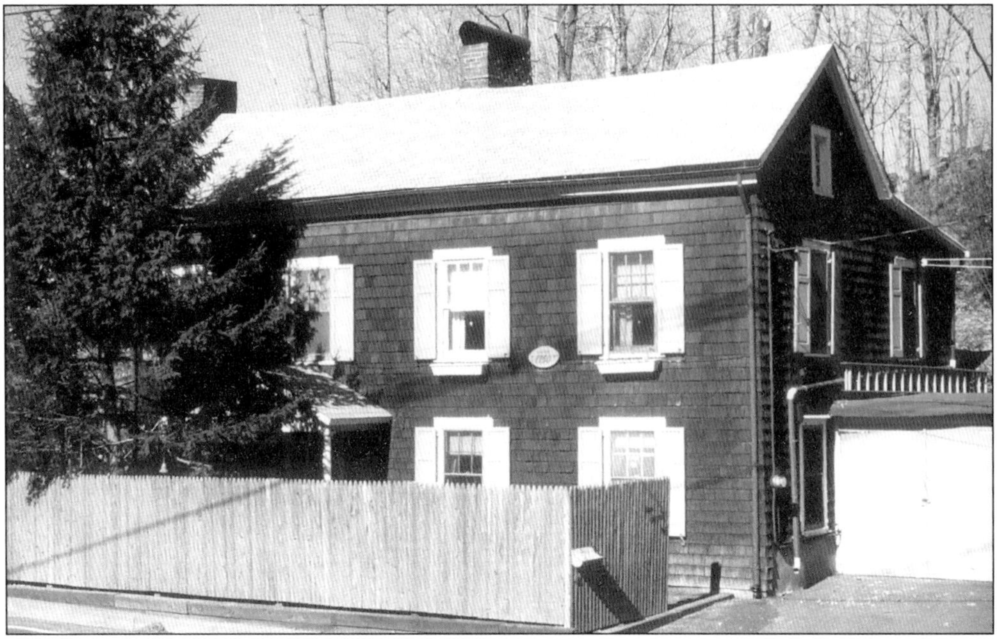

978 Somerset Street. This house was built around the same time as the Washington House, somewhere between 1732 and 1750. The big fireplace in the dining room was used for cooking and as a source of heat. The original portion of the house fronting on Somerset Street is brick-lined for insulation.

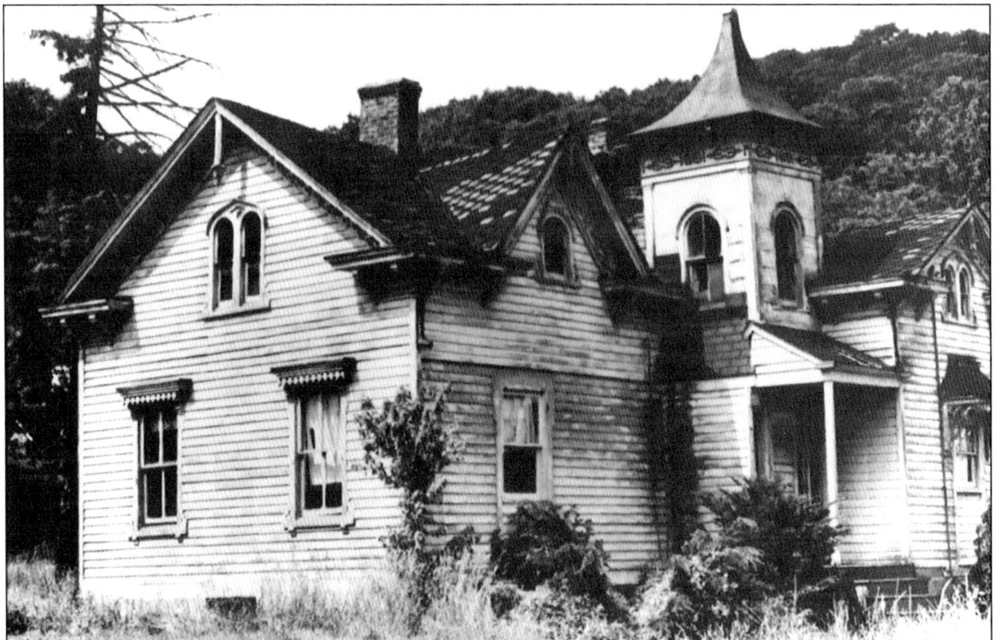

The Miles Homestead. Home of Frank and Sardina Miles, this house was located between Somerset Street and Watchung Avenue on land that is now part of the Watchung Triangle shopping district. The Miles family originally owned the florist located nearby. Then called Miles Florist, it later became the Smith Floral Shop.

Five

SCHOOLS AND CHURCHES

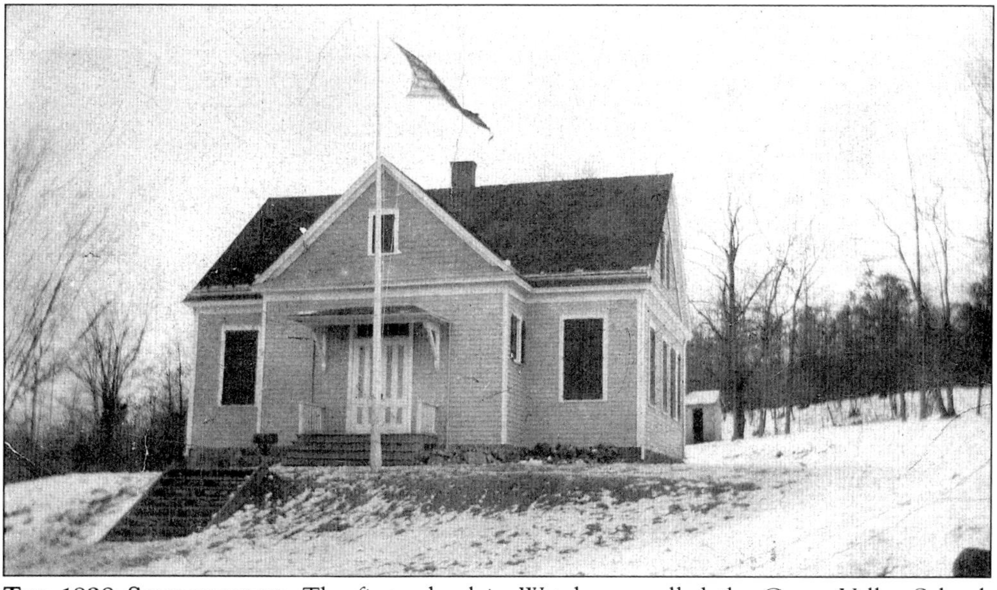

THE 1898 SCHOOLHOUSE. The first school in Watchung, called the Green Valley School, opened in 1851. In 1852, the building was enlarged. It was sold in 1859. A new site for a school was chosen in Watchung Center, and the new school, then called Washingtonville School, was built in 1859. In 1898, the structure was sold and moved, and a two-room schoolhouse, shown here, was built that same year.

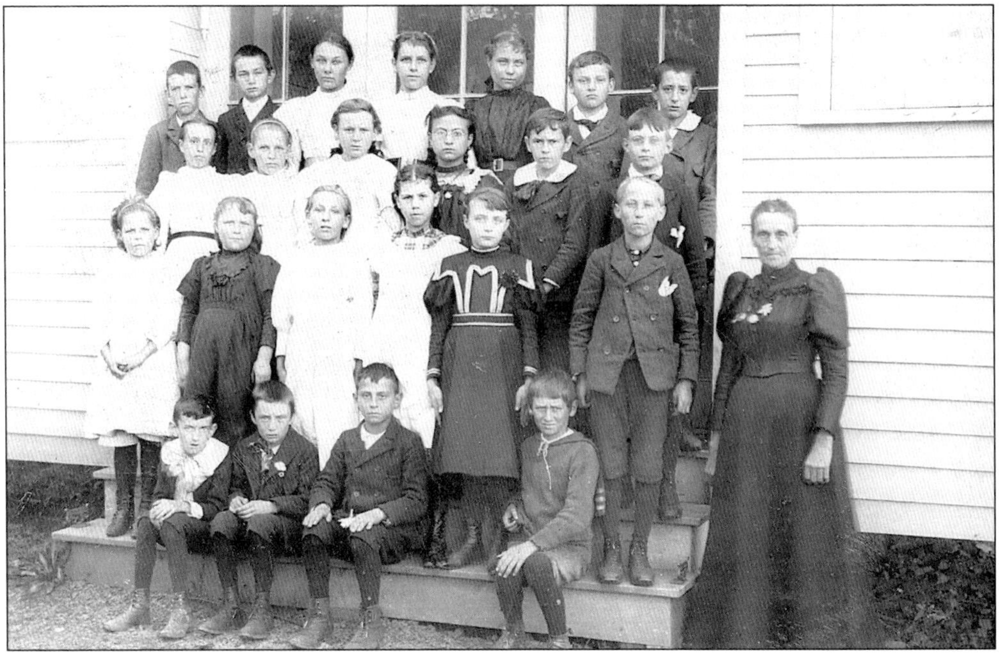

SCHOOLCHILDREN C. 1897. The first full-time teacher was Mrs. Higgins (far right), affectionately called "Granny Higgins." She was described as a strict old-fashioned schoolteacher loved by her pupils. Children in this photograph include the following: (first row) first boy on left, Willie Demler; (third row) first girl on left, Sadie Bodenheimer; second boy from right, Eddie Spier; (fourth row) fourth girl from left, Florence Bodenheimer.

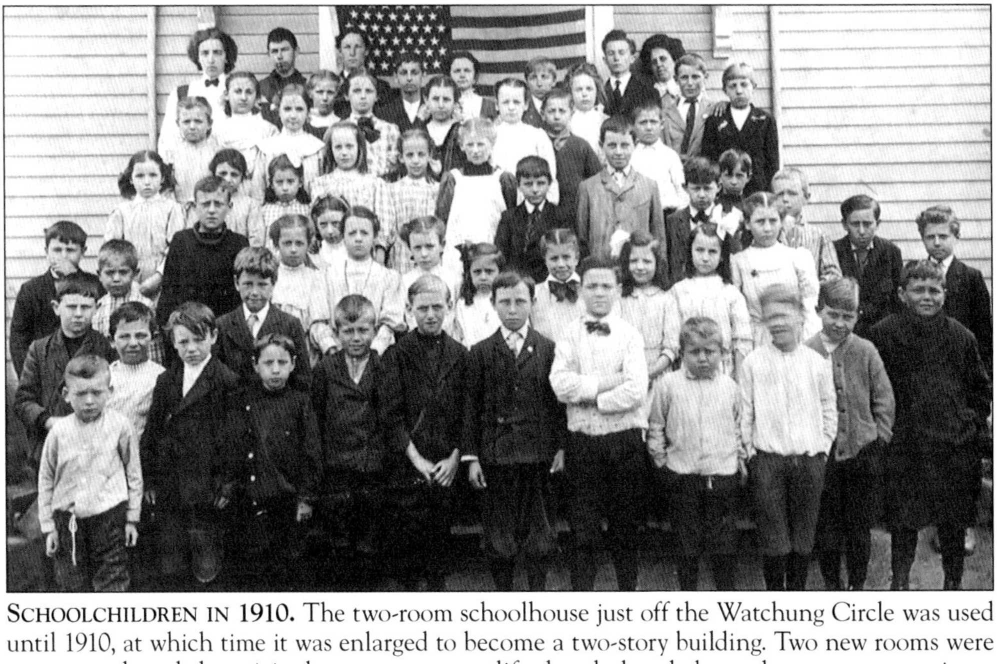

SCHOOLCHILDREN IN 1910. The two-room schoolhouse just off the Watchung Circle was used until 1910, at which time it was enlarged to become a two-story building. Two new rooms were constructed, and the original two rooms were lifted and placed above the new rooms using a system of pulleys. The Watchung School then had four separate classrooms, which were used for teaching kindergarten through eighth grade.

WALKING TO SCHOOL. George Mobus and Emile Perret are shown going to school in 1909. It is known that in the 1930s, a hot lunch of soup was prepared in the Pedeflous Restaurant, and PTA mothers and the teachers served the soup at the children's desks at noon. The teachers were Lavina Rounsaville (first and second grades), Betty Amstadt Sullivan (third and fourth grades), Dorothy Voorhees (fifth and sixth grades), and Edna Baldridge (seventh and eighth grades).

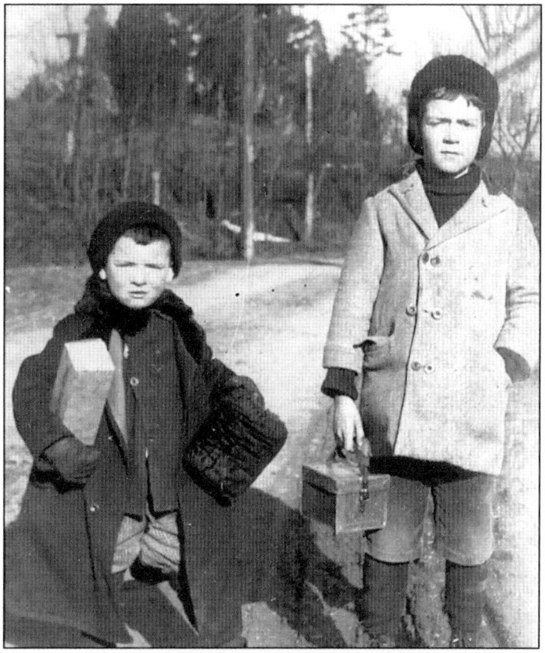

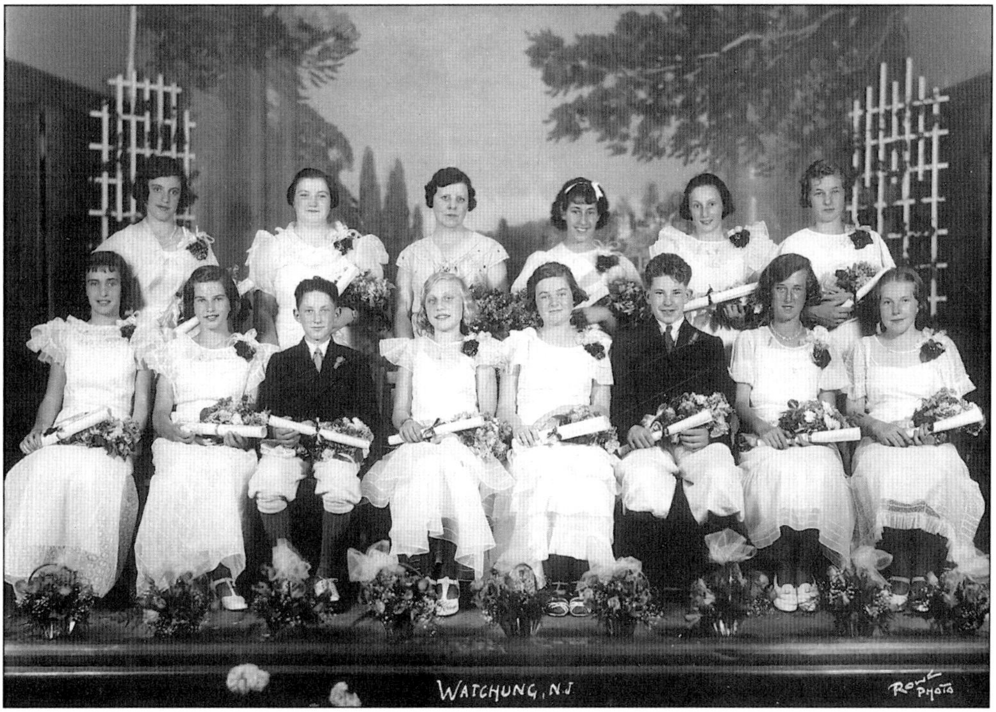

THE 1934 GRADUATING CLASS. The eighth-grade class of 1934 was the first class to hold graduation on the stage in the new borough hall. Shown in the photograph are, from left to right, the following: (front row) Jane Craigie, Marjorie Rendall, Tucker Fulcher, Marie Stober, Sally Pedeflous, Warren Neier, Mary White, and Lilly Olson; (back row) Elizabeth Janelli, Alice Ingraham, Mrs. Baldridge (teacher and principal), Irene Mirzaoff, Helen Arons, and Grace Haberle.

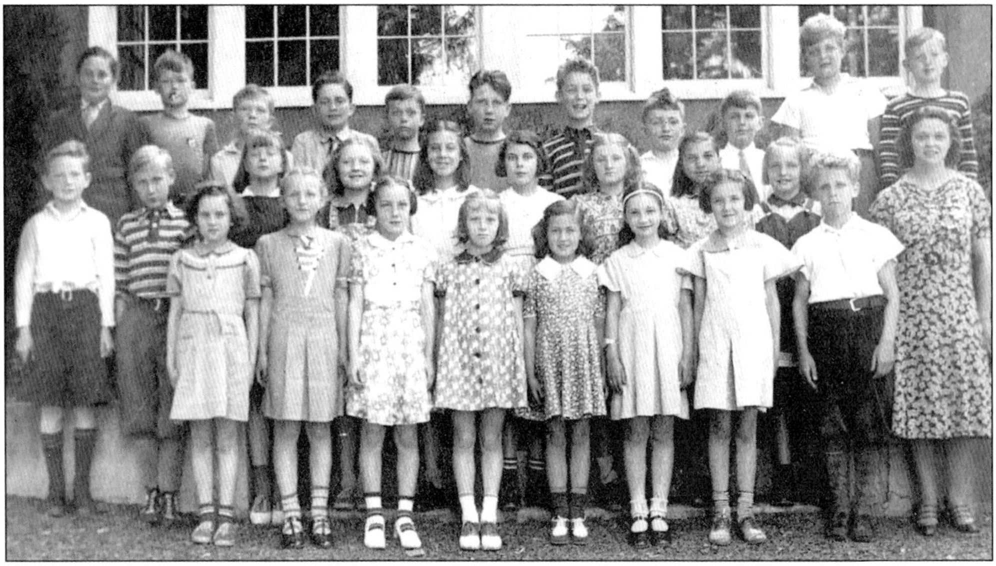

SCHOOLCHILDREN IN THE 1930S. Schoolchildren at the Watchung School in the 1930s are, from left to right, as follows: (front row) Mary Lou Crogg, Barbara Barrett, Virginia Ryan, Beatrice Van Ault, Gloria Ness, Sydelle Grobois, Barbara Adams, and Howard Graef; (middle row) Foster Brown, Joseph Meyersky, Katharine Wilmerding, Roberta Smith, Ann Underhill, Veronica Carrar, Virginia Ewing, Angeline Grievo, Charlotte Mathews, and Mrs. Sullivan; (back row) Richard Stites, Bruce Gavett, Fred Greves, Elmer Stites, Bob Gavett, William Shipley, Don Eaton, George Blackburn, Paul Gunderson, Norman Wakefield, and Fred Zaner.

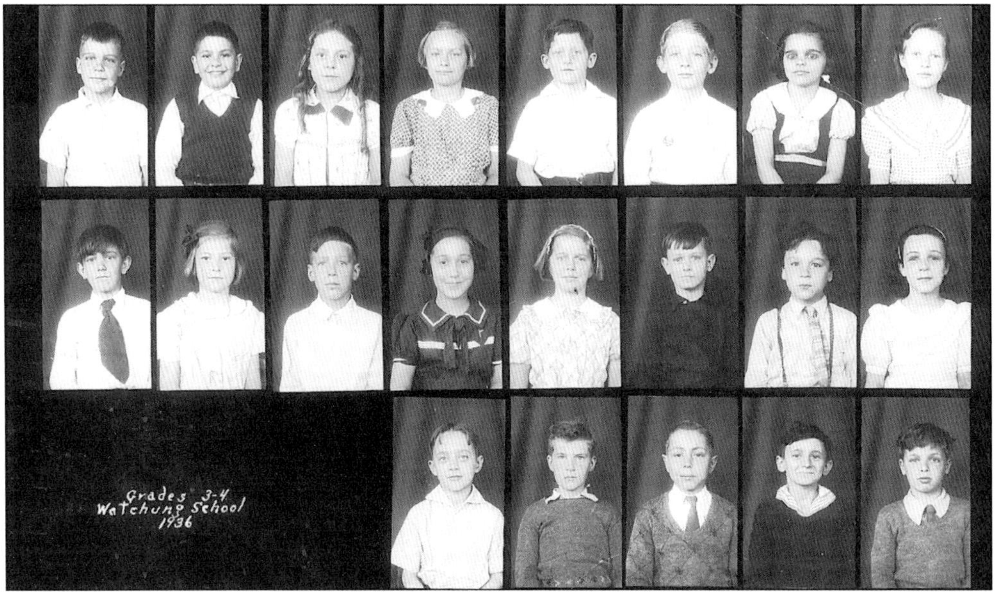

THIRD AND FOURTH GRADES IN 1936. Members of these classes in 1936 are, from left to right, as follows: (front row) Norman Snoden, Leonard Attlee, Jerry Loizeaux, Eugene ?, and unidentified; (middle row) Richie Hall, Eleanor Olsen, Thomas Douglas, Betty Neier, Augusta Wilmerding, Harold Lamson, Elmer Smith, and Emily Smith; (back row) Richard Armstrong, Rino Ghidella, Esther Burdick, Anna May Meyers, Arthur Dove, John Marshall, Mary Ann Bennett, and Ona Greves.

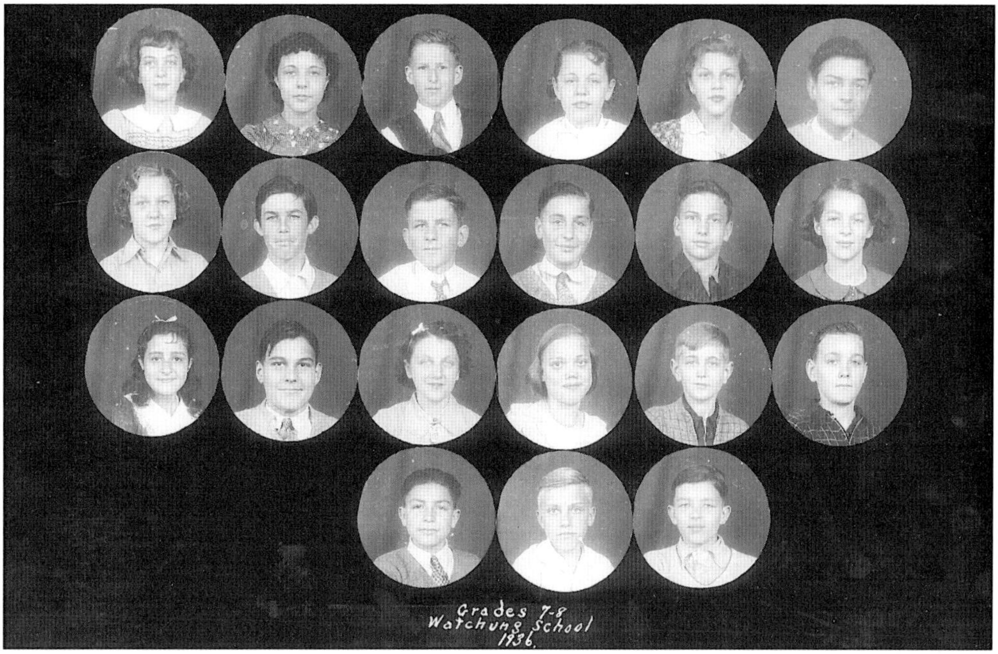

SEVENTH AND EIGHTH GRADES IN 1936. Members of seventh and eighth grades in 1936 are, from left to right, as follows: (first row) Salvatore Grievo, Water Stober, and Dale Flocker; (second row) Annie Lapelle, George Whitman, Elda Ghidella, Margaret Stober, Charles Neumann, and Myrdon Neumann; (third row) Marian Drake, Charles Nunn, Tony Santo, Bob Brown, Kenneth Gardner, and Marian Marshall; (fourth row) Marian Cragie, Eleanor Carrar, David Miles, Eleanor Rivell, Lois Genavero, and George Carrar.

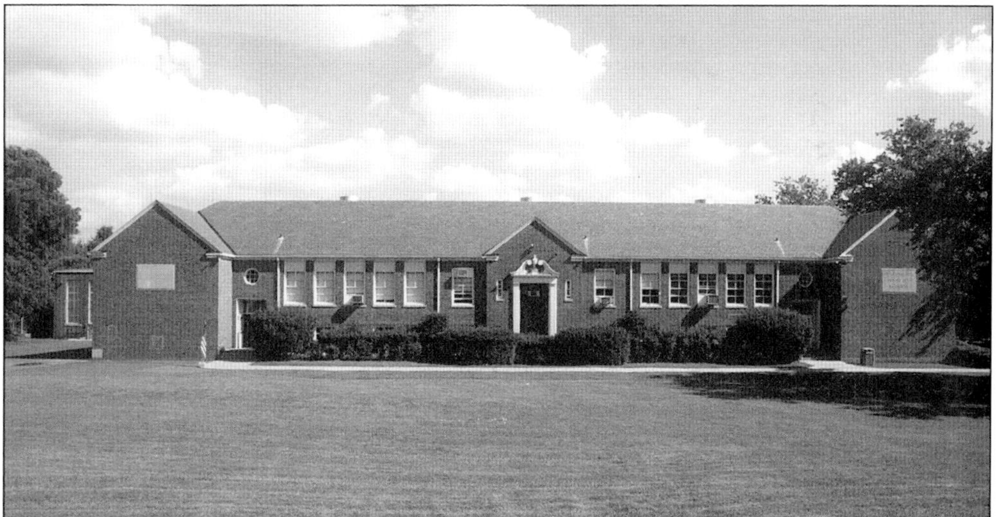

THE VALLEY VIEW SCHOOL. By 1948, enrollment in the Watchung School had increased to 175, and a new six-room elementary school, Watchung Borough School, was built on Valley View Road. In September 1963, when Bayberry School opened, the Watchung Borough School was renamed Valley View School, housing grades four through eight. For the 2000–2001 school year, there were 246 students enrolled at Valley View in grades five through eight.

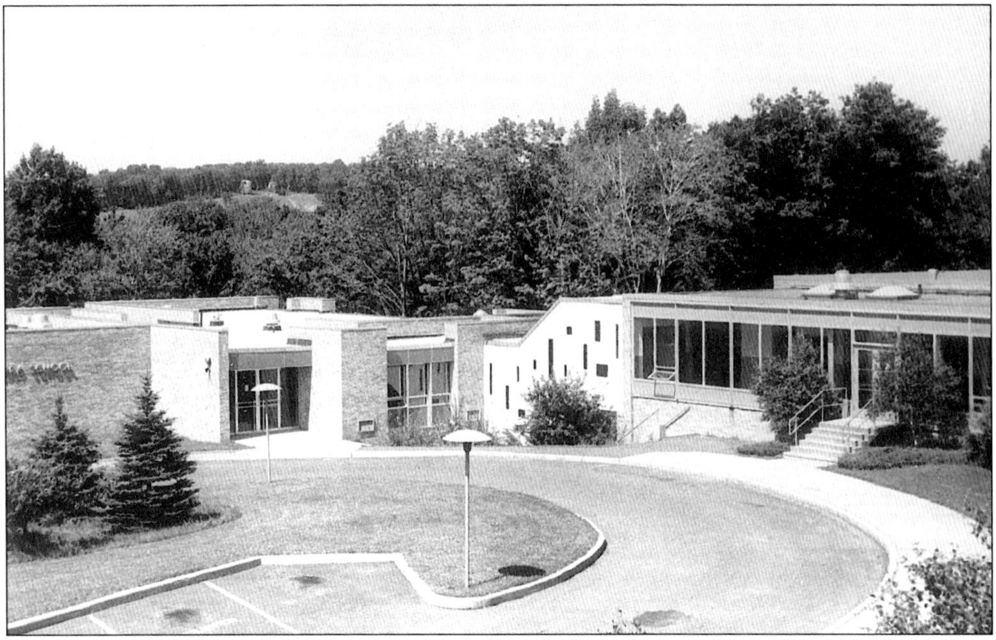

The Bayberry School. Located on a 15-acre site on Bayberry Lane, Bayberry School was opened in 1963, with an addition completed in 1968. For 2000–2001, there are 327 students enrolled at Bayberry in kindergarten through grade four. The Watchung Board of Education is currently facing a decision of how to accommodate a large projected growth in students.

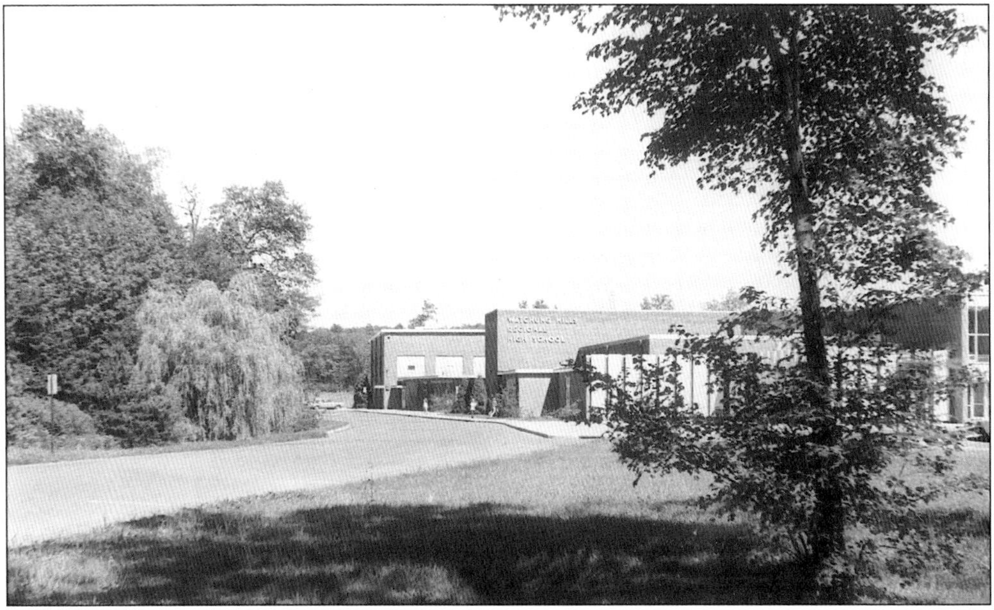

The Watchung Hills Regional High School. Watchung students used to attend Plainfield High School and, in later years, North Plainfield High School. In 1953, the North Plainfield and Bernardsville High School Boards of Education announced that after 1956, residents of the Watchung Hills area could no longer attend their schools as tuition students. Passaic and Warren Townships and the Borough of Watchung decided to establish Watchung Hills Regional High School, which opened in 1957.

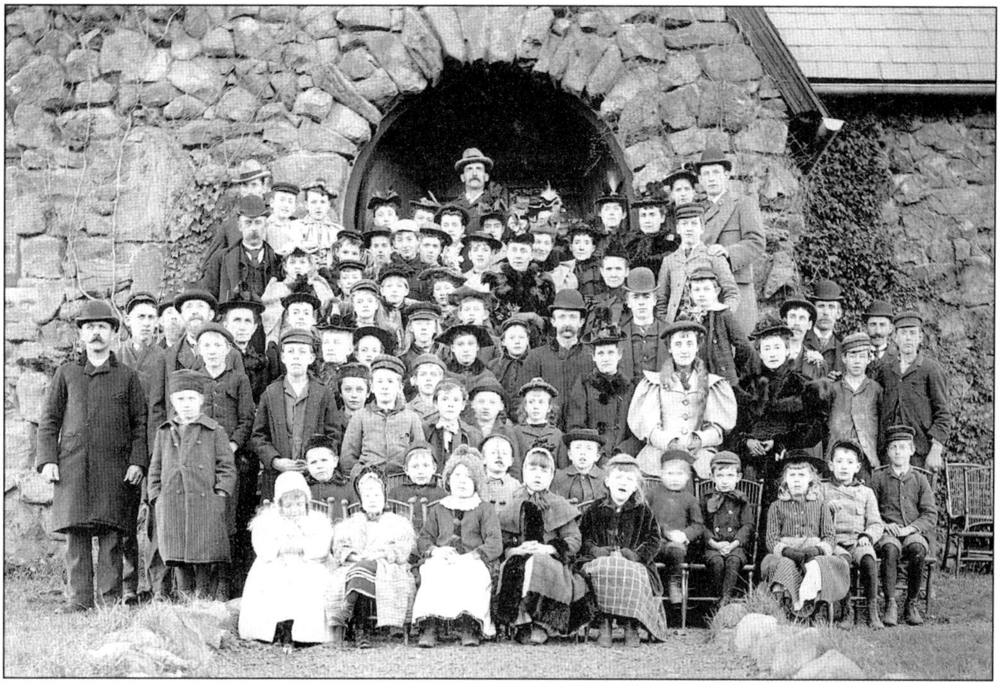

THE 1894 WASHINGTON VALLEY SUNDAY SCHOOL ASSOCIATION. The Washington Valley Sunday School Association began its service in 1851 in a private home. In later years, the Sunday school met in the then one-room schoolhouse. The Sunday school workers became convinced with the passing years that the Sunday school must have its own home. The group raised $2,000, and, although it was not enough to build the chapel they wanted, it was enough to get started.

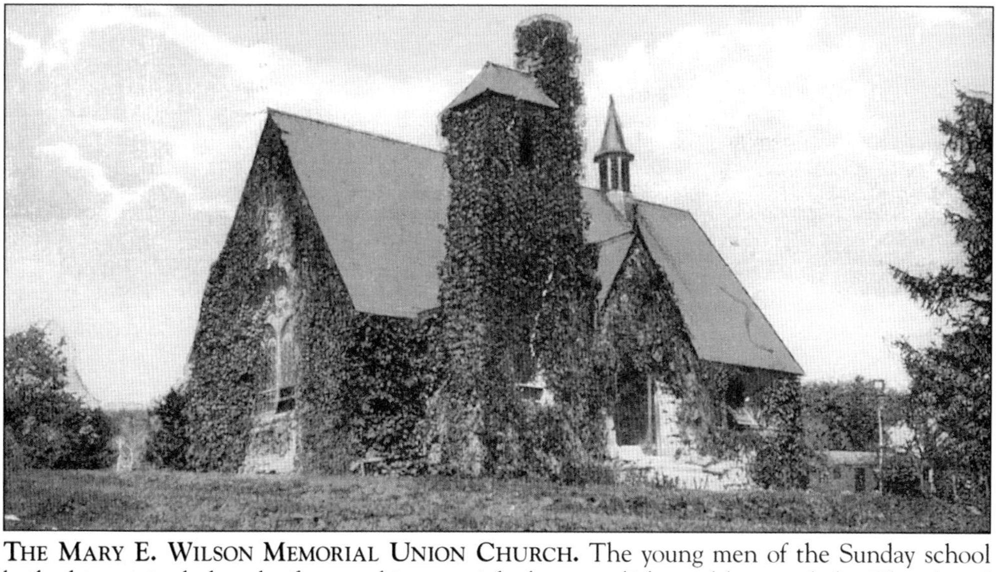

THE MARY E. WILSON MEMORIAL UNION CHURCH. The young men of the Sunday school built this original chapel, often working at night by moonlight and lantern light. The chapel was dedicated in 1890 and was used by the Sunday school until it was turned over to the church congregation organized by community leaders in 1914. The stone chapel still stands today at the intersection of Valley and Hillcrest Roads.

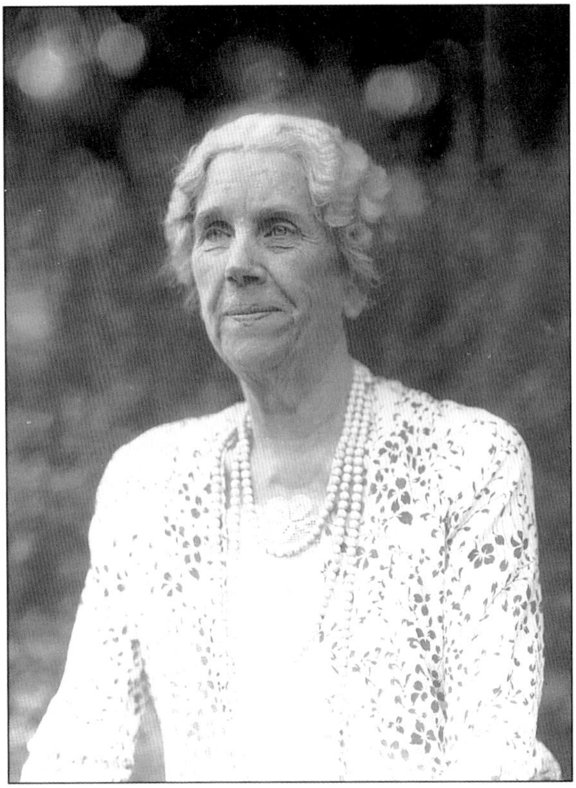

MARY E. WILSON. The work of the Sunday school members to build a chapel came to the attention of Col. John F. Wilson of North Plainfield. He offered a substantial donation of $3,500, if the chapel were named in memory of his wife, Mary E. Wilson, who had been especially interested in young people. In 1969, a new sanctuary and related facilities were dedicated, and the original building was once again referred to as the "Chapel," as it was called from 1890 until 1914.

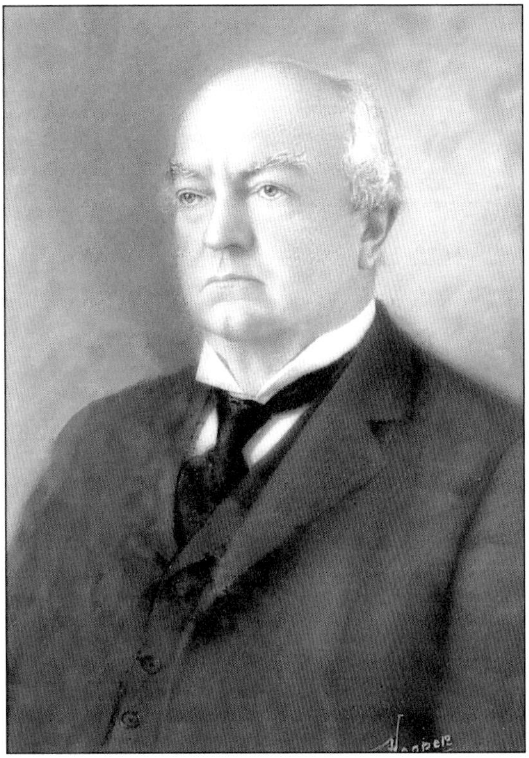

JOHN F. WILSON. Col. John Farmer Wilson, who lived on a plantation in Georgia prior to the Civil War, served during the war as a colonel in the Black Horse Cavalry for the state of Georgia. At the end of the war, Colonel Wilson gifted his plantation to his freed slaves and moved to Plainfield with his wife, Mary E. Wilson. In the 1870s, Wilson was an editor of the Plainfield newspaper and served as mayor of North Plainfield in 1895.

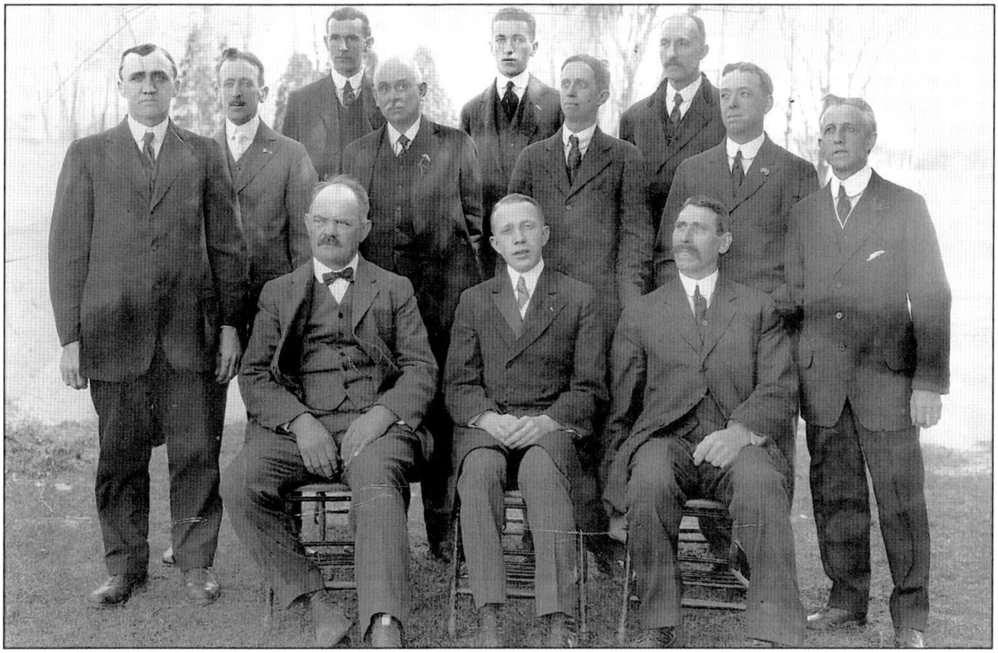

THE FIRST WILSON MEMORIAL BOARD. The members of the first board of Wilson Memorial Union Church, elected by the congregation in 1914, are, from left to right, as follows: (front row) Ephraim S. Ackor Sr., Rev. Mebane Ramsey, and George T. Winans; (middle row) John Mobus, Harry B. MacDonald, Henry R. Kennedy, George T. Hughes, Melvin H. Cleaves, and William E. Patte; (back row) Charles Edward Spier, Douglas W. Demler, and John Herrmann.

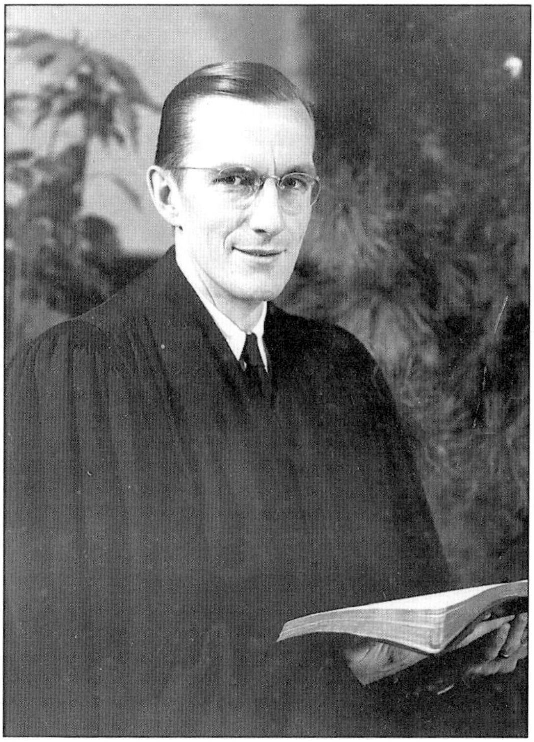

REV. RONALD OST. Shown in 1945 (his first year as pastor of Wilson Memorial Union Church), Rev. Ronald Ost served until he died in 1975 at age 60. Reverend Ost served as chaplain of the Watchung Rescue Squad, the Watchung Borough Council, and the Watchung Chemical Engine Company and as scoutmaster for Boy Scout Troop 32. The first minister of Wilson Memorial was Rev. Mebane Ramsey, who occupied the pulpit from 1915 to 1917.

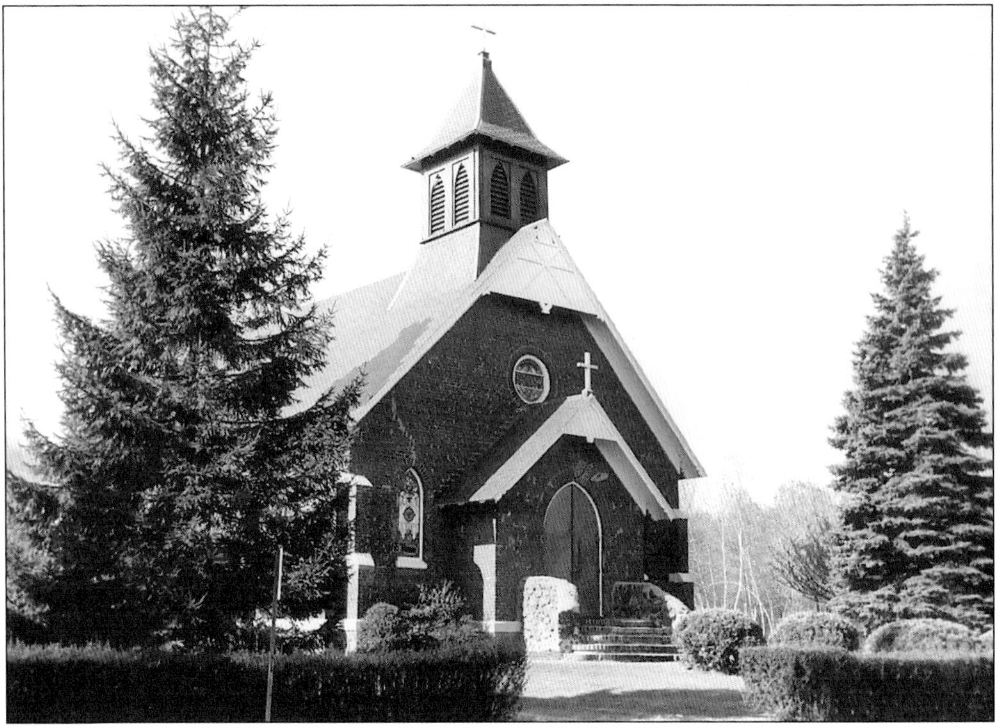

ST. MARY'S CHURCH ON STONY HILL. In 1847, the cornerstone was laid for a modest Catholic church on what is now Plainfield Avenue on Stony Hill. The initial church was too small to accommodate the growing congregation and, in 1877, the cornerstone for a new church (shown here) was laid. The parish predates any of the dioceses in New Jersey, having been incorporated in 1847 under the direction of the Diocese of New York.

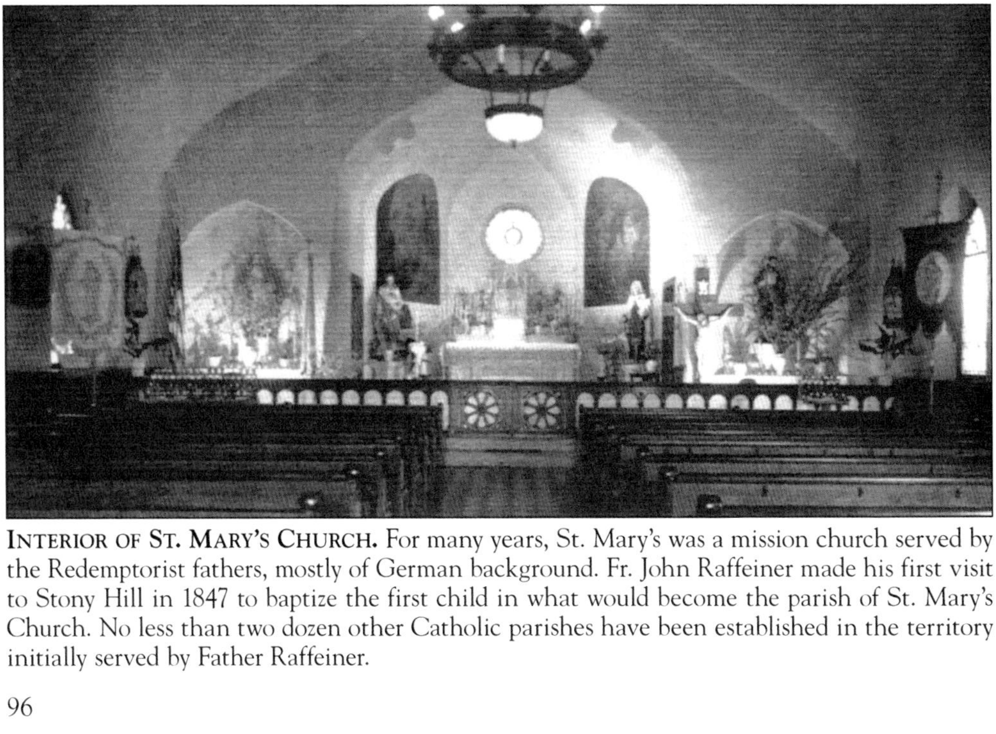

INTERIOR OF ST. MARY'S CHURCH. For many years, St. Mary's was a mission church served by the Redemptorist fathers, mostly of German background. Fr. John Raffeiner made his first visit to Stony Hill in 1847 to baptize the first child in what would become the parish of St. Mary's Church. No less than two dozen other Catholic parishes have been established in the territory initially served by Father Raffeiner.

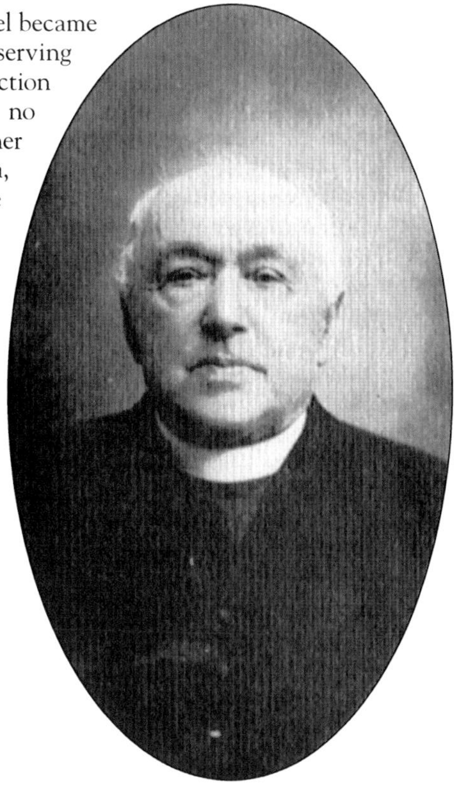

REV. JOHN SCHANDEL. In 1878, Rev. John Schandel became the first permanent resident pastor of St. Mary's, serving until 1904. In December 1880, the coal collection netted $13, which was apparently sufficient as no other coal collection was taken up that year. Another longstanding pastor was Msgr. Martin Madura, serving from 1942 to 1957. He developed the cemetery and initiated the education program for parish children.

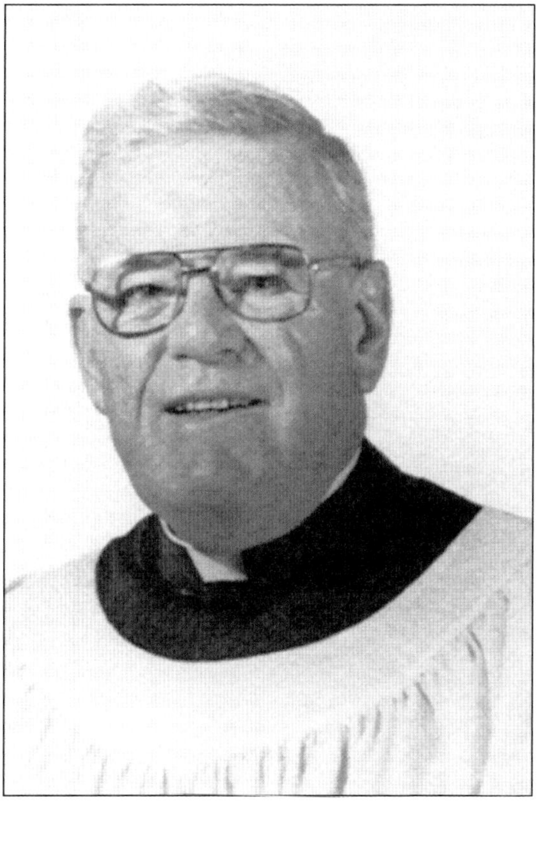

REV. CHARLES PLATT. In 1958, Rev. Charles Platt was assigned as chaplain of Mount St. Mary's Motherhouse and, with that assignment, was included the care of St. Mary's parish on Stony Hill. In 1966, Father Platt was assigned as the full-time pastor of St. Mary's. Under his direction, the parish experienced enormous changes, one of the most significant events being the purchase of 25 acres of land on Mountain Boulevard, opposite Brookdale Road.

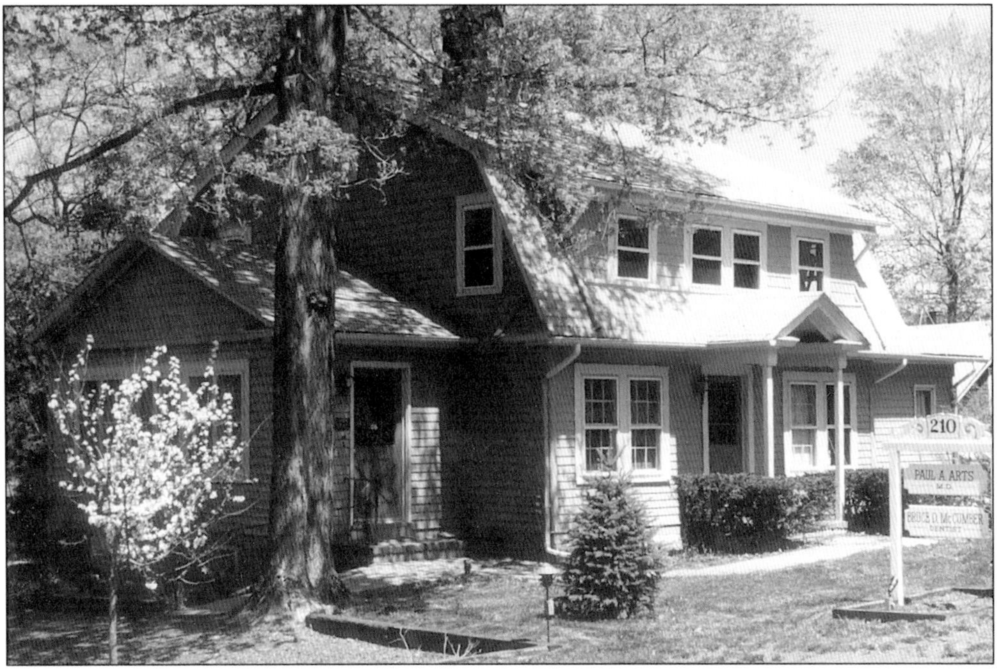

210 MOUNTAIN BOULEVARD. This house built c. 1826 was purchased by St. Mary's Church as a rectory in 1966. Picnics were held on the property to help raise finances needed by the parish for a new larger church. The new church was built at the top of a hill on the Mountain Boulevard property in 1971. In 1974, the old church was razed, with selected items being brought to the new church.

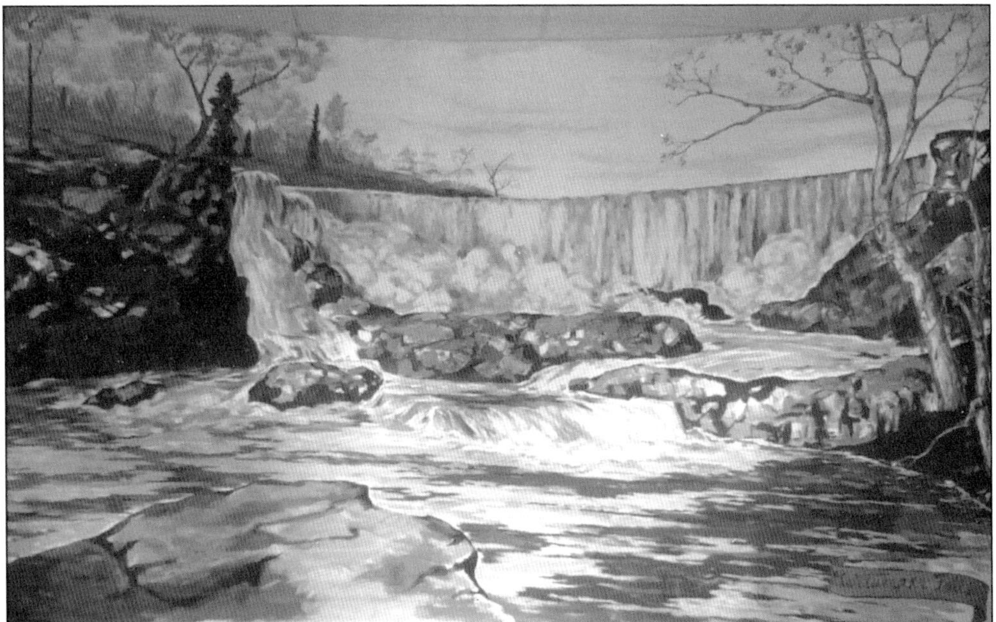

THE MURAL AT ST. MARY'S. Shown here in 1974, this mural of Wetumpka Falls serves as a backdrop for the stage in St. Mary's Stony Hill Hall, since renamed Father Platt Hall. The artist was Mildred L. Muse from Newark.

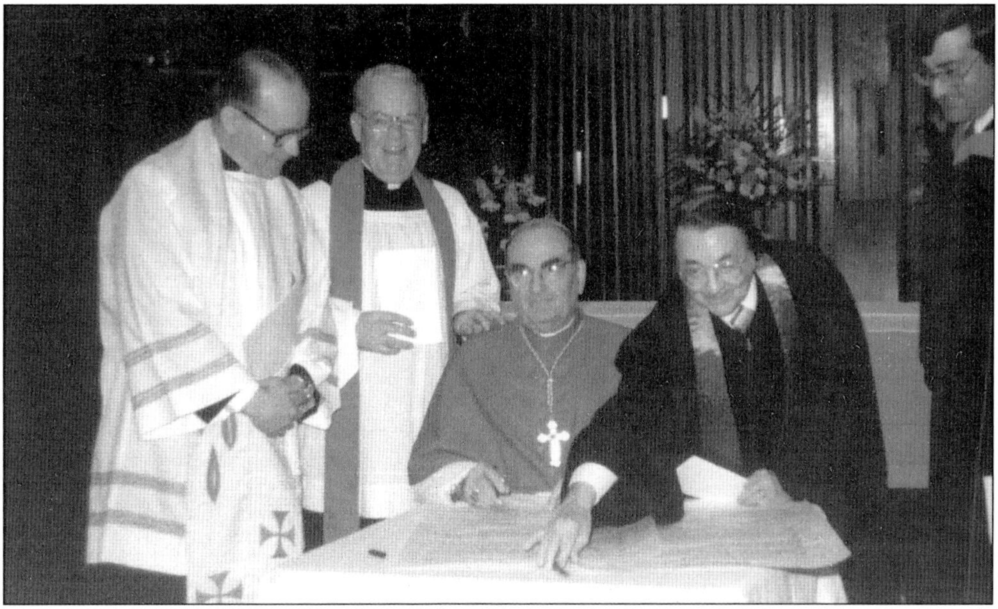

A COVENANT SIGNING. On January 22, 1978, a covenant was signed joining St. Mary's Church–Stony Hill and Mary E. Wilson Memorial Union Church in Christian unity. Shown, from left to right, are Rev. Joseph C. Shenrock, director of the Diocesan Commission on Ecumenical and Inter-Religious Affairs; Rev. Charles P. Platt, pastor of St. Mary's; Bishop George W. Ahr; Rev. Paul L. Stagg, general secretary of the New Jersey Council of Churches; and Rev. J. Ronald Miller, pastor of Wilson Memorial.

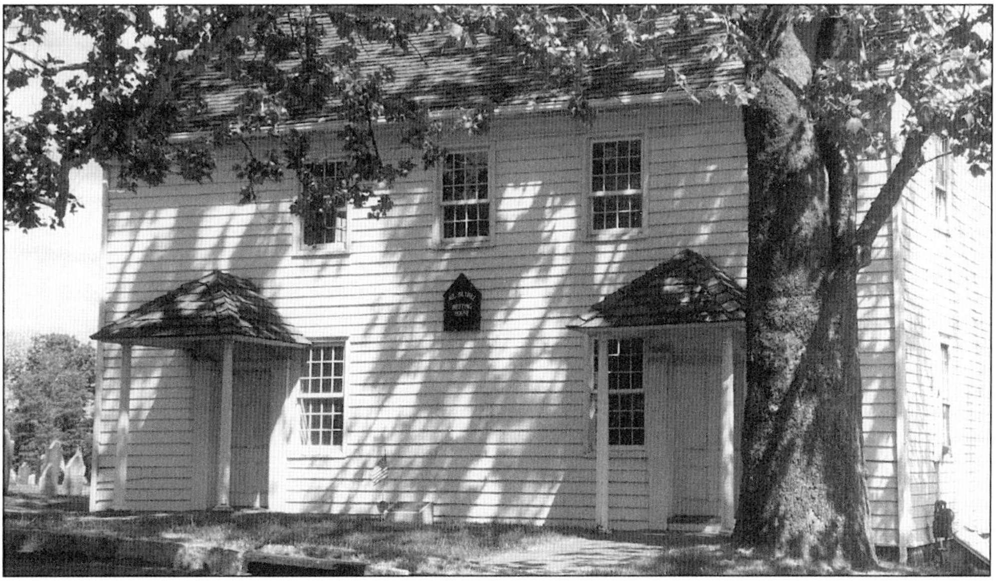

THE MOUNT BETHEL BAPTIST MEETING HOUSE. The original location of the Mount Bethel Baptist Meeting House was between the First and Second Mountains near the place where O'Connor's Restaurant now stands. The building was erected in 1761 and then disassembled and moved to this site in Warren in 1785. The headstone of Hannah Coon, who died in 1769, was found at the original site of the church and moved by the Warren Historic Sites Committee to the meetinghouse in 1995 for preservation.

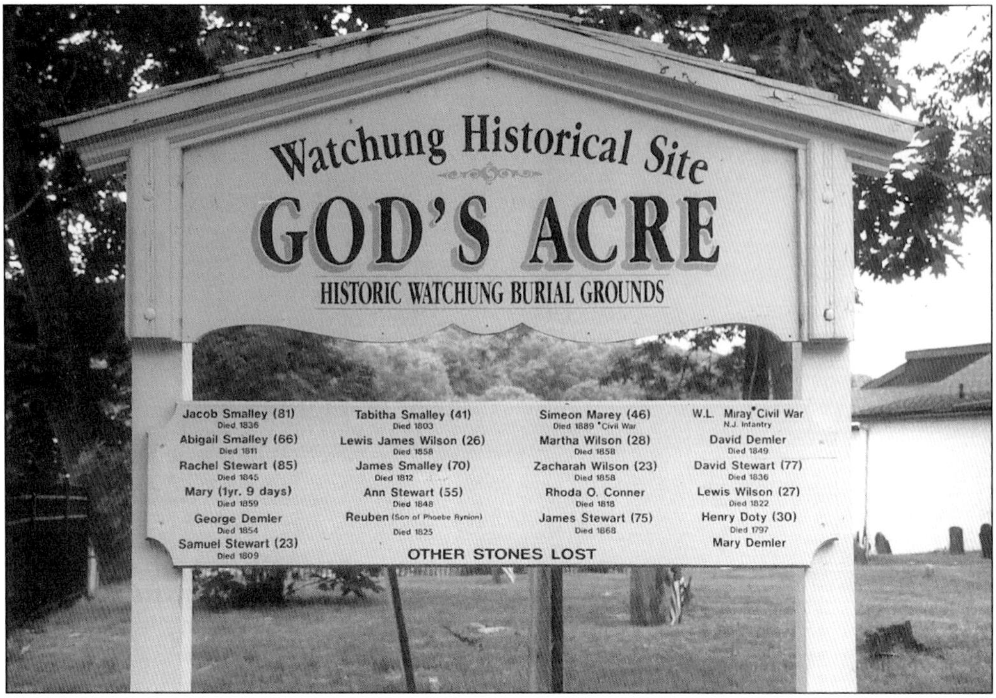

GOD'S ACRE. The cemetery overlooking Watchung Lake, called "God's Acre," contains graves dating from 1791 to 1858. The burying ground is located on what was formerly the Spencer farm. Buried within are some of Watchung's oldest families, including the Smalleys, Demlers, and Stewarts. The oldest stone, with a date of May 31, 1791, commemorates Henry Doty, who lived at 105 Brookdale Road.

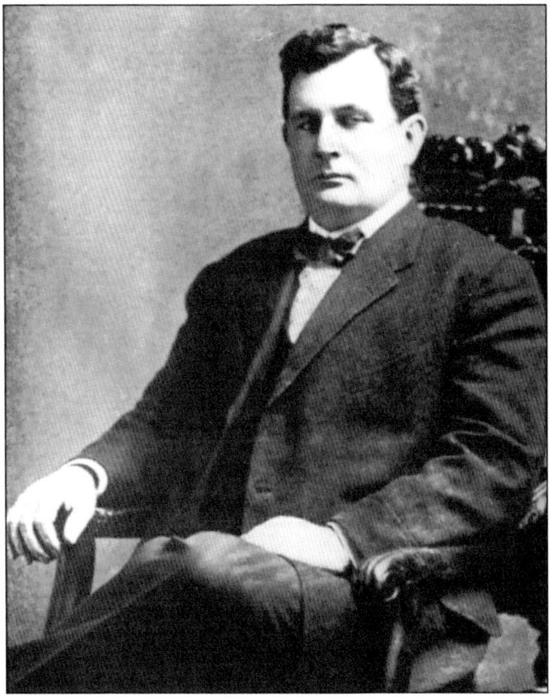

DAVID T. KENNEY. Plainfield inventor David T. Kenney entered his daughter Marie at St. Gabriel's Academy in North Plainfield in 1902. Working on a patent for the vacuum cleaner, Kenney requested the prayers of the Sisters of Mercy who taught at the academy for the success of the venture. Some time earlier, he had purchased 300 acres from the estate originally owned by John Taylor Johnston. When the cleaner was a success, he gave 40 acres of the land to the Sisters of Mercy in 1905.

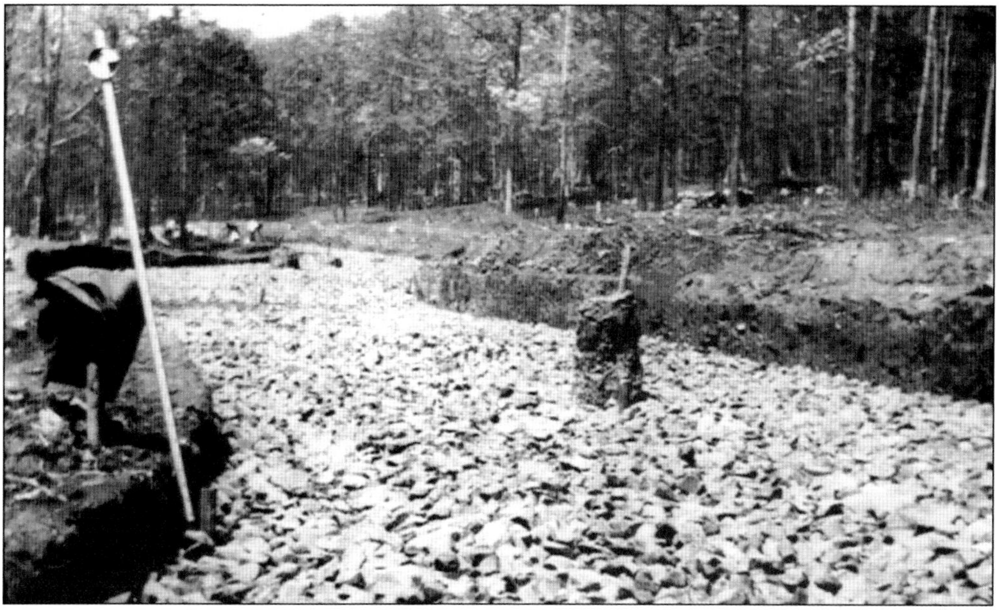

PREPARING THE MOUNTAIN. The First Watchung Mountain was to become the home for Mount St. Mary's College and Academy, with construction beginning in July 1906 when Mother Gabriel of the Sisters of Mercy turned the first spadeful of earth. A forest had to be cleared and acres of rock dug out. Due to the nature of the hill, the roadbed was laid out in a serpentine route, which remains today.

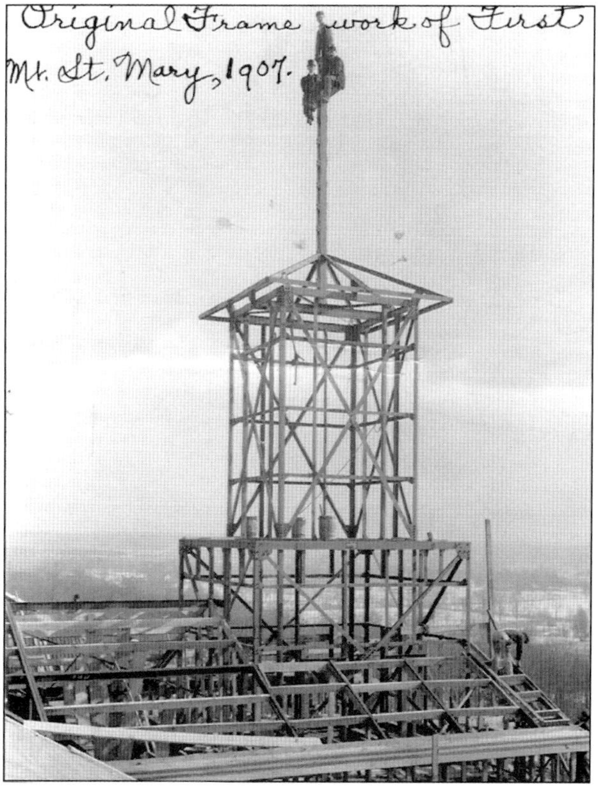

TOWER FRAMEWORK. Three men are shown in 1907 at the top of the tower framework for Mount St. Mary's. The architect was William E. Boring, head of the Columbia University School of Architecture. The Sisters of Mercy of New Jersey trace their lineage from the Order of Mercy founded in Dublin in 1831. Beginning with their first permanent location in Bordentown in 1873, their primary mission has been education.

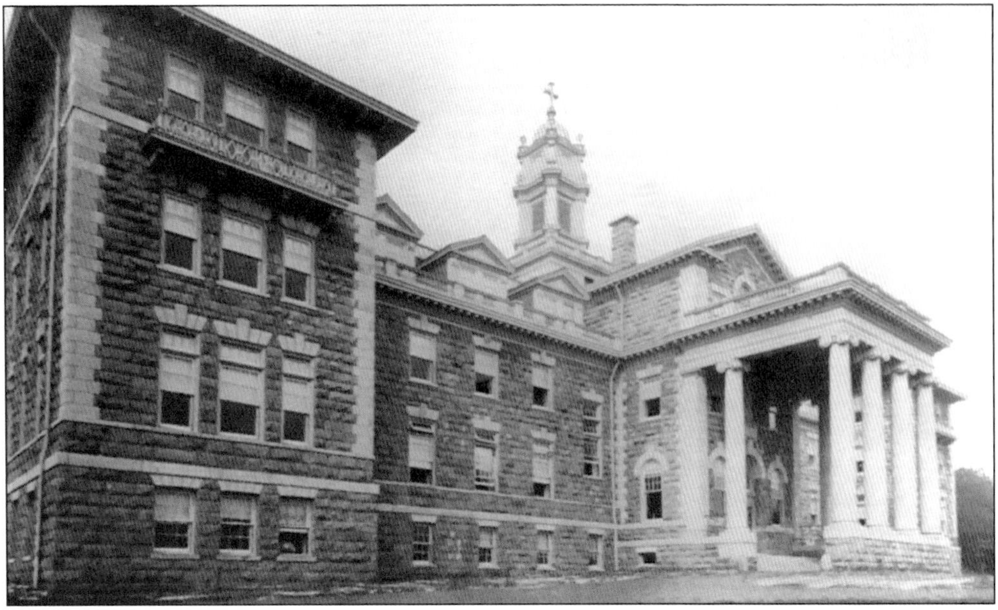

The 1908 Mount St. Mary's. In a building made of rough-cut buff-tinted Washington Valley stone, the college and academy formally opened on September 28, 1908. There were 62 students registered, 7 of whom were college students. With other land gifts and purchases, the property reached 124 acres. Later, the Sisters of Mercy sold land along Johnston Drive, where there are now private homes, and along Route 22, including land now owned by Sears.

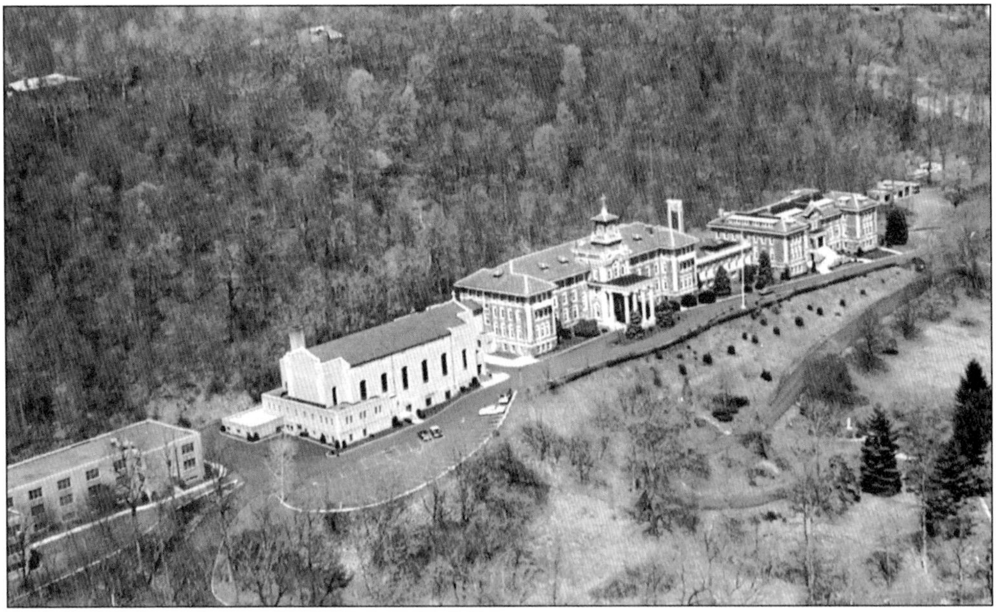

The Modern-Day Mount. This aerial view of Mount St. Mary's taken sometime after 1960 shows all the buildings currently located at the top of the hill. From left to right, they are St. Joseph Hall, part of St. Mary's Academy, built in 1960; the Chapel, built in 1955; the main Mount St. Mary building, rebuilt and reopened in 1912; and Gabriel Hall, built as part of the reconstruction and dedicated in 1913. In 1924, the college moved to Lakewood and was renamed Georgian Court College.

Six

Disasters

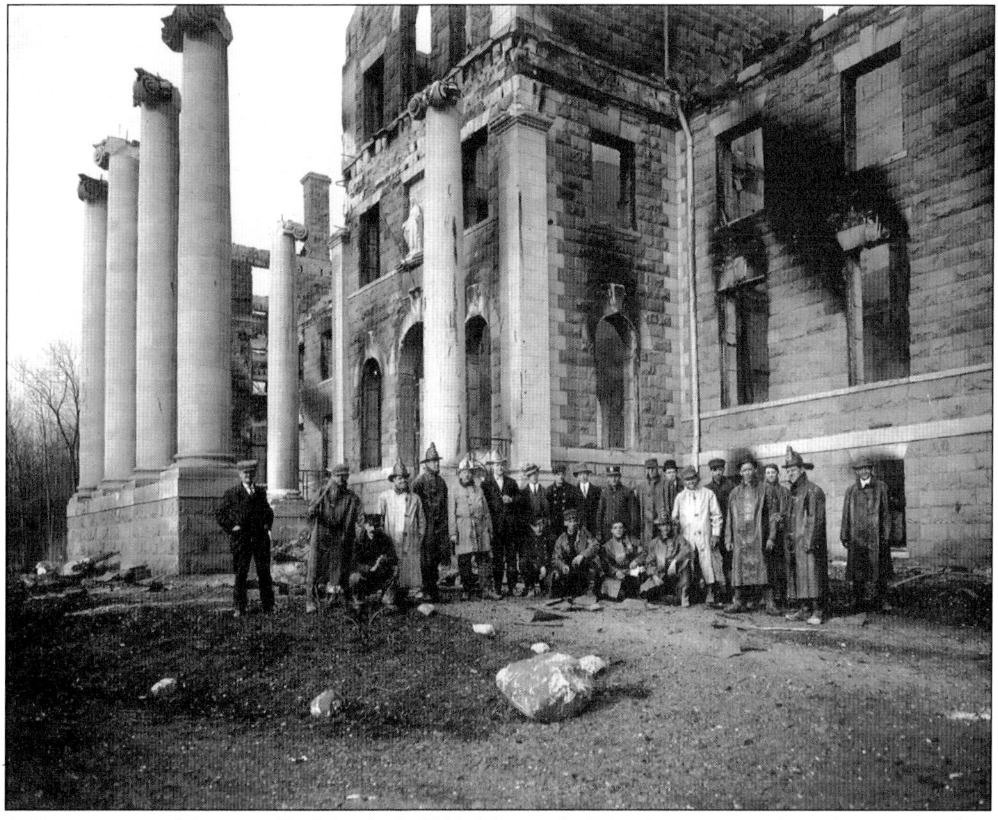

A Fire at the Mount. On March 2, 1911, Mount St. Mary's was swept by a devastating fire. No one was injured in the fire that two Sisters of Mercy discovered at 2 a.m. Engines arrived from Watchung, Plainfield, North Plainfield, and Scotch Plains, but the fire could not be contained. One by one the massive columns at the entrance snapped off.

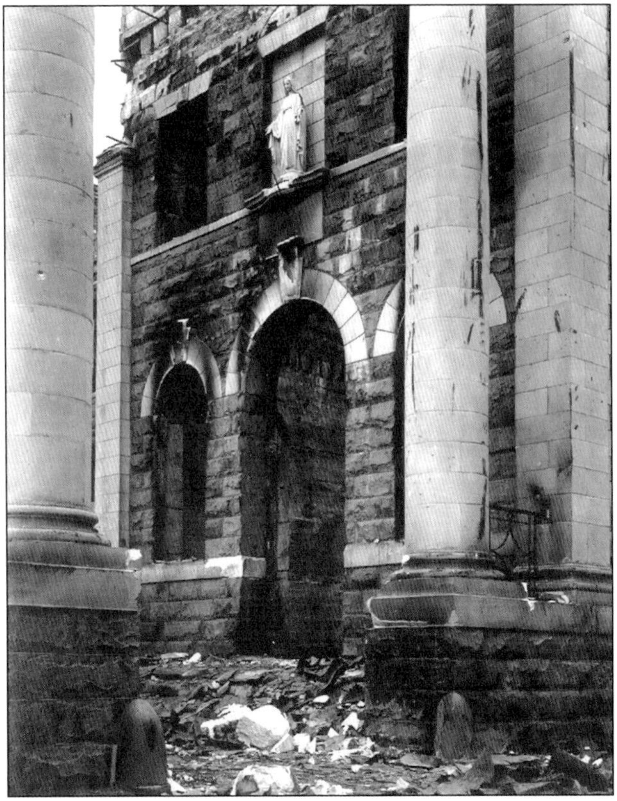

THE STATUE OF MARY. Beneath the demolished arches of the main entrance, a statue of the Virgin Mary stood unscathed despite the ravages of the fire around it. Temporary quarters for the school were found, and, within three weeks, classes resumed with every student returning. The decision was made to rebuild on an enlarged scale, and Mount St. Mary's reopened in September 1912.

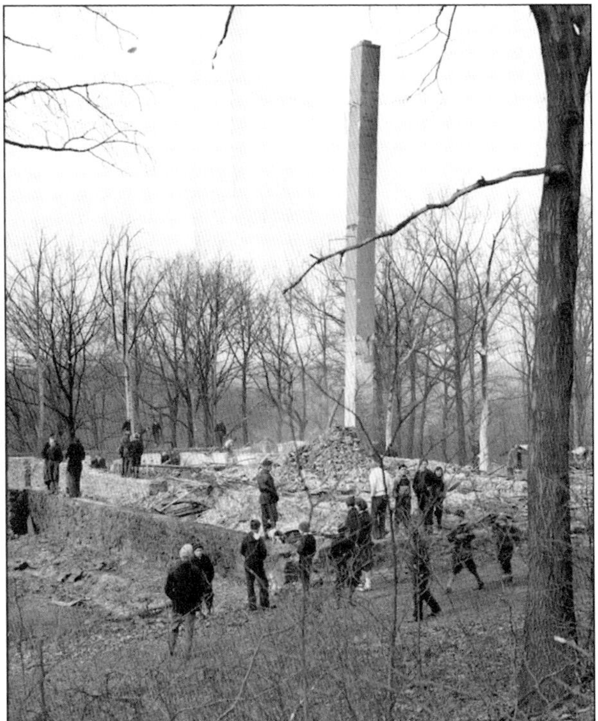

THE GROSSMAN SCHOOL FIRE. Shortly after the completion of Johnston Drive, the Mountain View Hotel was built on the corner of Johnston and what is now Oak Ridge Lane. The building was later used for the Grossman School, a school for children with special needs. After the school was closed, the building burned to the ground on December 29, 1937. The spectacular blaze was seen as far away as New York.

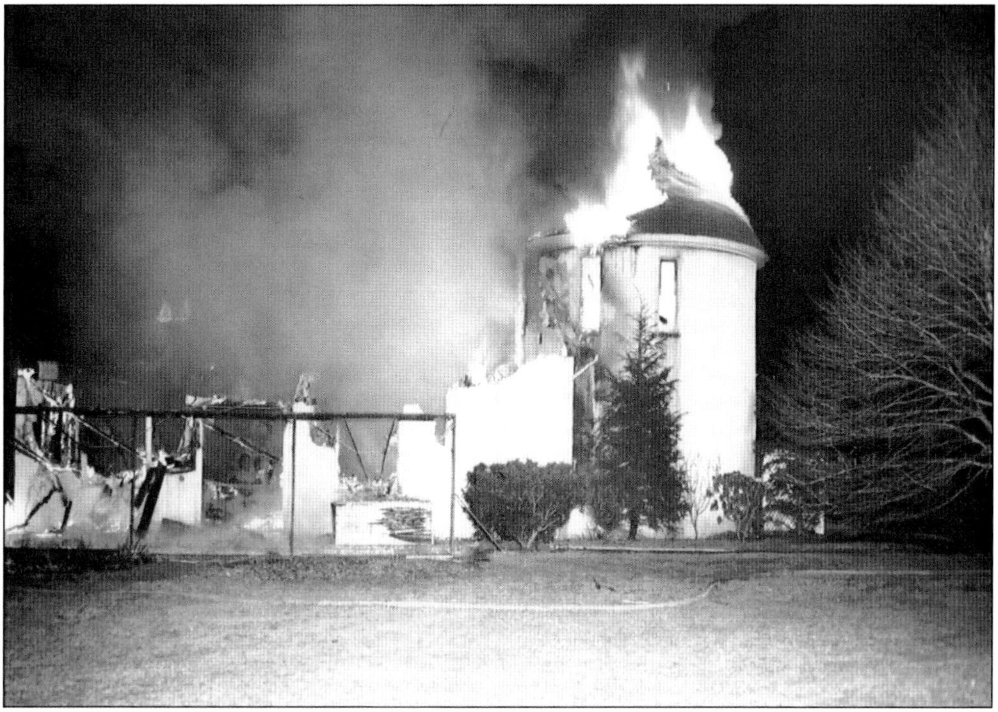

THE TWIN BROOKS FIRE. The Colonial-style clubhouse at Twin Brooks Country Club was damaged in a fire on March 9, 1945. The northwest wing, which included the kitchen and a silo, were leveled by the blaze. The club, located on the former Ackor farm, was originally built in 1926 by members of the Hydewood Golf Club and named Watchung Valley.

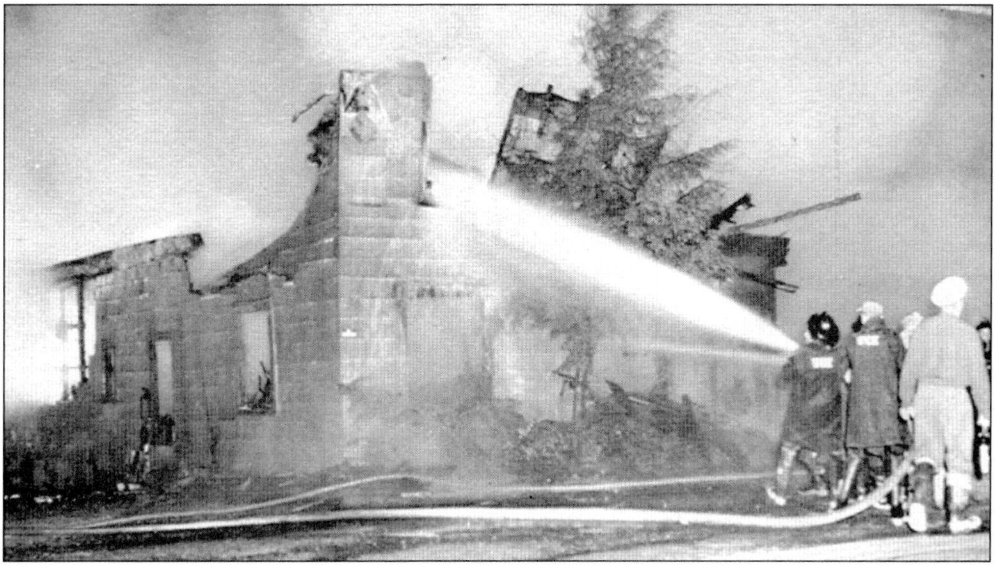

THE HALL'S FREIGHT TERMINAL FIRE. A group of Watchung firemen is shown fighting a fire on May 11, 1957, at Hall's Freight Terminal on Mountain Boulevard. One truck driver who was sleeping in the building was trapped and died in the flames. The only Watchung fireman to die while on active duty was G. Edward Snoden, who died while fighting a shed fire on March 6, 1950.

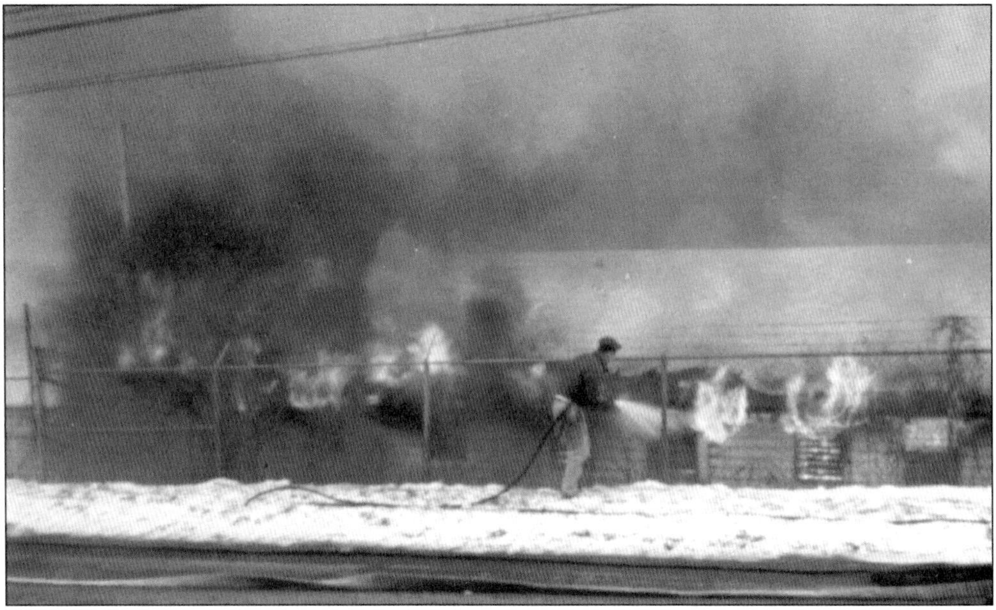

A Bathhouse Fire. On December 30, 1961, a wooden bathhouse on the property of the Watchung Lake Swim Club burned to the ground. The bathhouse contained a number of boats, sliding boards, and other swim club equipment. The firemen drew water from the lake and were able to save nearby structures.

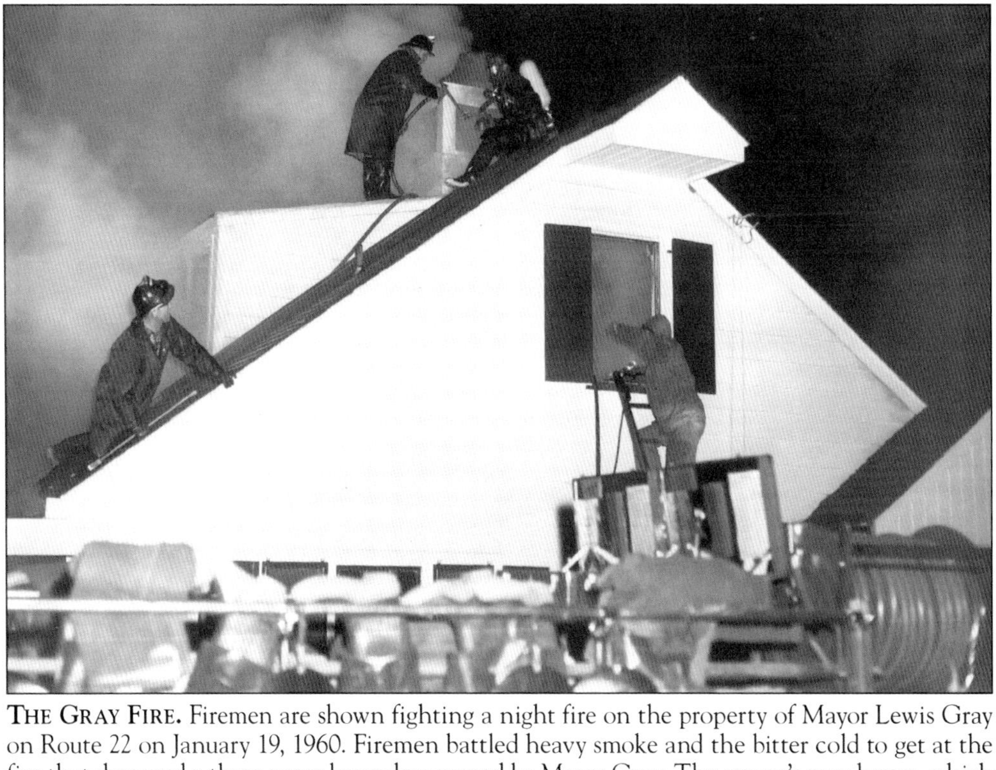

The Gray Fire. Firemen are shown fighting a night fire on the property of Mayor Lewis Gray on Route 22 on January 19, 1960. Firemen battled heavy smoke and the bitter cold to get at the fire that damaged a three-room bungalow owned by Mayor Gray. The mayor's own house, which was about 50 yards from the bungalow, was not damaged.

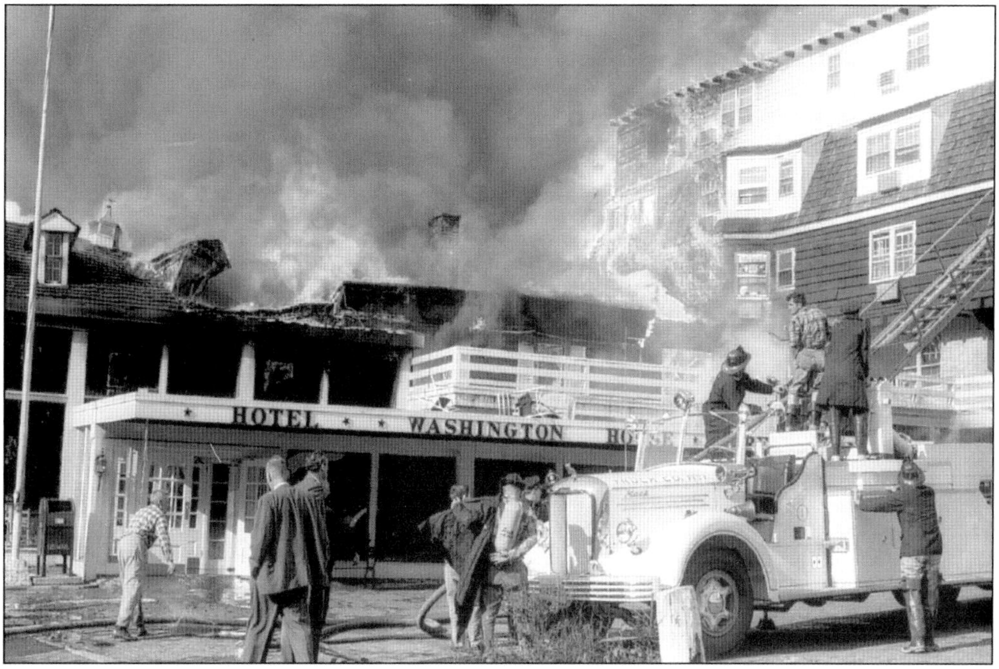

THE WASHINGTON HOUSE FIRE. In three violent hours, a roaring inferno of flame completely destroyed the Washington House Hotel and Restaurant on October 19, 1962. The blaze originated in the kitchen and then swept through the recently added five-story hotel section. Fortunately, there were no fatalities.

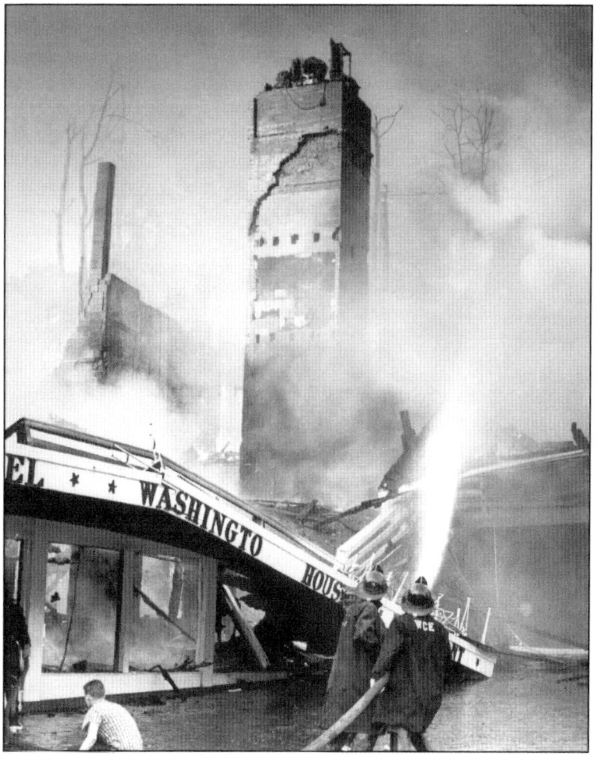

THE WASHINGTON HOUSE DEBRIS. In this photograph, the elevator shaft is seen rising out of the Washington House debris. Despite the efforts of more than 100 firemen who manned 17 pieces of heavy equipment, the fire leveled the entire structure. Aiding the Watchung Chemical Engine Company were fire units from the three Plainfields, Warren Township, Berkeley Heights, Green Brook, New Providence, Martinsville, and Mount Bethel.

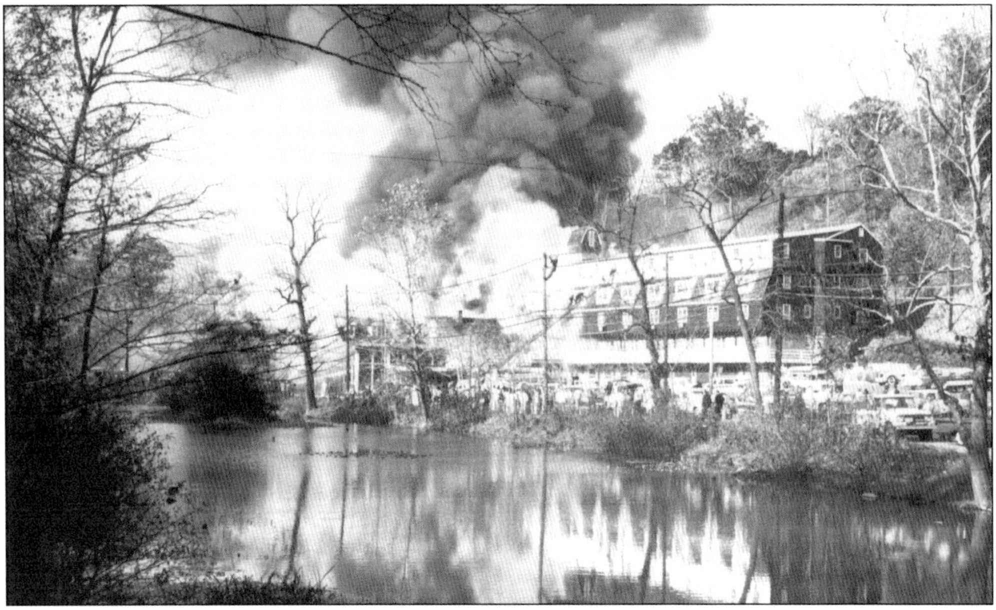

The Washington House Fire from a Distance. Veteran observers termed this the worst fire in Watchung's history. Firemen were thwarted by the intense heat and the towering flames that, at times, reached heights of about 70 feet. Ironically, it was in the very building that they valiantly tried to save that the Watchung Chemical Engine Company was formally organized in 1910.

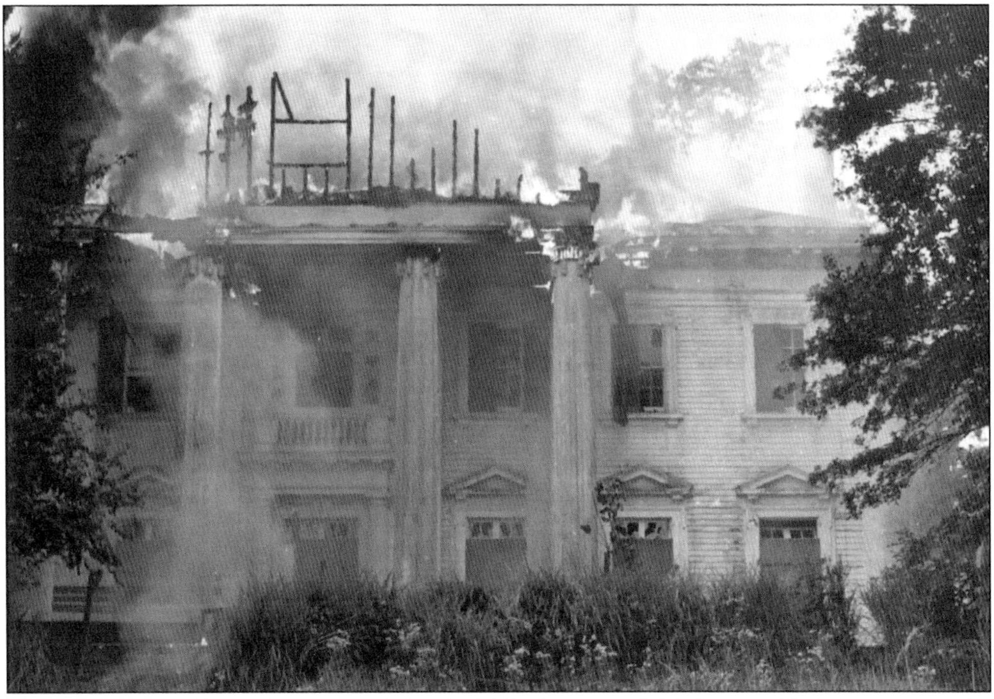

The Hydewood Hall Fire. On July 26, 1963, fire gutted Hydewood Hall, located at the base of the First Watchung Mountain, north of Route 22. The building had been slated for demolition.

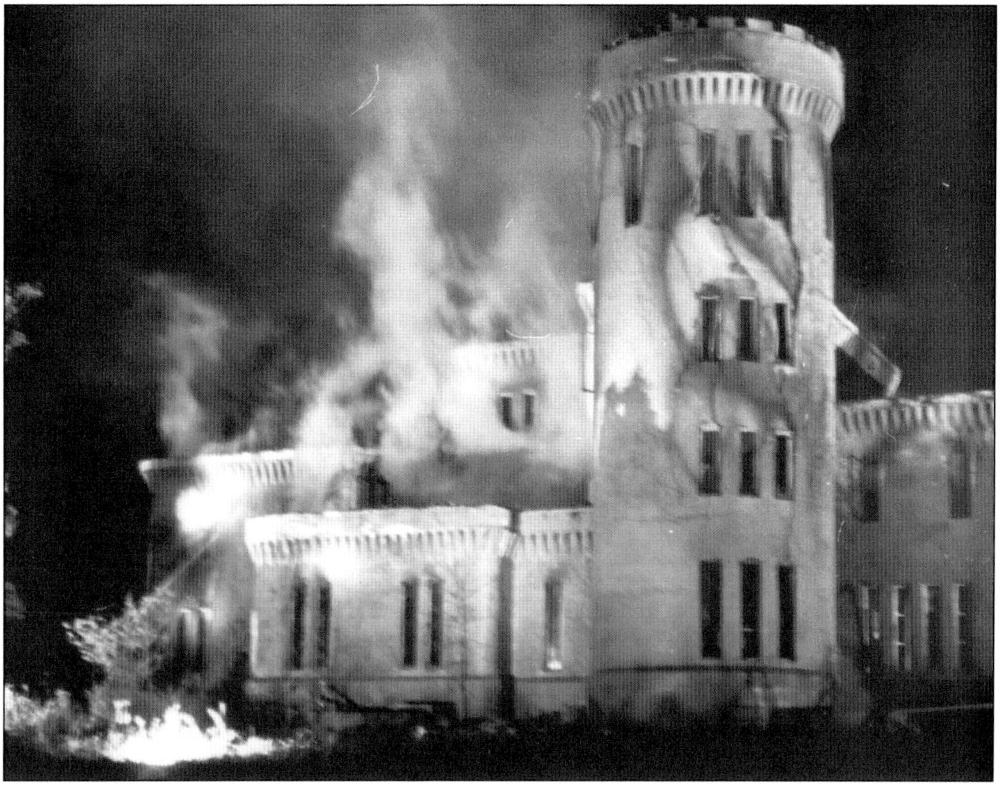

The Castle Fire. On October 26, 1969, the Moldenke castle was damaged in a fire. The fire began just hours before wreckers were due to destroy the castle. In early October, the owners had opened it for inspection, and more than 4,000 visitors toured the landmark.

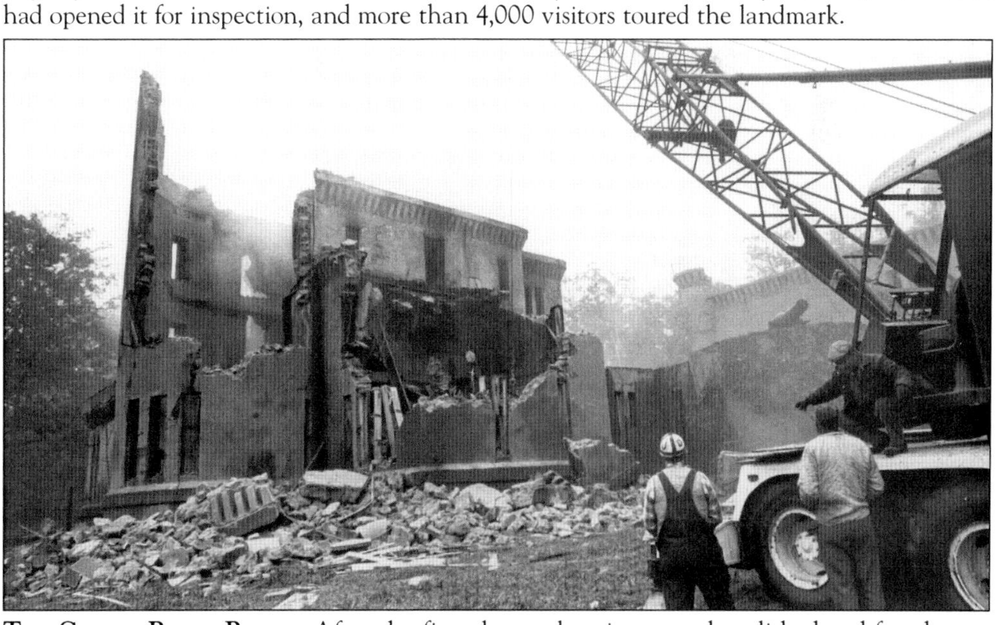

The Castle Being Razed. After the fire, the castle ruins were demolished and four homes built in place of the castle. The castle neighborhood, centered on Sherwood and Elsinore Drives, continues to be called the "Castle Tract."

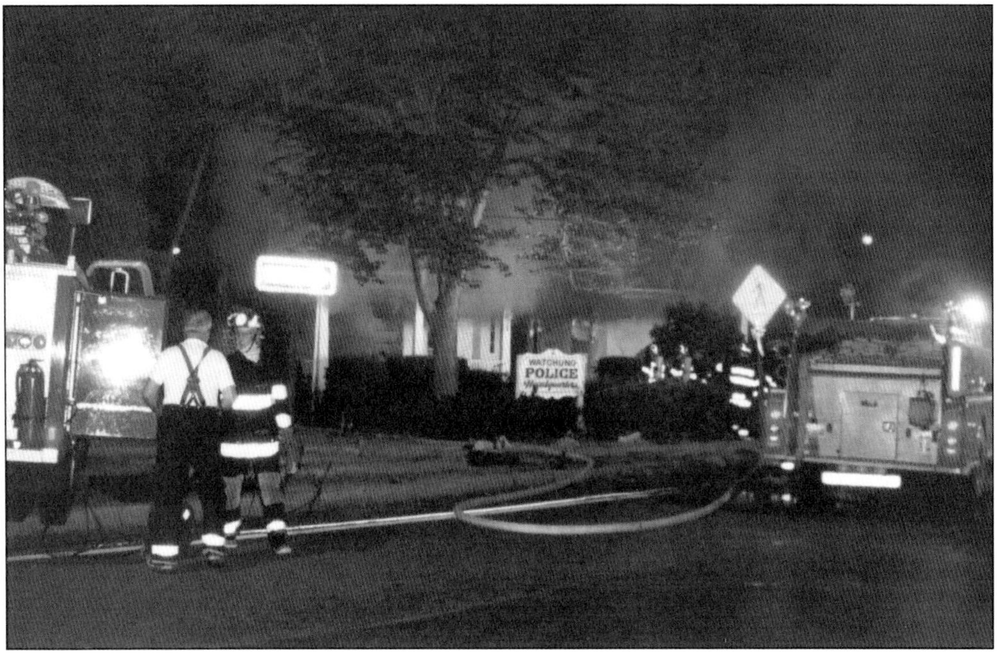

THE POLICE HEADQUARTERS FIRE. On June 3, 1991, Watchung police headquarters in the Texier House on the Watchung Circle was severely damaged. As a result of the fire, the police department occupied temporary quarters for nine years, first at the former Lockheed property on Route 22 for six years and then in trailers located between the borough hall and the firehouse for three years.

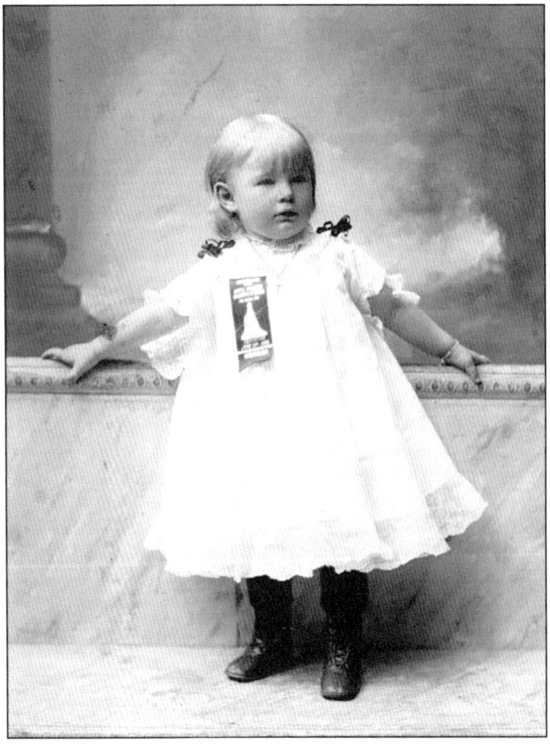

GENERAL SLOCUM SURVIVOR. At the age of six months, Adella "Tiby" Liebenow (Wotherspoon) became the youngest survivor of a horrible fire that destroyed the excursion steamer *General Slocum* in New York's East River in 1904, killing 1,030 passengers. The calamity claimed the lives of Tiby's two sisters, two aunts, and two young cousins. At the age of 18 months (as shown), Tiby unveiled the Slocum Monument in Lutheran Cemetery. Several years later, after her father died, she and her mother moved to Watchung. Tiby celebrated her 97th birthday on November 28, 2000.

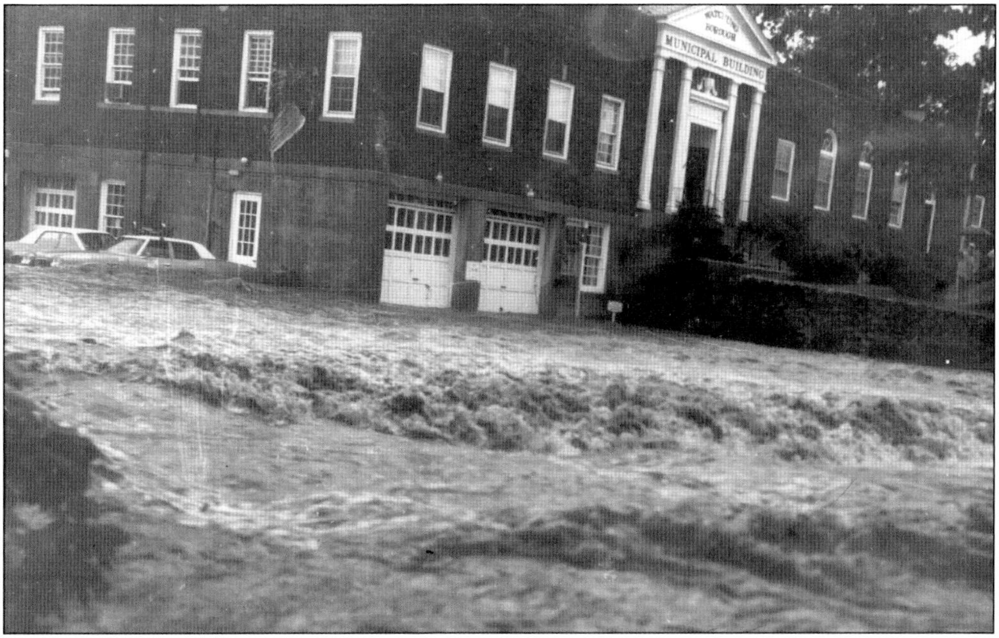

THE 1973 FLOOD. On August 2, 1973, a raging flash flood swept through Watchung and North Plainfield, claiming the lives of five people. This view of the flood, looking from the Watchung Police Department headquarters in the center of the Watchung Circle, shows the municipal building. The damages in Watchung were estimated at $700,000.

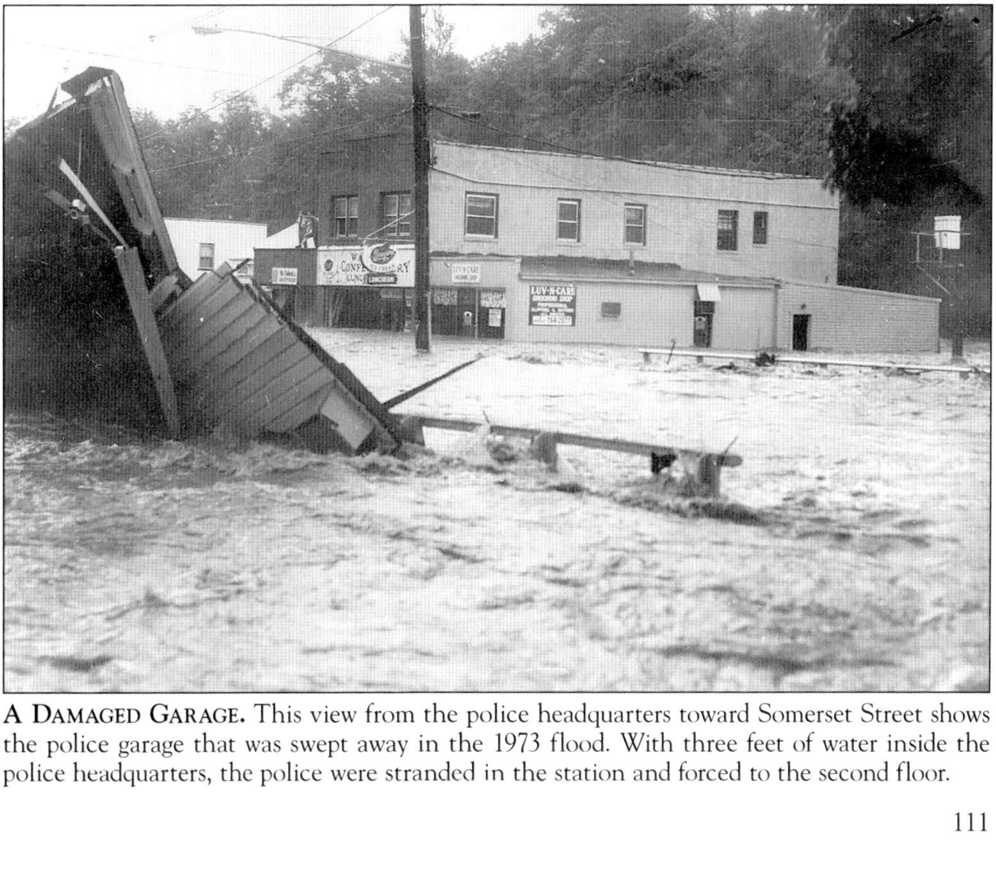

A DAMAGED GARAGE. This view from the police headquarters toward Somerset Street shows the police garage that was swept away in the 1973 flood. With three feet of water inside the police headquarters, the police were stranded in the station and forced to the second floor.

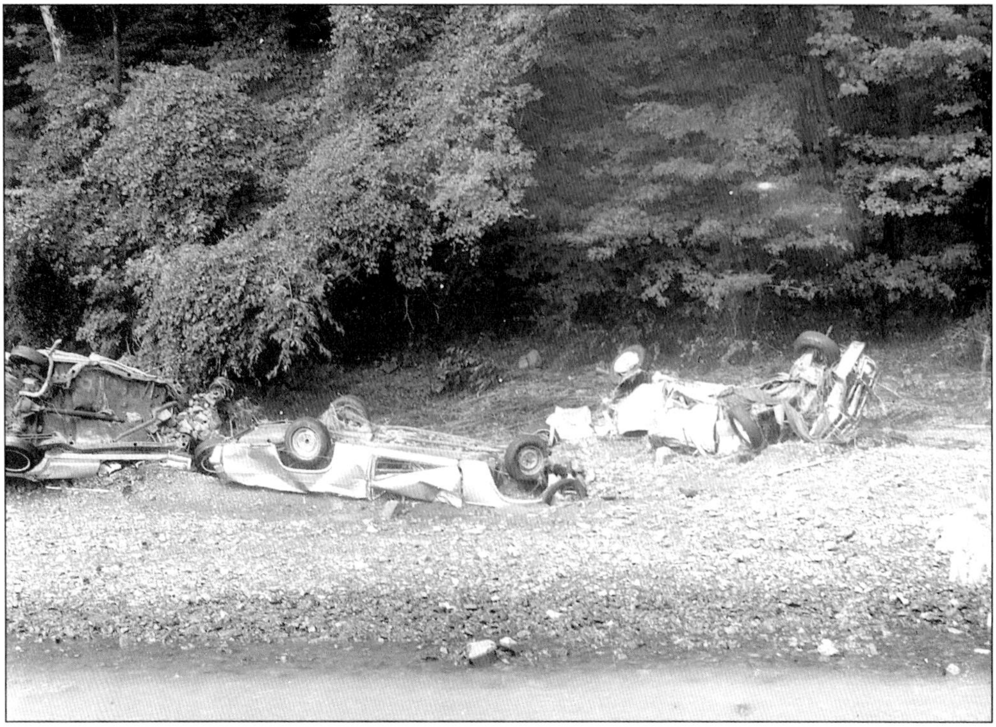

THE AFTERMATH. After the 1973 flood, these cars were found on the far side of Stony Brook, washed down from the Watchung Circle. The flood caused severe damage along Somerset Street, destroying Wetumpka Falls. The Wetumpka Falls had survived terrible floods in 1889 and 1938.

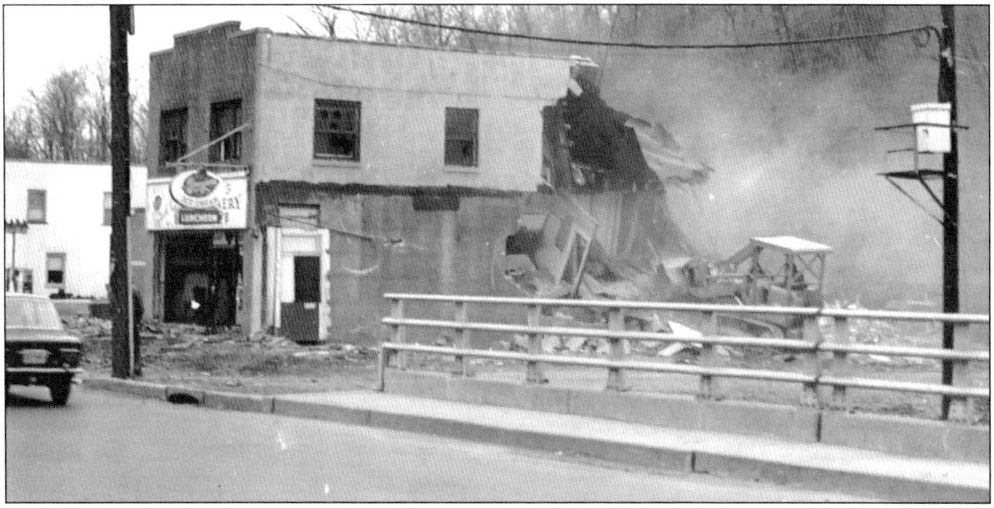

THE DEMOLITION. Following the August 1973 flood, this grocery store on Somerset Street was razed. The area was later converted into a small park.

Seven

COMMUNITY LIFE

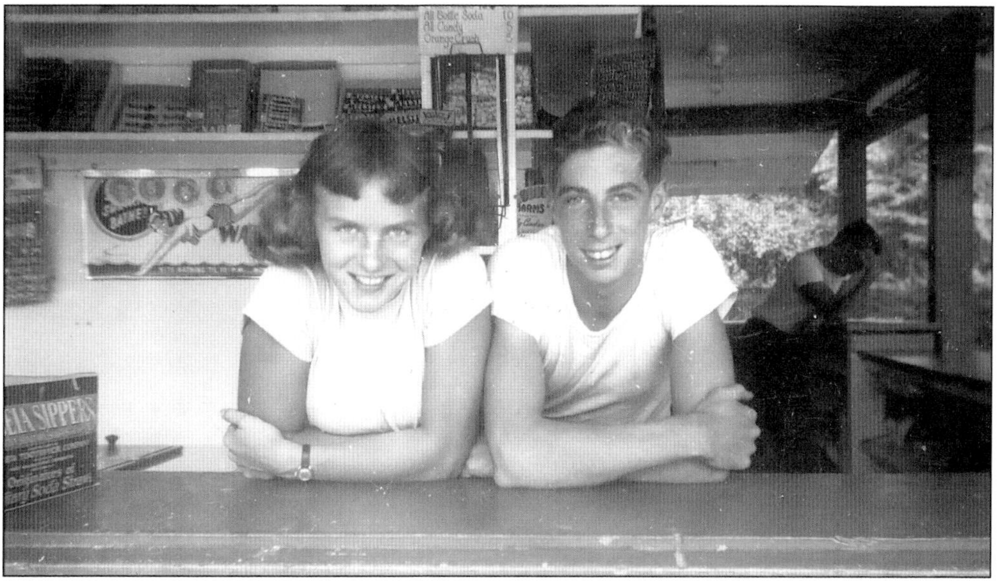

THE WATCHUNG LAKE REFRESHMENT STAND. In 1930, Watchung Lake was converted into a bathing facility. The Watchung Lake Swim Club soon became a popular hangout, with two police officers directing traffic on weekends. Local teens, such as Barbara Barrett (Diem) and Jerry Roberts (shown here in the 1940s), used to work at the refreshment stand.

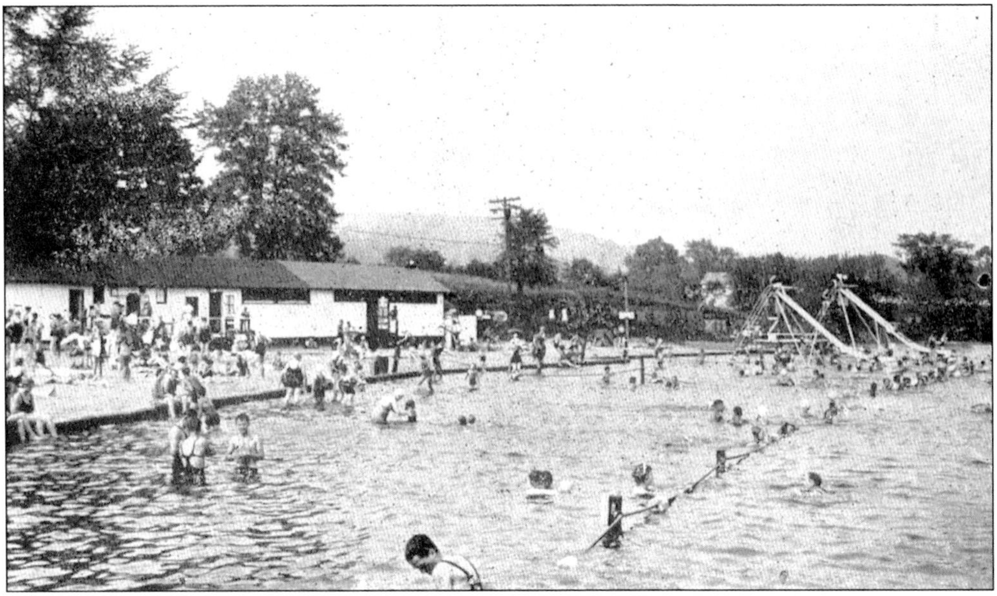

A Bathing Beach. As advertised in 1937, the lake facilities included a "white sand beach, flood lights for night bathing, water slides, free parking area, and free seats for spectators." That year, adults were charged 40¢ on weekdays and Saturdays and 75¢ on Sundays and holidays; for children under 12 years of age, the prices were 15¢ and 25¢, respectively.

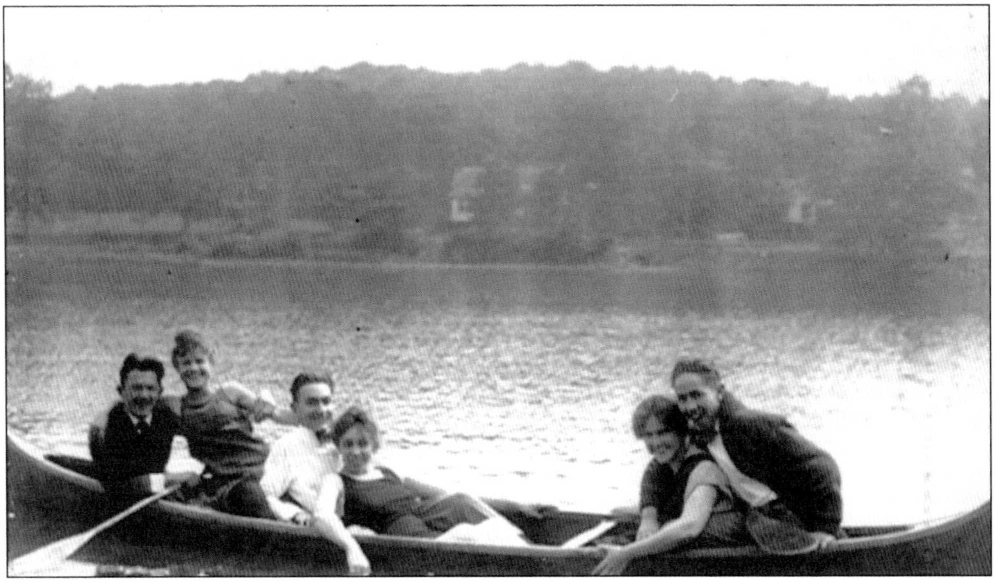

Canoeing on Watchung Lake. Members of the Texier family are shown canoeing on Watchung Lake c. 1915.

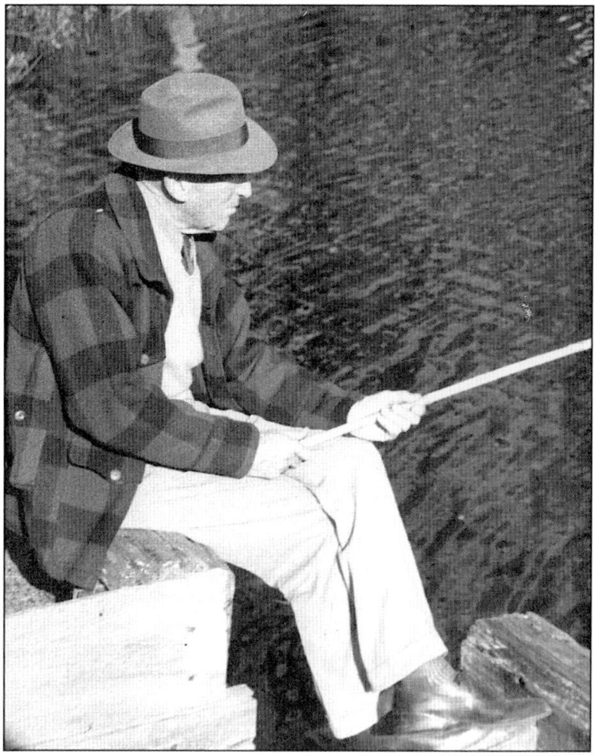

Fishing at Best Lake. Watchung's first mayor, Harry MacDonald, is shown fishing at Best Lake. Fishing continues to be popular both at Watchung Lake and Best Lake. When Watchung Lake was still used for ice harvesting, children used to fish from the wooden walkways that were used to harvest the ice. They would sell what fish they caught for 5¢ each.

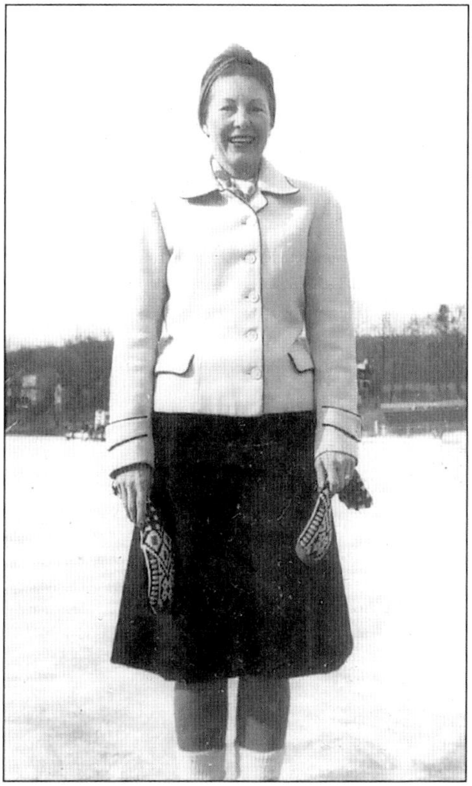

Skating. Tiby Wotherspoon is shown skating on Watchung Lake in 1930. When the ice became rough, skating was stopped and firemen would spray water over the ice to make it smooth again. In addition to skating, popular winter activities included bobsledding down the Dugway (now Hillcrest Road), tickley bender, dominoes and checkers, taffy pulls, square dances, and quilting parties.

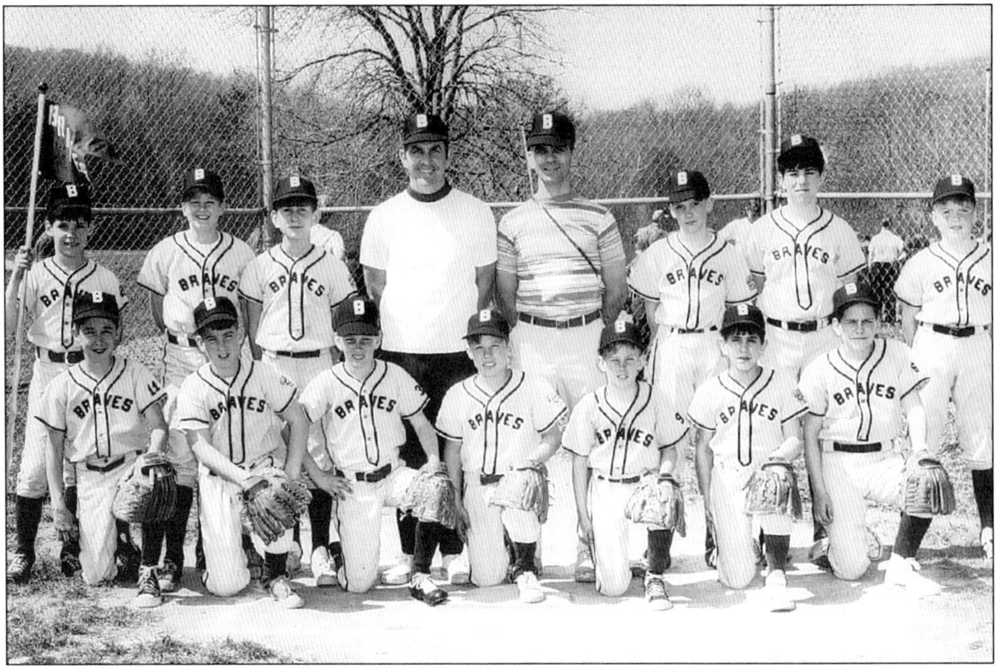

THE WATCHUNG BASEBALL ASSOCIATION. Stories of a baseball club in Watchung that played on a field owned by the Underhills date back to 1912. The Watchung Little League, known for many years as the Watchung Baseball Association, was started in 1962. When the association was formed, there were no Little League fields in the borough. By 1964, there were three fields and a fourth was being prepared.

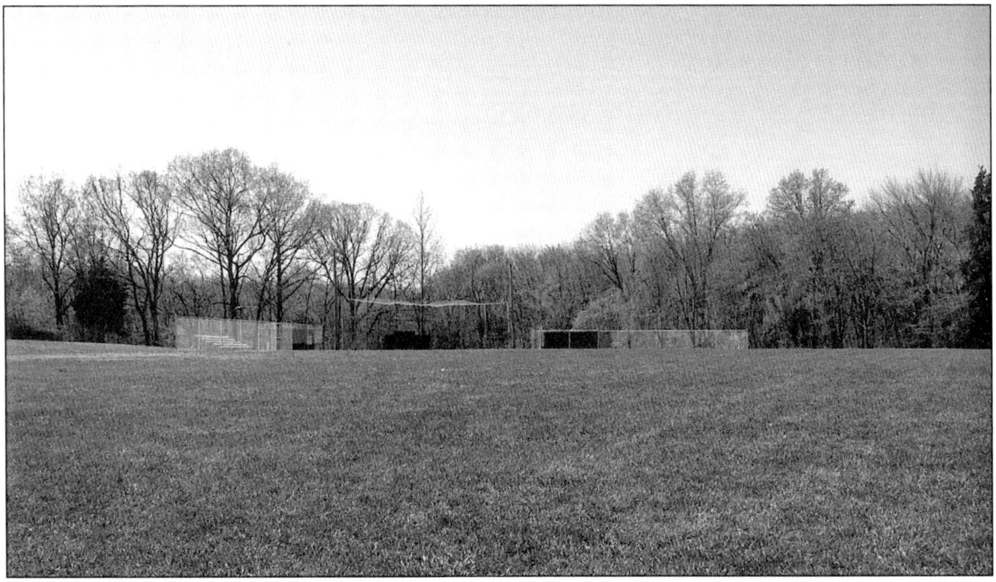

PHILLIPS FIELD. In 1975, the Phillips Field Development Corporation, a nonprofit organization, was formed to raise funds and manage the physical changes needed to improve the former Phillips farm to provide additional recreational facilities for the borough. The land, owned by the Watchung Board of Education, is now used primarily for baseball, softball, and soccer.

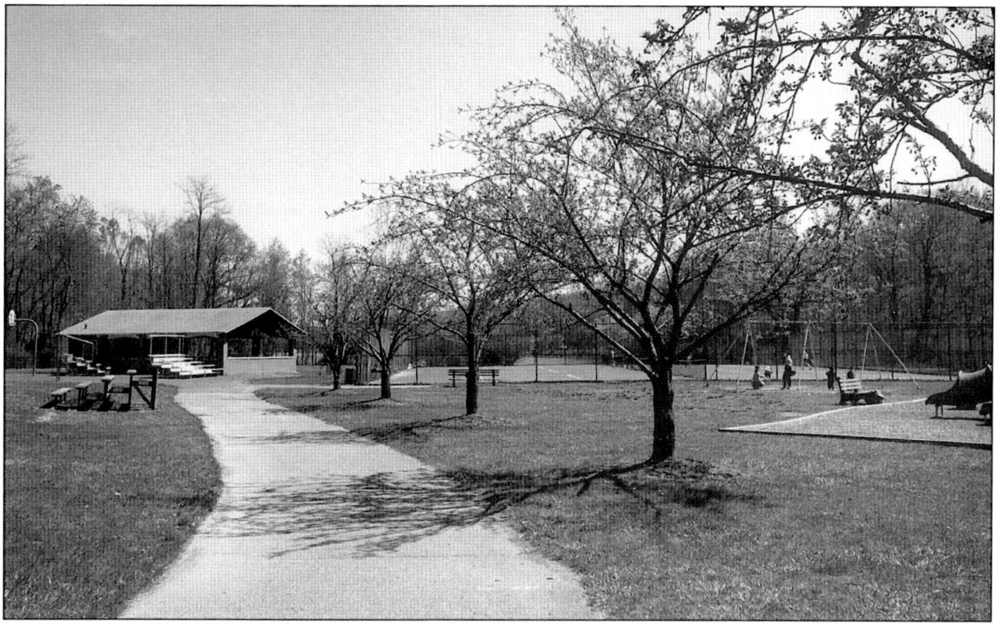

MOBUS FIELD. The Watchung Recreation Commission, established in 1940, supervises and maintains Mobus Field, where there is a closed pavilion that was built in 1963, a baseball field, a children's playground established in 1964 and refurbished in 1970, and three tennis courts that were set up in 1966. Located on land that had been owned by the Plainfield Lumber Company, Mobus Field was named in honor of brothers Dave and Woodrow Mobus and dedicated on May 30, 1967.

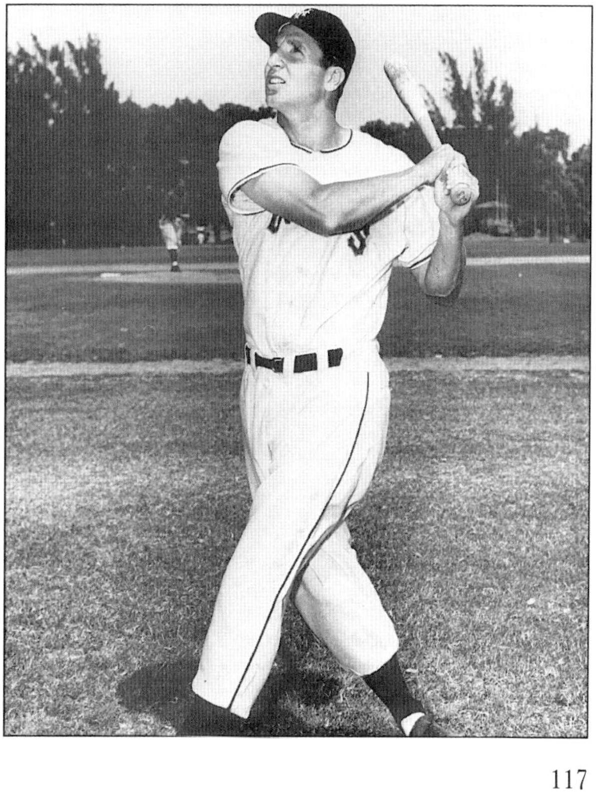

BOBBY THOMSON. In the 1951 playoffs for the World Series, Bobby Thomson made baseball history with "the Shot Heard 'Round the World." In the bottom of the ninth with two men on base, he hit the home run that won the game and the playoff series for the Giants against the Dodgers. Since 1958, Thomson has lived in Watchung, where he coached Little League and led the league's umpires in the 1970s. He is shown here at spring training in St. Petersburg in 1951.

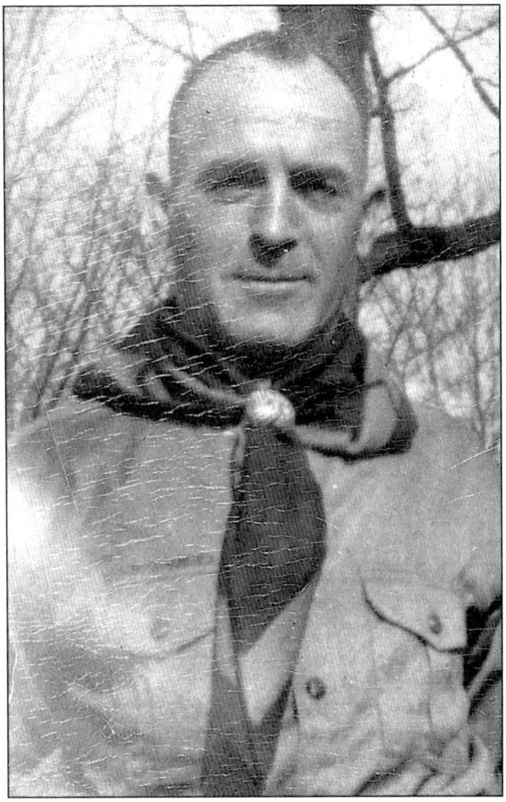

DAVE MOBUS. Watchung Boy Scout Troop 32 was formed in June 1937, sponsored by Wilson Memorial Union Church. From its inception, it has been an outdoor troop, investigating, improving, and exploring local woodland trails and remote mountains and lakes. Among his many community activities, Dave Mobus served as scoutmaster from 1949 to 1958. The Mobus family came to the Watchung area in the mid-to-late 1800s.

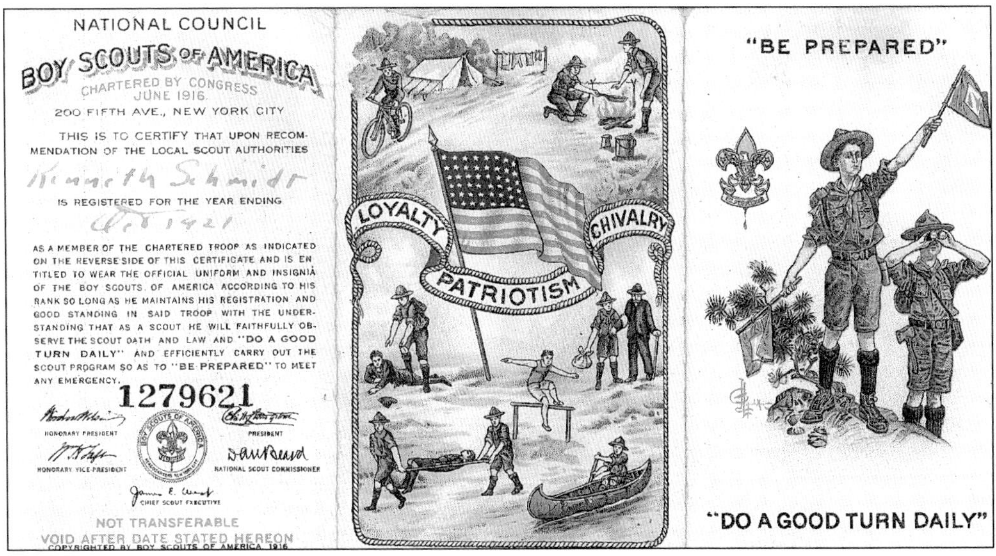
NATIONAL COUNCIL
BOY SCOUTS OF AMERICA
CHARTERED BY CONGRESS JUNE 1916.
200 FIFTH AVE., NEW YORK CITY
THIS IS TO CERTIFY THAT UPON RECOMMENDATION OF THE LOCAL SCOUT AUTHORITIES
Kenneth Schmidt
IS REGISTERED FOR THE YEAR ENDING
Oct 1921
AS A MEMBER OF THE CHARTERED TROOP AS INDICATED ON THE REVERSE SIDE OF THIS CERTIFICATE AND IS ENTITLED TO WEAR THE OFFICIAL UNIFORM AND INSIGNIA OF THE BOY SCOUTS OF AMERICA ACCORDING TO HIS RANK SO LONG AS HE MAINTAINS HIS REGISTRATION AND GOOD STANDING IN SAID TROOP WITH THE UNDERSTANDING THAT AS A SCOUT HE WILL FAITHFULLY OBSERVE THE SCOUT OATH AND LAW AND "DO A GOOD TURN DAILY" AND EFFICIENTLY CARRY OUT THE SCOUT PROGRAM SO AS TO "BE PREPARED" TO MEET ANY EMERGENCY.
1279621
HONORARY PRESIDENT
PRESIDENT
HONORARY VICE-PRESIDENT
NATIONAL SCOUT COMMISSIONER
CHIEF SCOUT EXECUTIVE
NOT TRANSFERABLE
VOID AFTER DATE STATED HEREON
COPYRIGHTED BY BOY SCOUTS OF AMERICA 1916

"BE PREPARED." As a boy, Ken Schmidt was a Boy Scout in an earlier Watchung troop that failed to survive. This was his 1921 member registration card, when he was 12 years old. He later served as the secretary and treasurer of the first troop committee for Troop 32, which still serves Watchung today.

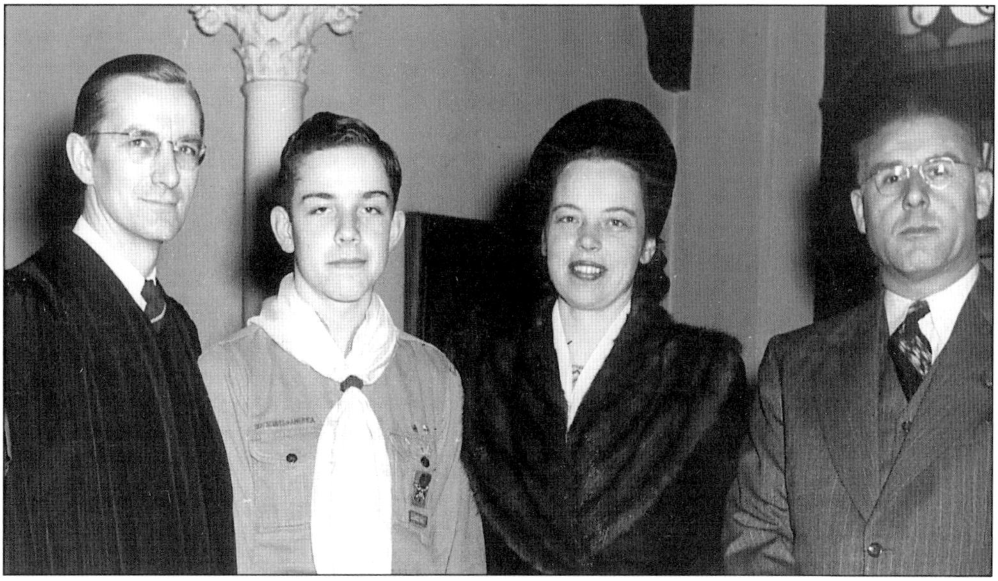

The First Eagles. In August 1949, two brothers, Harry and Charles Beckwith, were the first to be awarded the rank of Eagle Scout in Troop 32. Shown in 1948 when Harry received his Life Scout award are, from left to right, Rev. Roland Ost; Harry Beckwith; his mother, Ruth Beckwith; and his father, Al Beckwith. Harry also received the first Medal of Courage awarded by the Plainfield Disabled American Veterans for overcoming his deafness. In its 64-year history, Troop 32 has awarded the Eagle rank to 66 scouts, including the author.

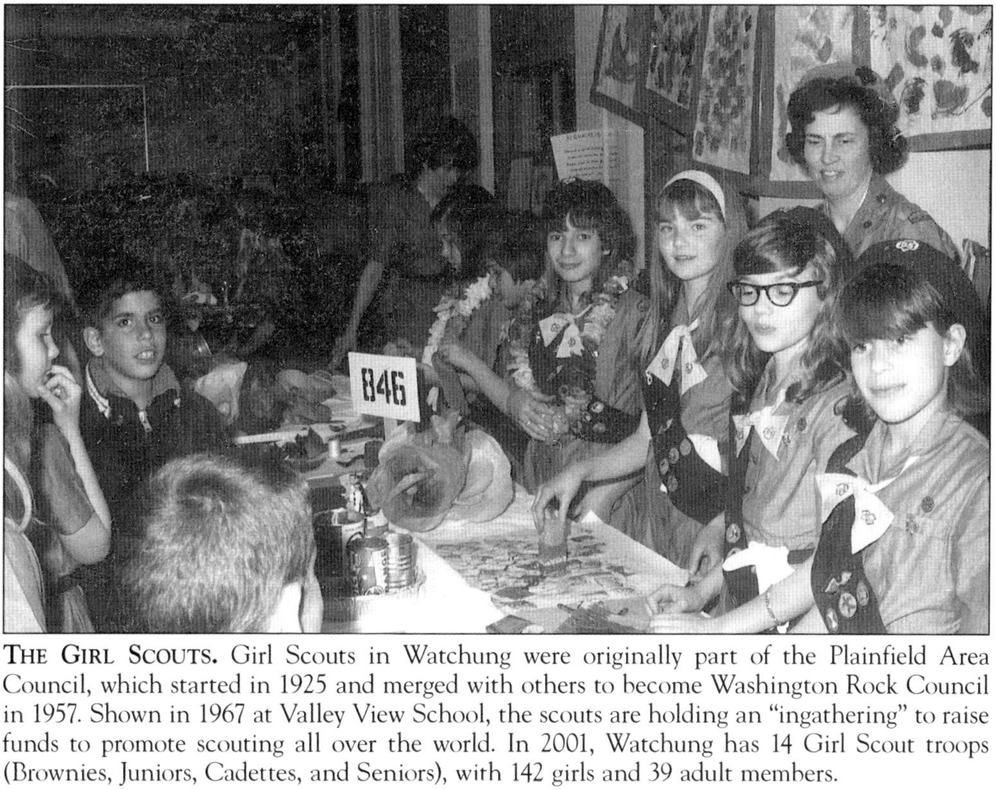

The Girl Scouts. Girl Scouts in Watchung were originally part of the Plainfield Area Council, which started in 1925 and merged with others to become Washington Rock Council in 1957. Shown in 1967 at Valley View School, the scouts are holding an "ingathering" to raise funds to promote scouting all over the world. In 2001, Watchung has 14 Girl Scout troops (Brownies, Juniors, Cadettes, and Seniors), with 142 girls and 39 adult members.

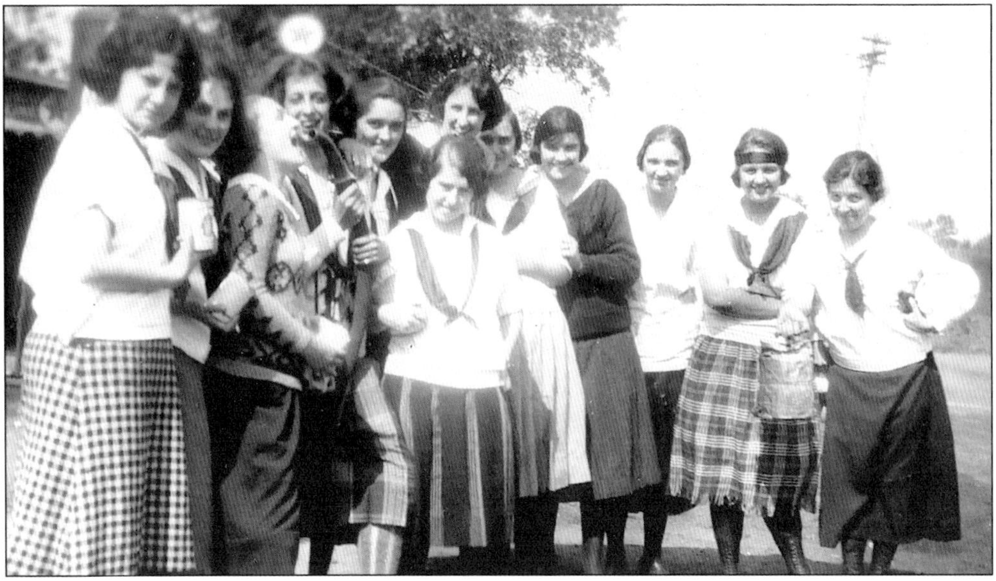

The "Gnuhctaw Club." Some girls belonged to the "Gnuhctaw Club" c. 1915, which is Watchung spelled backwards. Helen Schmidt got the members together, including Helen MacDonald, Mary Rose Eaton, Marie Merrill, Margaret Demler, Ruth Kennedy, and Tiby Liebenow. They enjoyed hiking and camping trips.

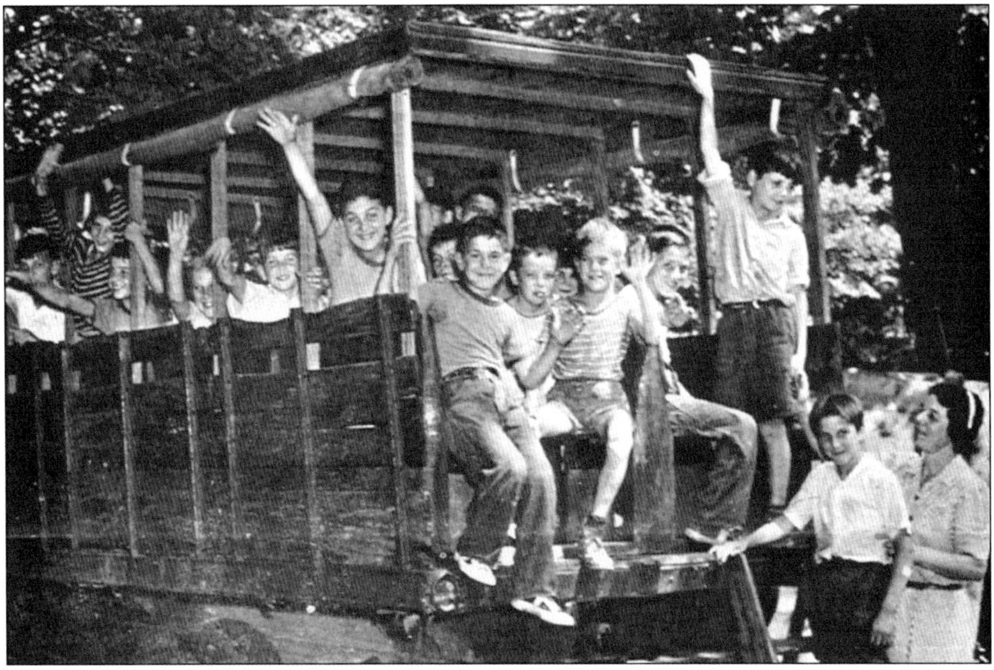

Camp Endeavor. In 1911, Camp Endeavor for underprivileged children was opened on Johnston Drive by the Union County Christian Endeavor Societies. Jesse Lounsbury, working with his wife, Helen, ran the camp from 1922 until his retirement in 1964. Beginning with a few tents, the facilities were expanded to include a swimming pool, playgrounds, dormitories, and a dining room. After the 1971 season, the camp merged with Camp Brett and moved to Hunterdon County.

THE OPTIMISTS CLUB. Established in 1965, the Optimists Club of Watchung sponsors an annual fishing derby at Best Lake, a geography bee, a photography contest, an oratorical contest, and an athletic awards banquet. This Native American statue, purchased early in the club's history, lists each new president's name on one of the feathers of the headdress. The statue resides with the club president during his term of office.

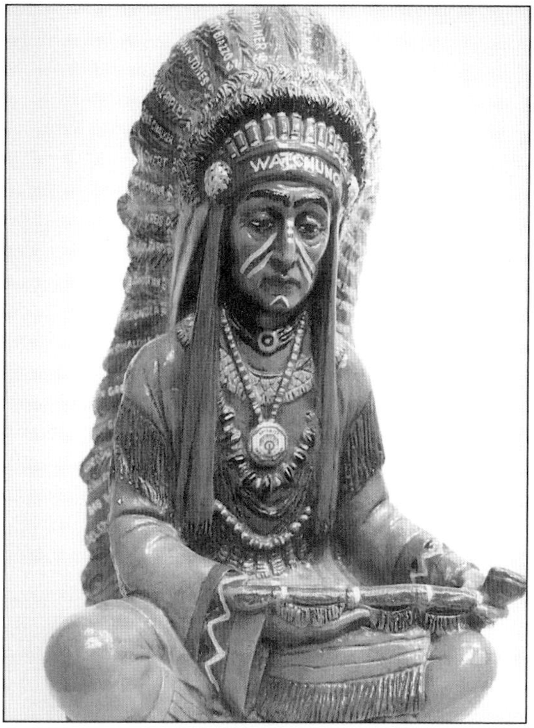

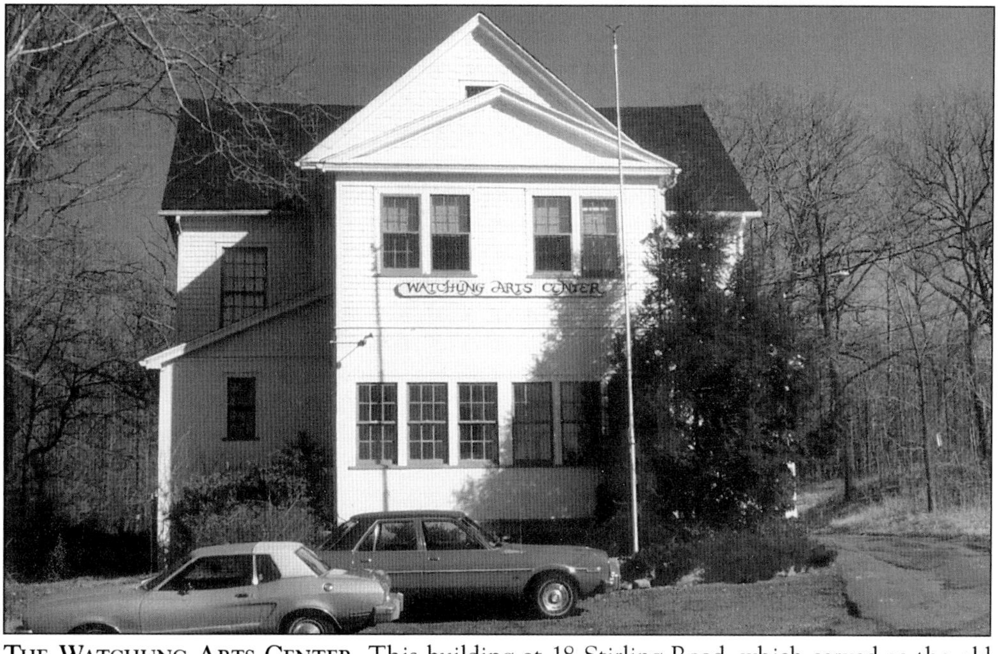

THE WATCHUNG ARTS CENTER. This building at 18 Stirling Road, which served as the old schoolhouse through the late 1940s, was then used as a library and recreation center. The Watchung Arts Council, a nonprofit organization, began using the building in 1977 with the purpose of providing a diversified and active arts program. The Watchung Arts Center attracts thousands of patrons a year for performances and to attend classes in painting, photography, sculpture, and crafts.

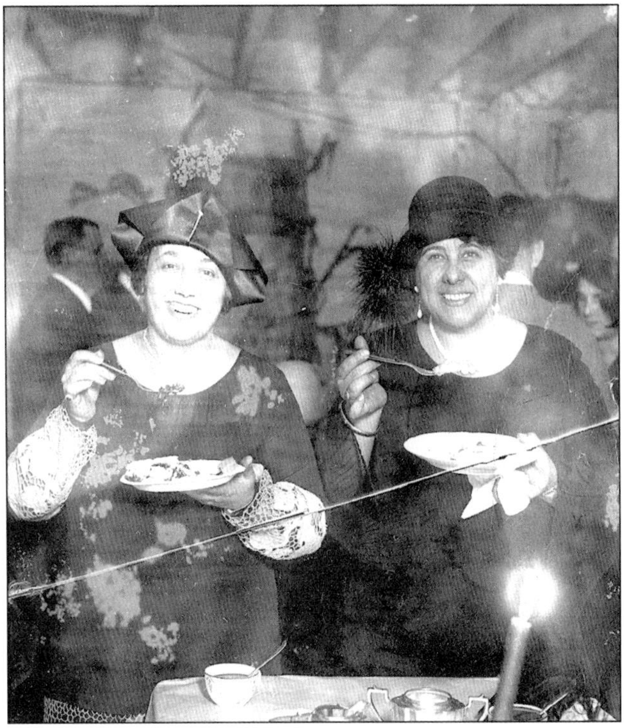

A PIE-BAKING CONTEST. Mrs. August Mirzaoff and Mrs. James Siccardi are shown in the early 1920s at the annual pie-baking contest held at the Old Mill. On December 15, 1935, the New York Times reported, "The annual pie-baking contest is a civic event of major importance in Watchung, New Jersey." That year, Mrs. M.H. Cleaves was the winner with a pumpkin pie, with honorable mention going to Mrs. Harry MacDonald. Grace Viebrock's crullers were also justly famous.

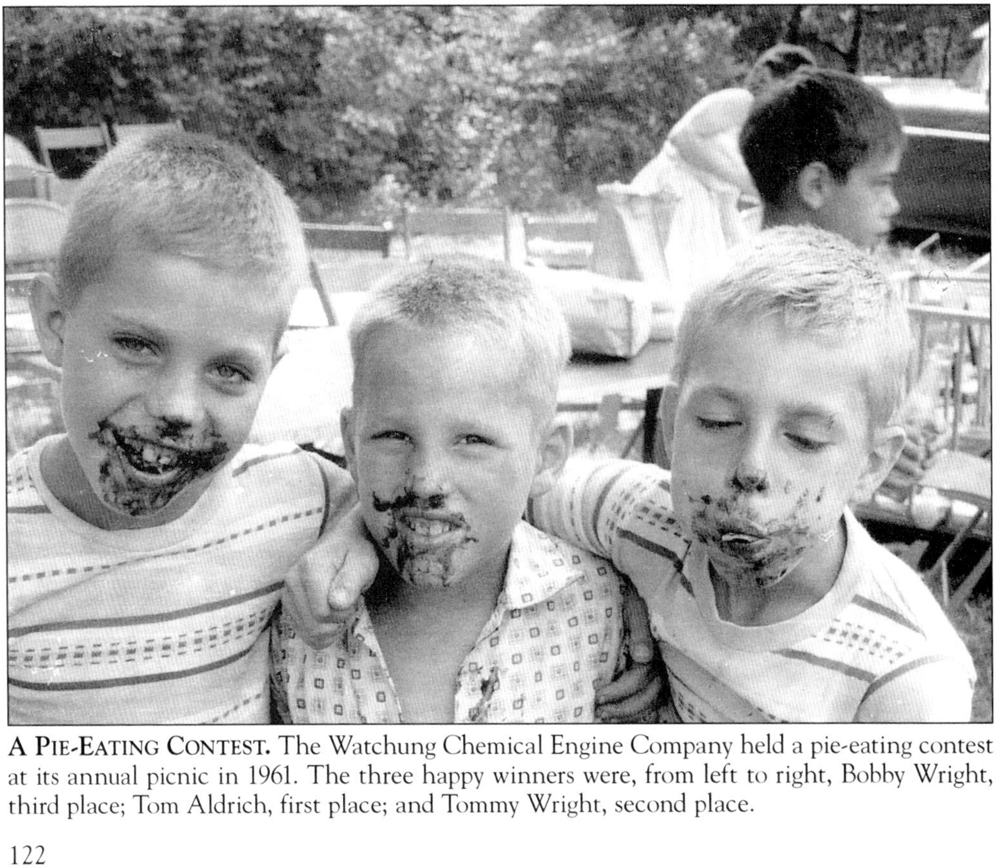

A PIE-EATING CONTEST. The Watchung Chemical Engine Company held a pie-eating contest at its annual picnic in 1961. The three happy winners were, from left to right, Bobby Wright, third place; Tom Aldrich, first place; and Tommy Wright, second place.

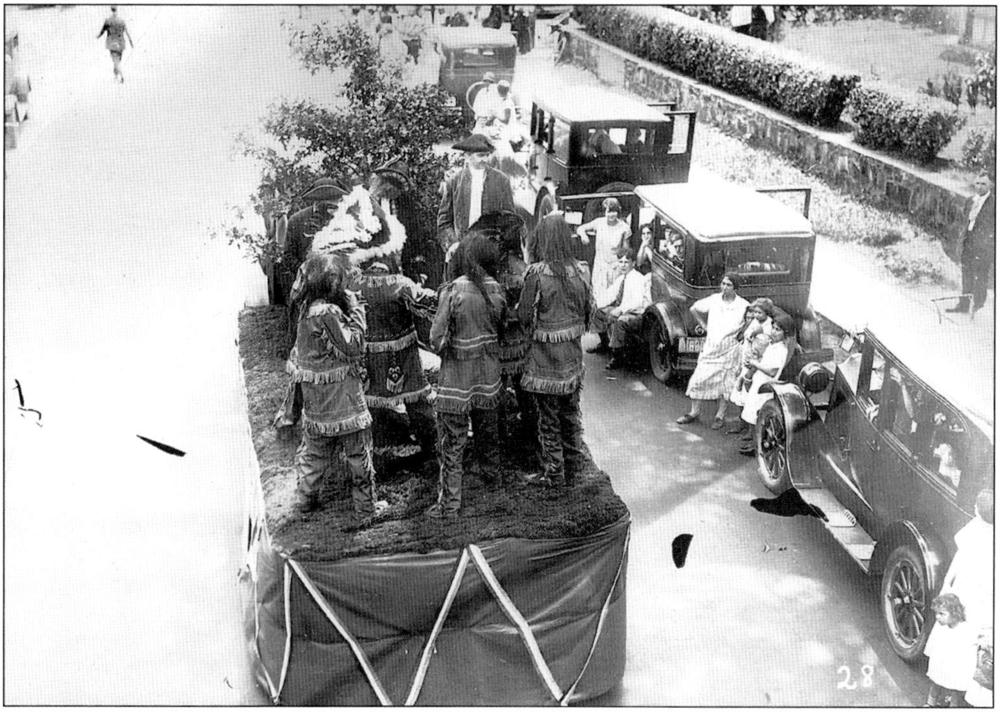

A Fourth of July Parade. This 1928 float in the Fourth of July parade shows Native Americans and settlers, probably reenacting the *Indian Legend of Watchung.* Modern-day community events include a Memorial Day town picnic, summer concerts, and a Halloween party.

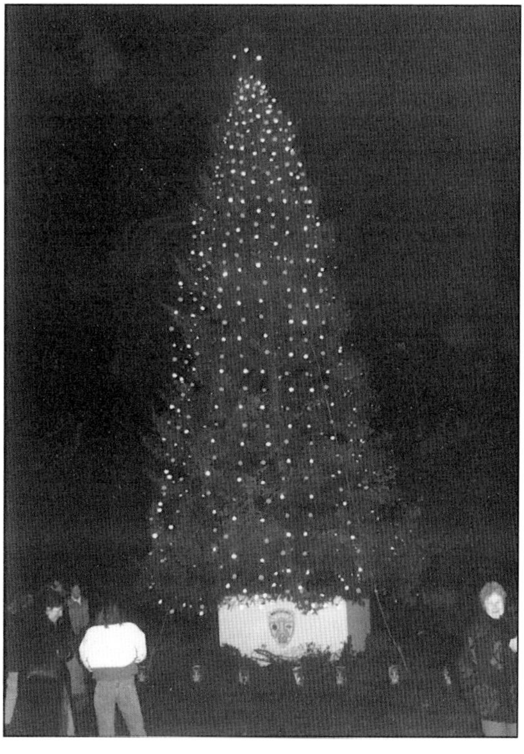

The Tree of Lights. A tree-lighting ceremony held in early December has become an annual town event in recent years. The "tree of lights" is sponsored by the Watchung Rescue Squad as a fundraiser. The tree in the center of the village green area is used for the event.

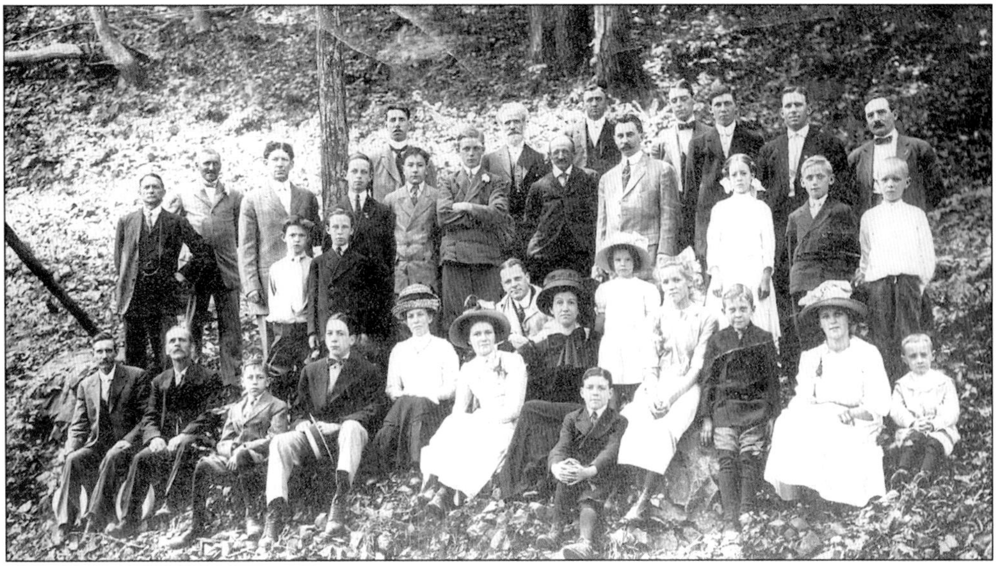

WATCHUNG RESIDENTS C. 1910. Although it is not certain what event brought these residents together, the photograph contains members of well-known Watchung families, such as Mobus, Schmidt, and Texier. The boy in front with his hands on his knees was Emile Perret, born in 1899. His family came to Watchung c. 1845. The man in the back row, fourth from the right, was Bill Anderson. This photograph was taken at about the time he wrote and directed the first *Indian Legend of Watchung* pageant.

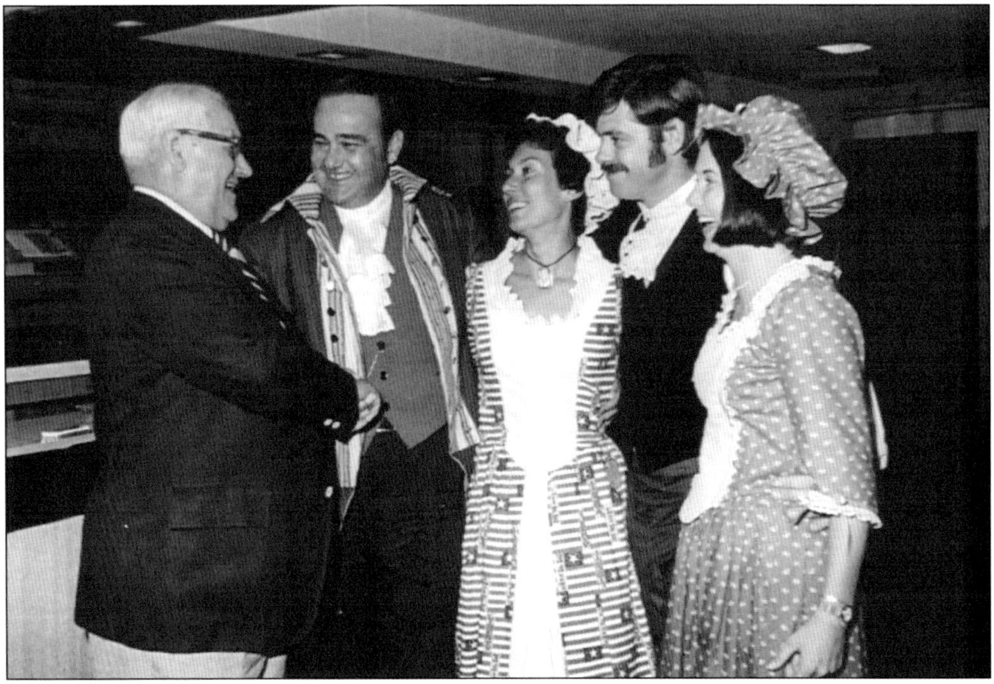

THE BICENTENNIAL CELEBRATION. Mayor Ken Schmidt (left) is shown with Bob Lippman, Norma Lippman, Jim Rittenhouse, and Lois Rittenhouse, who performed as part of the 1976 bicentennial celebration. The year 1976 also marked Watchung's 50th year of incorporation, and items were placed in a time capsule buried near Best Lake to be opened in 2026.

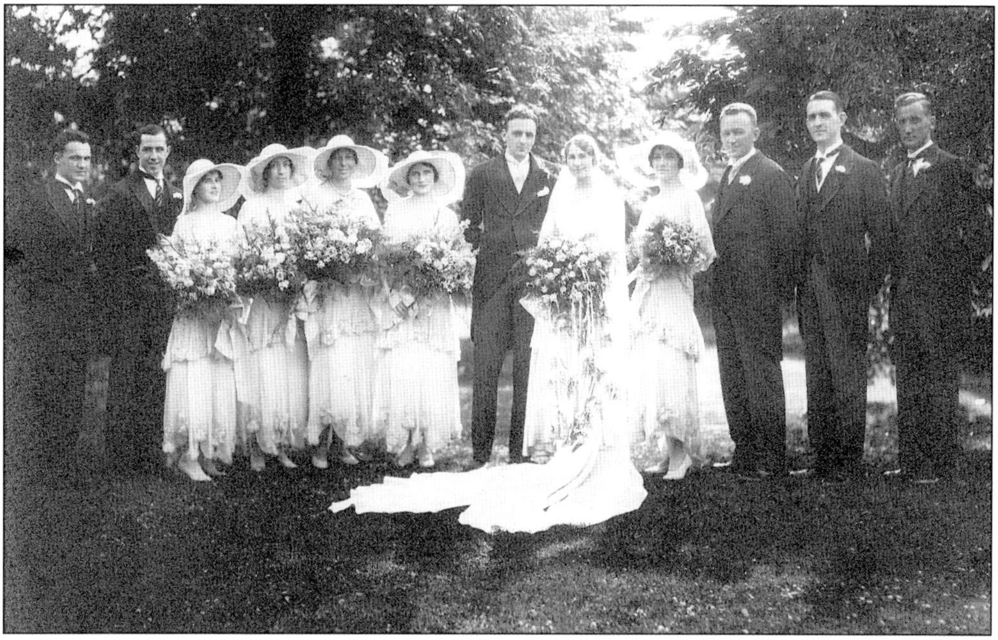

THE WOTHERSPOON WEDDING. Tiby Liebenow and James Wotherspoon from New York were married in 1930 in Wilson Memorial Chapel. After they were married, the couple got an apartment in Plainfield. In 1939, they bought land in Watchung and started building a house in 1941.

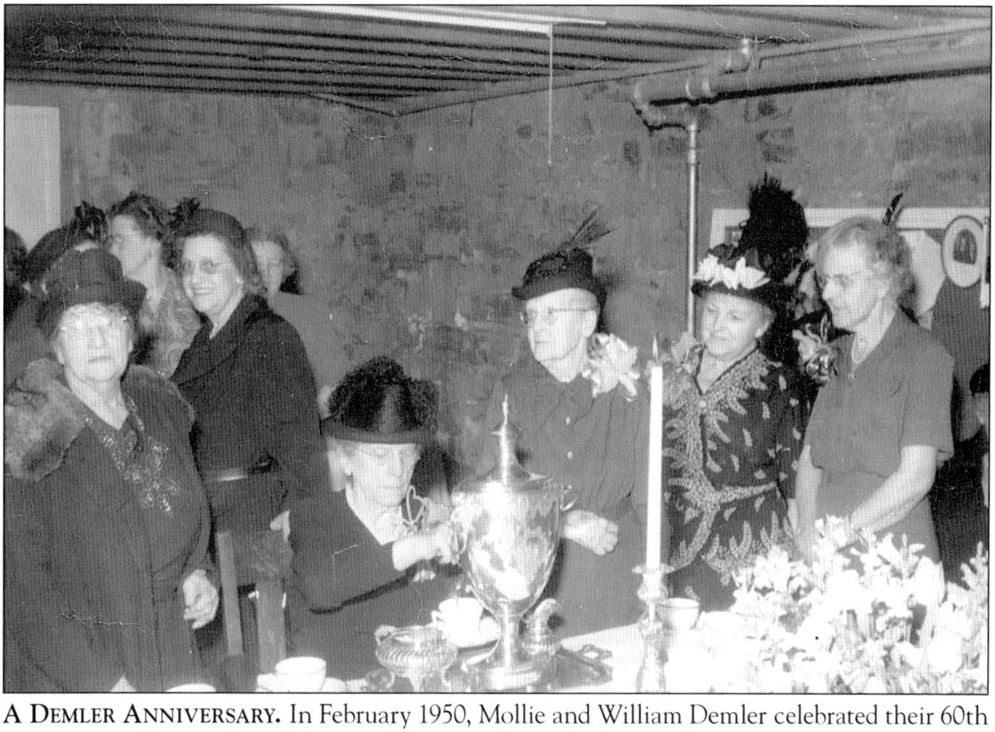

A DEMLER ANNIVERSARY. In February 1950, Mollie and William Demler celebrated their 60th anniversary. Shown, from left to right, are Sadie Bodenheimer (with glasses), Mollie Demler (seated), Mrs. Henry Bodenheimer, Mrs. Charles Miles, and Mrs. George Hughes.

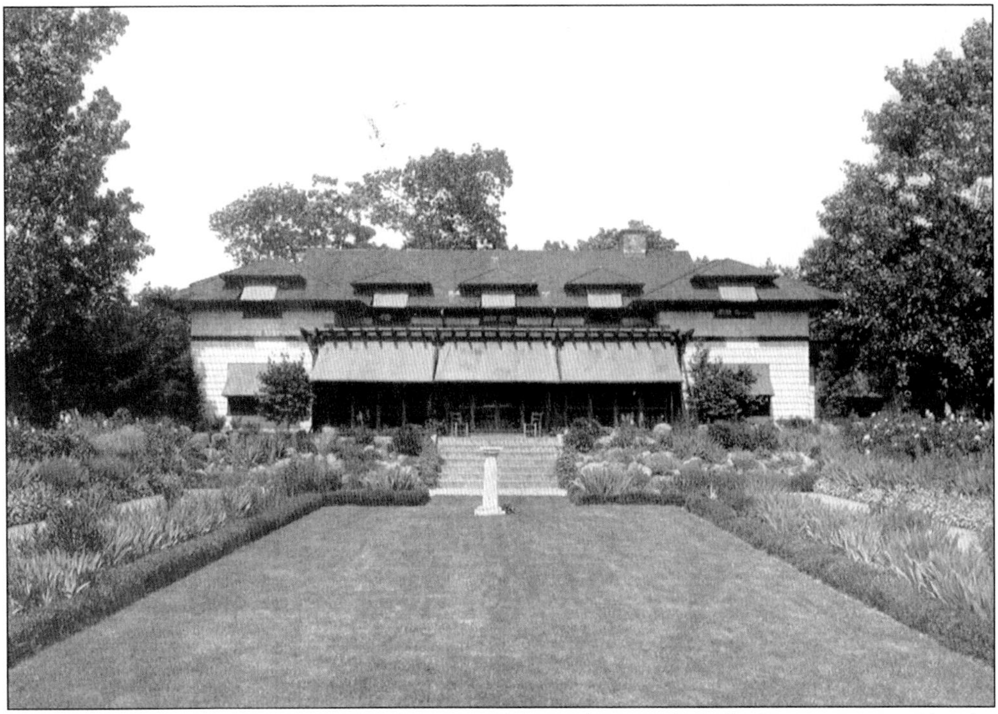

THE SALVATION ARMY HOME. This house, still located on High Oaks Drive, was used by the Salvation Army as a retirement home or rehabilitation center. At that time, High Oaks was a dirt road serving as a driveway to this building.

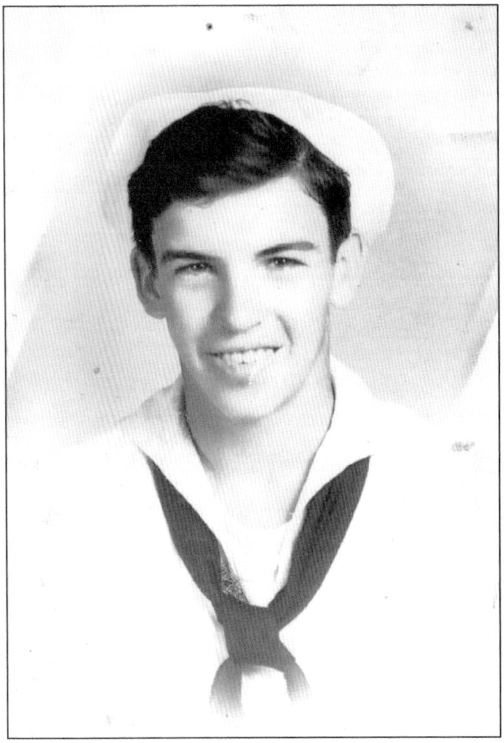

LEROY NUNN. Son of former Police Chief Elmer Nunn, Leroy Nunn enlisted in the U.S. Navy on March 6, 1943. He was one of four Watchung residents who died in service during World War II, the other three being Douglas Demler Jr., David Dickson, and Donald Fredericks. Nunn was killed on August 19, 1944, at the age of 17.

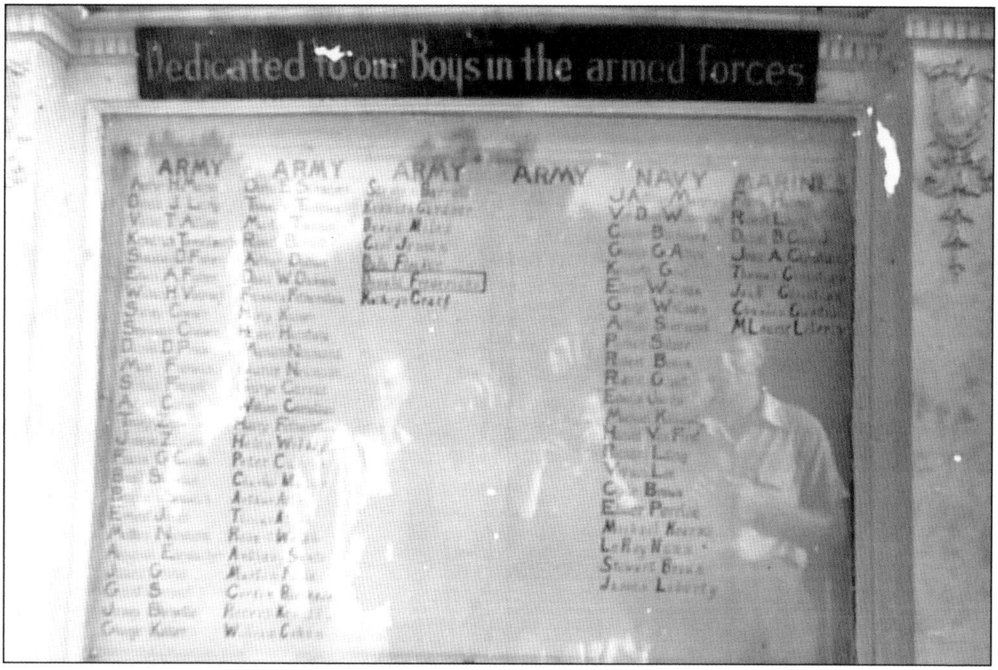

"DEDICATED TO OUR BOYS IN THE ARMED FORCES." This long-lost war memorial was a handwritten board that stood in front of the borough hall. This photograph of the honor roll was taken in 1944. The people in the reflection are Opie Jack, Barbara Barrett, Ann Underhill, Betty Pagel, Harold Brown, and Eddie Pabst.

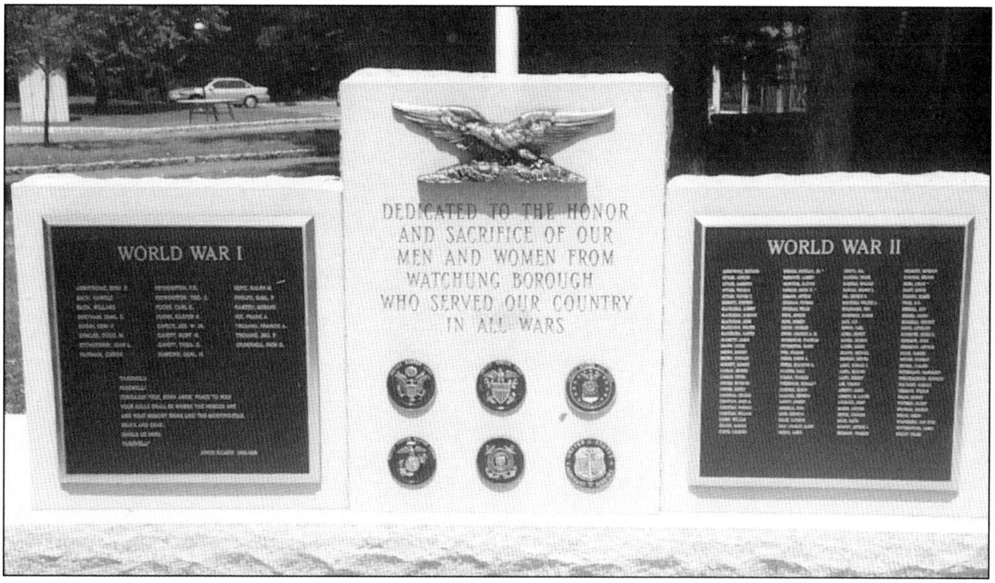

THE NEW WAR MEMORIAL. A new permanent war memorial was dedicated on Memorial Day, May 28, 2001, in front of the Texier House on the Watchung Circle. Each branch of the military—U.S. Army, U.S. Navy, U.S. Air Force, U.S. Marines, U.S. Coast Guard, and U.S. Merchant Marines—has its insignia on the monument. There is a bronze plaque with the names of 23 World War I veterans from Watchung and another listing of 108 Watchung residents who served in World War II.

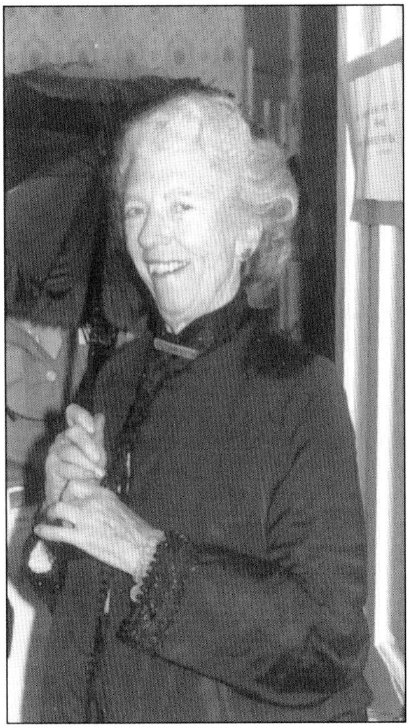

THE BICENTENNIAL ROOM. A member of one of Watchung's oldest families, Margaret Demler, dressed in family heirlooms, is shown in 1979 at the Bicentennial Room in the Watchung Public Library. The room is sponsored by the Watchung Historical Committee and contains a diorama of Watchung Center, as well as historical photographs, clothing, and other artifacts donated by town residents. The Watchung Historical Committee was founded in 1964 by Mr. and Mrs. Paul Runyon.

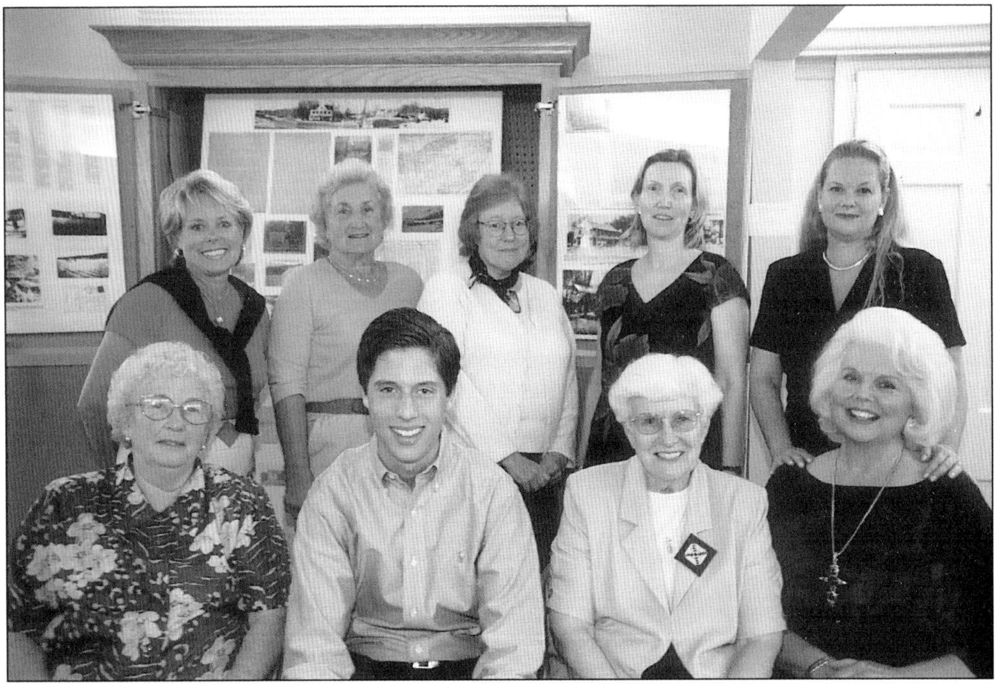

THE WATCHUNG HISTORICAL COMMITTEE. Present and former members of the Watchung Historical Committee, which provided access to its extensive photograph collection for this volume, are shown in a 2001 meeting with the author. Shown, from left to right, are the following: (front row) Betty Aldrich, David Page, Barbara Diem, and Ginny Cooper; (back row) Emi Havas, Phyllis Blackadar, Muriel Jacobs, Susan Feibush, and Catherine Ilchert.